I06I7055

Sensing Speech

*A How-To Manual for Those Wishing to Speak
General American English Easily, Articulately and
Expressively through a Feeling-based Process*

by

Jonghee Shadix & Nancy Krebs

Edited by

Deborah Kinghorn

An LTRI publication

First published in the USA by the Lessac Training and Research Institute (LTRI)
60 Seaman Avenue #1D, New York, New York 10034
www.lessacinstitute.org

Cover design and Book Layout: Selma Schiller

ISBN 979-8-9913943-0-7 (paperback)

Printed and bound in the United States by
Ingram Publisher Services ("IPS"), Nashville, TN

Contents

---

[1] *The Use and Training of the Human Voice: A Bio-Dynamic Approach to Vocal Life* by Arthur Lessac ©1997 McGraw-Hill Higher Education Publishing pg. 160

Acknowledgements

It is a fact that no book is solely written by the author or authors. Many talented and supportive individuals collaborated along the way to give birth to this new book. The authors wish to gratefully acknowledge the following contributors:

Dr. Julia Austin, the former Director of the Professional Development Program in the Graduate School of the University of Alabama at Birmingham, for the language editing on Jonghee Shadix's original manuscript; Nancy Abney and Jennifer Greer, the former co-faculty members at the Professional Development Program in the Graduate School of the University of Alabama at Birmingham; and all of Jonghee Shadix's students who attended the English Pronunciation and Intelligibility Training classes and workshops in the Professional Development Program in the Graduate School of the University of Alabama at Birmingham; her beloved husband Harry Shadix, her children Grace Shadix and Naomi Shadix; colleague Yuanlei Nikki Zhao for writing the Foreword to this manual; Aimee Blesing for her photos and illustrations; Syaiful Ariffin and Eric Berryman for their photo contributions; Crystal Robbins for her contributions; the peer reviewers; and those who gave so much of their time to read and assess this manual.

A special thank you to the entire Lessac Master Teacher Team, and E. Nelson Hudgins for his constant supply of love and encouragement.

Dedicated to:

The memory and legacy of Arthur Lessac,
founder of Lessac Kinesensics,
without whom this book would not exist,
and to all the students who attended the
Pronunciation and Intelligibility Classes
at the University of Alabama at Birmingham,
under the tutelage of Jonghee Shadix.

Foreword

Jonghee and Nancy have written an important and unique book - a book that should be embraced by English learning enthusiasts and owned by anyone working on acquiring General American English or teaching English to L2 speakers.

Picture this for a moment: a Chinese child around the age of 5 is glued to the screen of an analogue TV in her home in China. The seven dwarfs have just finished work in the coal mine and begin to chant 'hi ho' excitedly on their way out. To this little girl, the tune is merely made up of foreign sounds and melodies that match the vivid imagery of the tale of Snow White. Many replays later, she is able to hum along to the songs, and occasionally mimic the characters' verbal expressions and pitches.

My introduction to English began at a young age when I first watched Walt Disney's *Snow White*. The English language sounded foreign to me, but I enjoyed the animation and music. And then, as a part of the education system in China in the early 90s, I started to receive formal English tuition at the age of eight (8). Two years later, I moved to Australia to join my dad, and spent the 'integration' process predominantly at a local primary school, putting whatever English and communication skills I already possessed to the test. With my limited vocabulary and expressions, I found it extremely challenging to have any conversations with my classmates. I constantly panicked when I couldn't express myself and had difficulties making friends.

The children in my class often carried items that showed off their favourite pop idols and their latest album releases. Desperate to find ways to fit in, it wasn't long before I started to follow pop culture through the radio and weekend music TV. Music and songs immediately introduced an ease and joy to learning English for me, which led to enunciating, speaking, and expressing myself in English with more confidence and clarity. The feeling-based process of language acquisition mentioned in this book really spoke to me. We are sensory beings, and learning to feel and be guided by sensations associated with the vocal apparatus became a solid foundation to my work with voice and speech. Arthur Lessac's Kinesensic Voice Training paints the images of how speech, languages, and melody work in a way that anyone could understand.

Nancy was the first one to ignite my interest in treating speech sounds in English and Mandarin (my mother tongue) as *music making*, whether they were sustained like string instruments or tapped like drumbeats. She was my teacher of Lessac Kinesensic Voice Training before I undertook an MFA in Voice. Nancy was consistent and passionate, and helped me discover a mindful, intuitive, and enjoyable way to speak and communicate. Through *playing* of speech sounds, to communicating with a sense of vibrations at the points of articulation, I overcame some of my own challenges in communicating with more clarity and tone both in English and Mandarin. Take, for example, the /r/ in *rose*. I used to roll my tongue tip quite far back to make this sound, and it often felt laborious until Nancy guided me towards an efficient way to aim for this speech sound. I was delighted to have learned that clarity does not always mean working the articulators harder. To this day Nancy continues to inspire my career in teaching as I spread my work around the world, especially in my work with L2 speakers.

While I have not met Jonghee, I can relate deeply to her pursuit in making the learning of General American English more accessible to learners. Jonghee has articulated the struggles of L2 speakers, that English was often taught to them for academic purposes and not for practical use. I remember spending most of my English tuition classes in the format of call and response and sometimes we simply listened to a pre-recorded tape. There was an absence of ease or confidence in my speaking even though I was drilled with information, and so learning a foreign language felt passive and mechanical. This resulted in a lack of command, with a lot of second guessing when I needed to use English to communicate my intentions at the beginning of my time in Australia.

Jonghee is so aware of the learners' experiences that this book is written with a lot of care, understanding and the recognition of the learners' linguistic backgrounds and their unique challenges. Both Jonghee and Nancy recognise that learners have often been taught to rely on their listening skills to acquire English, without an understanding of why certain speech sounds can be more challenging to grasp than others. Therefore the chapters have been structured in a way that learners are invited to explore, speculate, and play with the carefully curated word lists, sentences, and short stories.

With a pedagogical approach that is non-suppressive, learning can feel fun and easy. Playful and organic discovery of speech contact points and shaping creates an awareness of the differences between a learner's first language and their understanding of General American. Because this wisdom is self-generated, the benefits are deeply embodied, thus more effective and longer lasting.

With their combined teaching experience in English Pronunciation and Intelligibility and Lessac Kinesensic Voice Training, the authors have set the chapters up in a way that allows easy and organic transition into the next exploration, but each chapter is a course in itself. The authors are able to offer such treats as 'useful tips' in every chapter, drawing the learner's attention to the observation and sensing of pronunciation rather than just listening. Rhythmic flow or fluency of the language is also addressed in this book under 'The Music of Expressive Speaking' in Chapter 3, moving clear speech to the next level. Finally, there is a wealth of valuable diagrams and photographs here, ranging from the anatomy of speech to photos of facial shaping for vowels.

In their simple yet unpatronising writing, I read two experienced practitioners relaying 'best practice', with references to lectures, conversations or common misconceptions explained. To the user, this book is a revolutionising tool to improve the clarity of English pronunciation and helps us all as we journey between learner and communicator. Because they write so clearly and with such humanity, this book is not only an essential reference book but constantly reminds us that the journey of speech making is a craft that anyone can invest in.

Yuanlei (Nikki) Zhao
Voice Coach, singer, performer
Melbourne, Victoria, Australia
May 8, 2024

Preface

Sensing Speech: A 'How-To' Manual for Those Wishing to Speak General American English Easily, Articulately and Expressively through a Feeling-based Process by Jonghee Shadix and Nancy Krebs is the first manuscript published by the Lessac Training and Research Institute (LTRI) under its newly expanded program for publishing innovative works around different applications of Lessac Kinesensics (LK). This new program encourages artists, researchers, scholars, and trainers to submit work that situates applications of LK within a pluralistic and global landscape while acknowledging that unique applications of LK might be perceived differently based on various life worlds, lenses, needs, wants, desires.

Within this process, the authors submitted their manuscript to the LTRI Research Team, who then initiated a rigorous process of blind review by experts in the field. Once feedback was provided, the LTRI Director of Research met with the authors and participated in various dialogues around the recommendations made, including discussing differing tensions within the field of Teaching English to Speakers of Other Languages (TESOL) specific to language, linguistics, and accent acquisition. Once the changes were accepted within a final review process, the authors and editor met with LTRI production team members to discuss art layout and marketing strategies for publication.

The value of the manual is that it offers accent acquisition within a TESOL context via a LK process of sensing and feeling. In particular, the manuscript gives the user awareness and skills to be able to decide when to make the shifts towards a General American accent and when to celebrate and apply their own accent or accents without a focus on accent reduction. While the authors value that some people will want to choose to maintain their own idiosyncratic vocal sounds and patterns, including accents when speaking English, they also recognize that other people may have the desire to shift their English pronunciation to a more General American accent that is either used or valued within mainstream communicative contexts within the United States or other areas where General American English is in use.

For those interested in exploring this shift, this manual shares how to sense and shape pronunciation differences and provides the reader with pronunciation options to acquire, should they so wish to explore. While the overarching aim of this manual is to empower those in the academic and professional fields of the United States who possess a different First Language (L1) than English it also benefits those who wish to acquire an 'American accent', including those studying General American English and those wishing to feel more confident in speaking General American English. Above all, the manuscript provides the reader the opportunity to develop skills that allow 'personal choice' in the articulation and expressiveness of English.

Sean Turner, PhD,
Managing Director
Lessac Training and Research Institute

Introduction

Dialogue: **Lessac Speech Training—an effective tool for clear communication**

Masaki: Ms. Jonghee, how did you find out about the Lessac Training and what made you want to share it in this class--English Pronunciation and Intelligibility Training?

Jonghee: As an English pronunciation instructor, I discovered a limitation in conventional pronunciation teaching textbooks, which generally used the concept of mimicking teachers or CDs for learning pronunciation.

Masaki: So, what was lacking in that method?

Jonghee: This method assumes that the language learners have the same linguistic experience as their teachers and can generate the target sounds in the speech just by "following" or "echoing" their teacher or listening to a CD.

Masaki: What would be the reasons for that?

Jonghee: In general pronunciation or phonology (the study of speech sounds) classes, teachers might be able to introduce the concepts of English phonology, but concepts alone might not actually bring about the changes in their students' pronunciation and their comfort level when speaking English.

Masaki: Why would you say that?

Jonghee: General American English-speaking facilitators might not have the same linguistic experiences as their students with various language backgrounds. There may be many sounds and sensations that are not experienced in the first languages of their students. Because of that, the learners have difficulty exactly mimicking the target sound that the teacher is asking of them. And the teachers might not have the strategies to help students make choices to acquire the General American accent.

I was in the same boat when I began teaching my Chinese students with Korean, English, Spanish, and Arabic language backgrounds. I was shocked at how much the English pronunciation of Chinese speakers differed from the English language as well as from other language speakers, and I didn't know how to help them effectively. I felt frustrated and inadequate. This prompted me to search for better strategies to help my Chinese students.

Masaki:	So, you found the Lessac Training?
Jonghee:	I was fortunate to be a *cross-pollinator* of knowledge, which means, I was and still am curious and interested about knowledge from different academic fields. So, to satisfy my curiosity as to how some Americans help their students gain clearer speech, I was led to take a voice class for theatre actors offered by the Theatre Department of the university where I was teaching. Luckily, the approach that our instructor used for that class was Lessac Training. So, the first day of that class is etched in my mind--the first step on a historic journey to use the Lessac Kinesensic Training for reducing the language distance between the learners' First Language and English for more effective General American English speaking and communication.
Masaki:	So, what happened in that class?
Jonghee:	The most exciting thing that took place in that class was something that I had never experienced before—to sense and feel the lip-opening shapes and sizes for each vowel sound; to feel the vibrations, and to feel the movements of my tongue, lips and teeth for each consonant sound—all the exact skills I needed to demonstrate for my Chinese students.
Masaki:	Can you share more about why knowing the Lessac concepts were so important to you as a pronunciation teacher.
Jonghee:	As a non-native English-speaking pronunciation teacher with an MA-TESOL (teaching English to speakers of other languages) background, I was well aware of the impact of the differences between a learner's first and the target language.
	However, when I started teaching English pronunciation, most of my students were international graduate students and scholars, mostly with Chinese backgrounds. Through these students, I discovered differences in areas I had never expected--n, m, l and ng: which I thought were included in every language. But by teaching many other language users, I discovered that every language has a different equivalent for each English sound.
	Since the Lessac work presented speech training for universal intelligibility through *feeling sensations* rather than *imitation*, using it helped all my students from any language background learn to speak English clearly, especially GA English, which was proven in my classes-- semester after semester through the years.
Masaki:	And now we get to experience it too!

Why write this book?

The dialogue above describes the path Jonghee Shadix took, spending roughly 15 years teaching English Pronunciation and Intelligibility classes to international graduate students and scholars in the Professional Development Program of the Graduate School in the University of Alabama at Birmingham (UAB). In her journey of teaching English pronunciation to international graduate students and scholars, she discovered that many pedagogies did not serve her students well and began to search for a more effective system of teaching. Since her first language was Korean, she could empathize and sympathize with the students' discomfort when they could not understand or be understood by first language English speakers. She vowed to herself to find a better way to give her students the choice to make shifts in their pronunciation of English when they thought it necessary or helpful.

She discovered the Lessac Voice and Body Training, otherwise known as Kinesensics, through the UAB Theater Department. This approach encourages first experiencing the **sensations** associated with **human language sounds**, thus identifying a multitude of consonants, vowels, and diphthongs, and then further exploring intonation, expressiveness, and fluidity in speech. This feeling-based bodyvoice approach provides speakers with optional pronunciation shifts that result in accent 'acquisition' rather than 'reduction', as advocated by other methodologies she had encountered.

This way of teaching and learning made sense to her, so she began to use her newfound skills to sense her own speech, and then to share this knowledge regarding potential pronunciation shifts with her students, who were mostly Chinese language speakers (more than 90% each semester), with a few students from Korea, India, and Japan, and with occasional different language speakers from various parts of the world. The make-up of her classes reflected national statistics. The United States attracts international students and scholars to its prestigious colleges, universities, language institutes, and communities each year, and a great number of those are from non-English speaking countries. For example, in 2019 alone, at least 1,095,299 international students enrolled in the US colleges and universities—among them, 431,930 were undergraduate students, and nearly and 377,943 were graduate students, with the largest number coming from China, India, and Korea.[2]

However, many of these talented people faced obstacles when communicating in General American English (GA)[3] (the typical version of English accepted by academics as representing the broadest interpretation of an overall American accent without specific regionalisms). Many of her students had learned English in their homelands as an academic subject, rather than as a medium for everyday communication. If they only learned English by translating English texts into their First Languages, or vice versa, they often lacked sufficient opportunities to develop their speaking skills in social or academic settings. In addition, they may have carried the pronunciation patterns of their first language (L1) over to their 2nd language (L2), that is, English; and thus were speaking GA with the accent

---

[2] https://educationdata.org/international-student-enrollment-statistics accessed 2019.

[3] After this introduction, we will most often refer to General American English as GA or GA English

11

from their L1. As a result, many U.S. speakers had difficulty understanding them when they were communicating the spoken word; and in turn, these international students, scholars, and professionals studying and working in the United States were not as freely able to understand U.S. speakers. So, countless highly educated people faced a major hurdle as they tried to adjust to life in the United States.

But when her students were introduced to the Kinesensic Training and applied its *feeling process* to acquire General American English, both Jonghee and her students immediately saw, felt, and heard the results. The training was transformational: her students' GA became increasingly fluent and intelligible to U.S. listeners in a very brief period of time. For her students, this was a hugely positive experience. This training also offered them options. They could *choose* when and how they wanted to shift. Word quickly spread about her classes around the campus. So many students wanted to take her classes each semester, her classes were completely full and waiting lists had to be maintained.

She created a series of lesson plans based on her understanding of Lessac Kinesensic principles. Because her former students reported increased confidence in their use of GA English due to this training, she decided to use those lesson plans as the basis for this manual. In 2018, she and her co-author, Lessac Master Teacher Nancy Krebs, combined their talents to create this manual that would feature Jonghee's teachings and the Lessac Kinesensic training.

If your goal is to gain confidence in speaking GA English, Jonghee and Nancy invite you to participate in this 'practical workshop", in which sensing and feeling the differences between your first language and GA English will guide you to distinguishing the idiosyncrasies in pronunciation, rhythm, and stress patterns in both.

To the reader of this manual...

This manual shares how to sense and shape pronunciation differences and provides you with pronunciation options to acquire, should you so wish. The aim of this manual is to empower those in the academic and professional fields of the United States who possess a different First Language (L1) than English. For your information, the following is a definition of *General American English*:

> **General American English** or General American (abbreviated GA or GenAm) is the umbrella accent of American English spoken by the majority of Americans and widely perceived, among Americans, as lacking any distinctly regional, ethnic, or socioeconomic characteristics. In reality, it encompasses a continuum of accents rather than a single unified accent. Americans with high education, or from the North Midland, Western New England, and Western regions of the country, are the most likely to be perceived as having General American accents. The precise definition and usefulness of the term General

American continue to be debated, and the scholars who use it today admittedly do so as a convenient basis for comparison rather than for exactness. Other scholars prefer the term Standard American English.[4]

Who can benefit from this book?

Students studying General American English who *wish to acquire* an 'American accent' can benefit by using this book as a resource because it is designed to be a *practical workshop*, in which a challenge or obstacle is presented at the beginning of each unit or chapter through the use of dialogues or vignettes. Each chapter will then guide you through instructions, explorations and 'practicing with awareness' with word lists, sentences, paragraphs, and conversations crafted to solve the obstacle posed at the beginning of the chapter. Our hope is that you will develop the skills that give you the gift of *choice*—the choice to have articulate, expressive, and confident General American English speech, accomplished by 'sensing and feeling' your way through these pages.

What is Lessac Kinesensic Voice Training?

Arthur Lessac, the originator and developer of this approach to bodyvoice training, was one of the leading voice pedagogues of the 20th century—and into the 21st. He is the author of two seminal texts: *The Use and Training of the Human Voice: A Bio-Dynamic Approach to Vocal Life*[5], and *Body Wisdom: The Use and Training of the Human Body*[6]. Over the many decades of his teaching, he formulated and then expanded upon his basic premise of 'organic instruction', which means discovering within us the sensations that guide us to optimal functioning within context, thereby giving us choices. This led to the development of what he named *Kinesensics*, a term created from 'kine', meaning movement/motion; 'esens', meaning the essence, the study of, or the nature of; 'sens', meaning inner life or spirit; and 'sic', meaning familiar events or occurrences. In short, it is a process that allows us to learn first from ourselves and life experiences, and then to apply what we've learned to make the unfamiliar familiar: in fact, to learn new knowledge. By engaging with this manual, you will develop an experiential awareness of the familiar speech and prosody of your first language while acquiring the knowledge and skills to shift to that which is found in GA English. This sensing and feeling process will allow you to experience small distinctions between the two languages, offering you choices when you opt to speak GA English in various contexts.

---

[4] Wikipedia, the free encyclopedia, https://en.wikipedia.org/wiki/General_American_English, 12/13/2023.
[5] *The Use and Training of the Human Voice: A Bio-Dynamic Approach to Vocal Life 3rd Edition* by Arthur Lessac, McGraw-Hill Higher Education Publishing © 1997, 1967, 1960
[6] Body Wisdom: The Use and Training of the Human Body, by Arthur Lessac, Lessac Training and Research Institute, ©2019

The purpose of this training is not to *reduce* your accent, but to enable you to *acquire* the skills that give you more options when speaking GA. The overall objective is for you to become self-reliant using this process to the point where you become your *own* teacher, your *own* guide. In this way, you will have the power to make shifts in pronunciation and expression when needed or desired.

For more information about Arthur Lessac, his work, and his books, please visit the Lessac Institute website.[7]

Using this manual for self-teaching

You can use this manual by yourself. The chapters are laid out as if you are taking a class. You can skip around or progress systematically through each chapter. Although some of the tasks invite a partner to carry on a conversation or dialogue with you, you can read both roles aloud on your own and carry out the explorations without needing anyone else.

Using this manual to facilitate a class

If you are an instructor of General American English (GA)[8] in a higher education TESOL[9] or SLA[10] setting, or teaching it as an additional language, you can utilize this book to facilitate for those who wish to acquire GA English pronunciation options for more effective communication with their listeners when they so desire. Most pronunciation classes in the United States or in other countries don't provide this unique kind of training. We believe the results will speak for themselves.

Notes: ....

....

....

....

....

....

----

[7] www.lessacinstitute.org

[8] For the purposes of identification, from this point onward, we will refer to General American English as GA or GA English. We will also use the term 'native English speakers' to identify those North Americans who have spoken English from birth.

[9] https://www.tefl.org/en-us/tesol/ Teaching English to Speakers of Other Languages

[10] SLA—Second Language Acquisition https://www.press.umich.edu/pdf/9780472034987-intro.pdf

IPA and Lessac Kinesensic Phonetic Symbols and Word Samples for all the sounds covered in this book[11]

Vowels & Diphthongs:

IPA	Lessac Kinesensic	Sample
[u]	#1	*food, school*
[oʊ]	#21	*old, bone*
[ɔ]	#3	*awful, fall*
[ɔɪ]	#3y	*boy, toil*
[ɔə]	#3n	*more, for*
[ɝ]	R (stressed)	*bird, fern, early*
[ɚ]	R (unstressed)	*never, father*
[ɒ]	#4	*fog, hot*
[ɑ]	#5	*f<u>a</u>ther, arm*
[aʊ]	#51	*cow, mountain*
[æ]	#6	*add, hand*
[aɪ]	#6y	*fly, side*
[i]	Y Buzz	*see, creep*
[eɪ]	+Y Buzz	*say, fade*
[ʊ]	N1	*took, could*
[ɪ]	N2	*tick, in*
[ɛ]	N3	*tech, settle*
[ʌ] or [ə] (unstressed)	N4	*tuck, love, enough*
[ʊə]	N1n	*poor, tour, cure*
[ɪə]	N2n	*peer, pier, dear*
[ɛə]	N3n	*pare, pear, chair*

---

[11] IPA symbols (International Phonetic Alphabet) *The Newbury Dictionary of American English*, Philip M. Rideout, ©Heinle & Heinle Publishers 1999

Consonants:

IPA[12]	Lessac Kinesensic symbols
[n] as in *none*	N
[ṇ] as in *student*	*N*
[m] as in *mom*	M
[v] as in *viva*	V
[f] as in *fluff*	F
[z] as in *zoo*	Z
[s] as in *sister*	S
[b] as in *bob*	B
[p] as in *pop*	P
[d] as in *dad*	D
[t] as in *tot*	T
[ʔ] as in *certain*	*T*
[g] as in *gag*	G
[k] as in *kick*	K
[dɬ] as in *cradle*	DL
[tɬ] as in *little*	TL
[θ] as in *thank*	*TH* (unvoiced)
[ð] as in *them*	TH (voiced)
[ʒ] as in *measure*	ZH
[ʃ] as in *shush*	SH
[ŋ] as in *sing*	NG
[l] as in *lily*	L
[j] as in *yay*	Y
[dʒ] as in *judge*	DZH
[tʃ] as in *church*	TSH
[dz] as in *friends*	DZ
[ts] as in *hats*	TS
[ɹ] as in *rarer*	R
[w] as in *wow*	W

Note: Throughout this manual, IPA symbols will be situated within brackets [θ] and Webster's Dictionary symbols will be within slashes */th/*. Lessac notation will be identified by special symbols for vowels and diphthongs, and the use of capital letters for consonants unless the consonants are within words and sentences.

---

[12] IPA is the acronym for International Phonetic Alphabet

Section A:

General American (GA) English
Consonants & Vowels
(The Music of Individual Sounds)

Chapter 1

Sensing & Playing Consonants
(The Music of the GA Consonants)

Dialogue:[13] Facing Challenges When Speaking English in the United States

Jonghee: So, what brought you to this class?

Sunny: I want to improve my GA English.

Jonghee: I can understand you fairly well.

Sunny: That may be true. But I want to speak GA English as clearly as my U.S. classmates or lab mates do.

Jonghee: You don't think that you do?

Sunny: Since my First Language of Chinese does not have many equivalent sounds of English, I just learned to pronounce English sounds and words as close to the way my teachers taught us in my English classes back in my country; but I did not realize that some of those sounds or words are quite different from the way Americans in the U.S. pronounce them.

Jonghee: I see. Did you know that in English the smallest unit of the language is called a phoneme, which is either a *consonant and/or* a *vowel*? But in Chinese, the smallest unit of the sound is a *syllable*, which is a combination of consonants and vowels, which cannot be divided further into smaller units such as consonants and vowels like we find in English.

Sunny: Yes, and in addition, I know that the majority of individual English sounds cannot be expressed in the written forms of the Chinese language because my language does not include some sounds that the English language contains. So, oftentimes, I cannot understand Americans when they speak quickly, and they cannot understand my English at times. So, I came to your class because some of my Chinese lab mates and classmates recommended it. I can tell that their English speaking has become much clearer to native English speakers now that they have taken this class, so I am here to improve my own English as well.

Jonghee: You came to the right place. In this class, we will explore together the secrets of possessing clearer and more expressive General American English speech. We will start with the consonants. If you create consonant sounds that are intelligible to those friends and colleagues who are listening to you, your communication will become much clearer to them in a very short time.

---

[13] Unless credit for passages is given, all dialogues, passages and stories have been created by Jonghee Shadix and shaped by Nancy Krebs

Sunny:	Clear consonants for clearer communication!

Jonghee: Yes. One thing we need to be aware of is that certain consonants are meant to be long, and other consonants, short. For example, n, l, m, ng, s, z, th, v, f, sh, zh, r, w and y can be 'long' or 'sustained', resembling a humming sound[14] or, if unvoiced, a hissing sound. The b, d, g, p, t, k, ch, dg, ts, and dz are not meant to be sustained, so they are 'short' or 'tapped', resembling the sound of a drumstick tapping a drumhead (the drumstick springs away from the drumhead).

Sunny: I see. What more do I need to know about consonants?

Jonghee: Some consonants are 'voiced' or vibrated, and others are without vibration, or 'unvoiced'. And different consonants are produced at different contact points in the oral cavity, as you can see here:

- Between the lips: b, p, m

- Between the tongue and the upper
  gum ridge: d, t, n, l, ch, dg, s, z, sh, zh, y

- Between the tongue and the soft palate: g, k, ng

- Between the teeth and the tongue: th (voiced and unvoiced)

- Between the teeth and the lower lip: f, v

- With rounded lips: r, w

- Sides of the tongue touching the
  inside of the back molars: r

- Exhaling with the root of the tongue
  slightly lifted: h

Sunny: So those are the *locations or points of contact* where consonants can be felt. What do you mean by the 'manner of articulation'?

Jonghee: Some consonant sounds are long, or sustainable, and some sounds are short, or 'percussive' by nature. We need to learn about both. Also, both native English speakers and L2 learners tend to include consonants clearly at the beginning of words and before vowels, but then may lose energy and forget, neglect, or ignore consonants in the middle or toward the end of words, phrases, or sentences, and often before another consonant

---

[14] Humming: to make a low, continuous, droning sound; https://www.dictionary.com/browse/hum; accessed 12/26/23. In Kinesensics, we vary the pitch of the hum, adding musicality and range to sustained voiced consonants.

sound, or before pauses and punctuations such as a period (.), comma (,), exclamation mark (!), and question mark (?). This phenomenon causes words to become unclear to listeners.

Sunny: I did not realize that. Are there ways to solve this problem?

Jonghee: Yes. All we must do is feel and include the consonants in each word as we speak in GA, and our speech will become clearer to whoever is listening.

Sunny: What causes us not to include our consonants within a word?

Jonghee: We often aren't aware that we need to feel and experience consonants throughout each word, or sometimes we just don't know how to create some English consonants.

Sunny: I see. So, what can we do about this 'lack of awareness'?

Jonghee: If a *problem* is identified, there is bound to be a *solution*. First, let's discover how to create each consonant, then recognize that some consonants are long and 'sustainable'; and other consonants are short and 'tappable'. In addition, in this workshop, I suggest that we identify those places within and between words that need consonants included as 'Sustainable Opportunities' or 'Tappable Opportunities'—meaning that we are giving ourselves an *opportunity* to experience the consonant, when before we might have forgotten them.

Sunny: I like the idea of having an 'opportunity'. That is such a positive and pleasant way to remind us to experience our consonant sounds.

Jonghee: That's right. In this chapter, you will be asked to *double-underline* the Sustainable Consonants in specific instances and to sustain them longer than your usual length. For example:

a.   Sustain the Sustainable Consonants *before another consonant*:
mind, Nancy, consonant, seldom, after, wishful, asterisk

b.   Sustain the Sustainable Consonants *Before a Pause or Punctuation*
He is learning to drive. Tina loves Tim, but he loves Jess.

c.   When we combine them together, we might observe this:
He is learning to drive. Tina loves Tim, but he loves Jess.

Sunny: So, I need to lengthen the sustainable consonants n, m, ng, l, f, v, s, z, sh, and zh before other consonants, pauses, or punctuation as if I am humming or feeling those sounds. For how long should I hum or sustain those consonants?

Jonghee:	As we explore the consonants in our class, I would suggest:

1. Reading the word list aloud for the 1st time, elongate the sustainable consonants 4 or 5 times longer than you usually would.

2. For the 2nd time, sustain the sounds twice as long as you typically would.

3. For the 3rd time and for professional or clear conversational speech, sustain just long enough to experience the feel of the sound being produced.

	Arthur Lessac, the creator of the *Lessac Kinesensic Training*, often reminded his students "If you FEEL it, your listeners will HEAR it."
Sunny:	I can picture what you're saying.
Jonghee:	And for the short and unsustainable (spring away or tapped) sounds, you want to *tap* the sound lightly and briefly at the point of contact.[15]
Sunny:	I understand the feeling of 'sustain' which means to hold the sound longer, but what does 'tapping' feel like in this case?
Jonghee:	Your question is a good one. Think of a drummer or a percussionist striking the head of their drum in rhythm. The drumstick springs away from the drumhead, like tapping. Or when you lightly knock at a door, you hear a tapping sound and your hand springs away. Or have you ever tapped your pencil against a desk and felt a little bit like you were drumming? The end of the pencil sprang away from the desk, lightly and quickly.
Sunny:	I see.
Jonghee:	You can feel that brisk tapping with certain consonants. This chapter is all about discovering the difference between consonants you can hum or sustain, and those you can tap. You may feel as if you are 'playing' the consonants like *musical* instruments, as if you are a musician. So, now let's feel the tapping of the tongue on the upper gum ridge (*hard palate*) for 't-t-t,' and then add voice for 'd-d-d.' Now spring your lips away from each other for 'p-p-p' and add voice for 'b-b-b.'
Sunny:	I think I have it. Let me see if I can find my own tapping— 'd-d-d, t-t-t, p-p-p, b-b-b, k-k-k, g-g-g.' You know, I cannot make these sounds longer even if I wanted to, right?

---

[15] The use of the terms "lightly and briefly" and other descriptors of percussive consonants are particular in this manual to GA English. In other languages, the pressure for producing the desired quality of consonant may vary.

Jonghee:	Right. Percussive sounds are short, and we cannot make them longer without altering them completely. We'll use a single underline to notate them. Let's review the important concepts here:

- Sustainable consonants: n, m, ng, l, f, v, s, z, sh, zh, th.

- Tappable consonants: b, p, d, t, g, k, ch, dg(j), ts, and dz

- **Sustainable or Tappable Opportunities:**
  1. before another consonant
  2. before a pause or punctuation (at the ends of words standing alone).

- **Not Sustainable or Tappable Opportunities:** at the beginning of words and before a vowel sound either within a word or before a word beginning with a vowel. (ex: hop up)

- **What about r, w, and y?** When these consonants occur in beginning and medial positions, they function as consonants. When sustained, these three consonants become vowel-like, which means they are no longer functioning solely as consonants. For now, we will exclude these consonants from our playable opportunity selections. We will engage with their special functions later in this manual.

Sensing language differences in order to achieve clearer communication in GA English contexts

Sunny:	Thank you for explaining the strategies for pronouncing GA consonants clearly and with a feeling of playing music! I also think I comprehend what it means to understand language differences for clear communication.
Jonghee:	You know, since every student who is learning GA English has a First Language that may be very different from it, it is typical to begin speaking English with the influences of the first language carried over. But, when we learn to feel the points of contact for consonants and be guided by the *sensations* of humming or tapping, we will then learn how to produce words that will sound more like our American friends and be clearly understood by our listeners.
Sunny:	That is exciting—and I am ready to recognize the language differences between my own language and the English language by first exploring GA consonants--through *feeling* the sensations, rather than by *imitating* anyone!
Jonghee:	Great! Just so you know, this chapter is organized according to the order of frequency that consonants occur in GA so you can start communicating more effectively right away. Let's get started!

Locations within our vocal 'apparatus' where the GA Consonants are created[16]

1. W, WH
2. P, B, M
3. V, F
4. TH, th
5. N, L, D, T, DZ, TS, Z, S
6. ZH, sh
7. R
8. G, k
9. NG
10. H

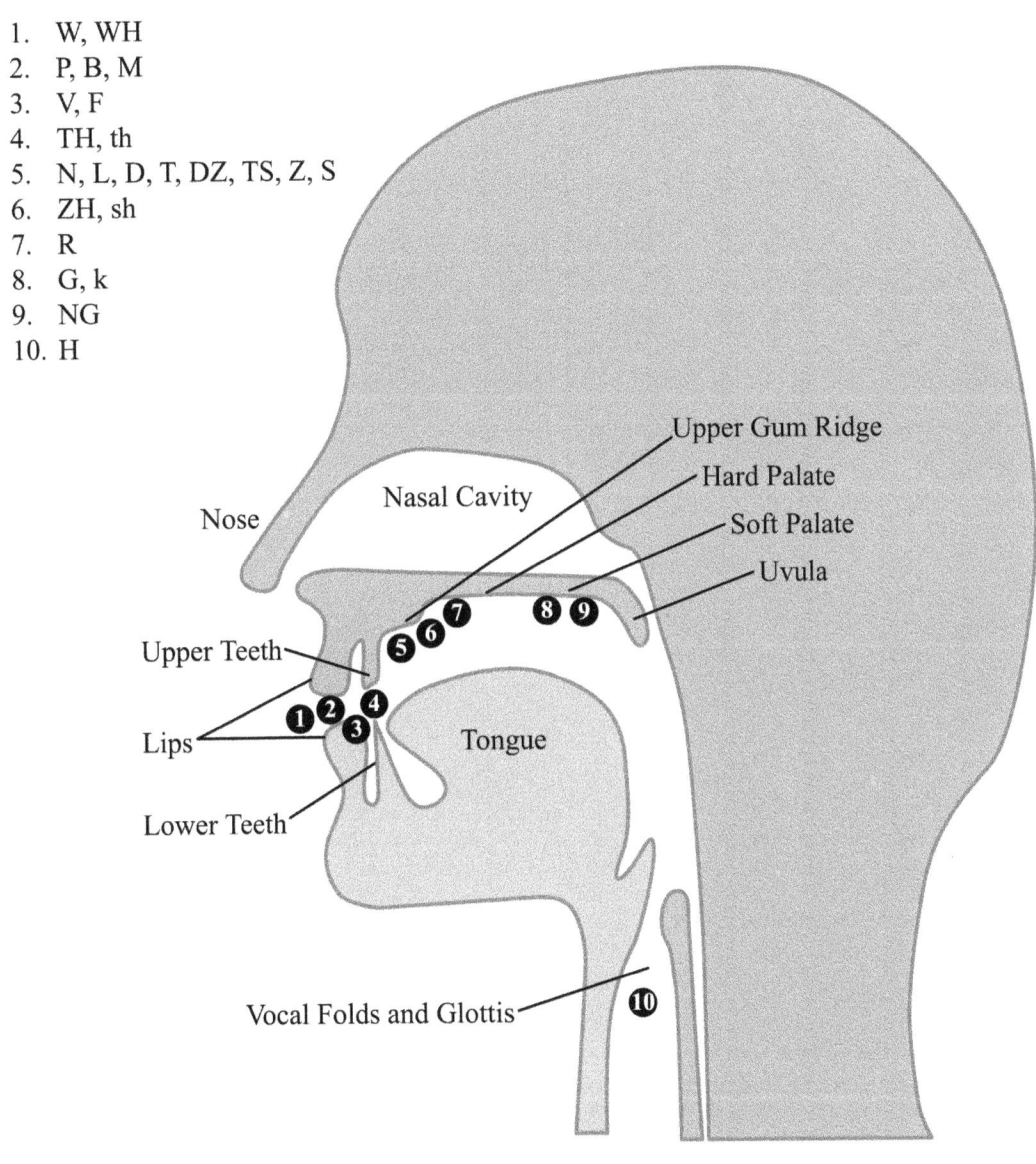

[16] Illustration: © 2020 Aimee Blesing based on an original illustration Laubach Literacy International ©1989

Human vocal organs and points of articulation for identifying parts of the tongue[17]

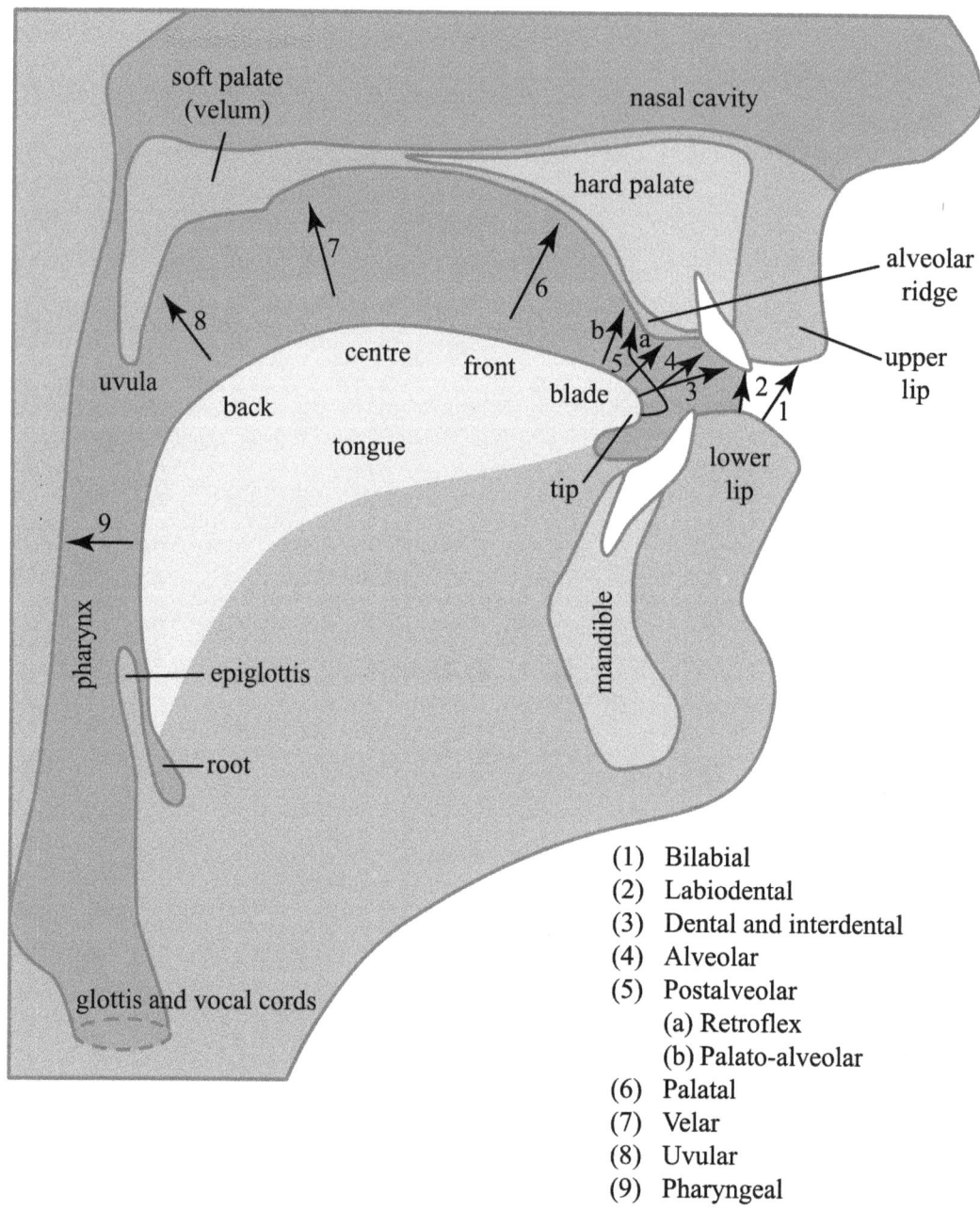

(1) Bilabial
(2) Labiodental
(3) Dental and interdental
(4) Alveolar
(5) Postalveolar
   (a) Retroflex
   (b) Palato-alveolar
(6) Palatal
(7) Velar
(8) Uvular
(9) Pharyngeal

© Encyclopaedia Britannica, Inc.

---

[17] https://www.britannica.com/science/phonetics August 9, 2021

The Sustainable Consonants

The N [n] as in *Nan*

The GA N is a sustainable, voiced consonant and, thus, can be hummed for as long as you can exhale. Because the N sound occurs frequently in the language, a clear N consonant will help to give you clear speech.

To create the N consonant:

1. First, place the relaxed, flat tongue blade rim (front of the tongue)[18] gently on the upper gum ridge (alveolar ridge/ hard palate), the ceiling of the oral cavity behind the upper front teeth.

2. Open and relax your lips comfortably.

3. Now, with your tongue in this position simply hum *(N~~~~)* and you will feel vibrations at the contact point where the tongue and upper gum ridge touch, which will also spread up into the nasal bone, and even to the forehead. This is your N consonant.

Useful tips:

- When you create the N consonant, you should be able to see the bottom of your tongue in the mirror, because the tip of your tongue is contacting the gum ridge behind the top teeth.

- The key to a clear N sound is relaxing the lips and allowing your **tongue blade front rim** to gently touch the upper **gum ridge** while the rest of the tongue rests gently near the floor of the mouth.

Notes: ....

....

....

....

....

---

[18] Refer to the illustrations on pages 23-24 from this point onward for clarification of locations and anatomy.

Sustainable 'Opportunities'

1. In speech, we typically have enough energy at the beginning of words for consonants to be clear. However, in the middle of words, at the ends of words and before other consonants, energy can be lacking, and so those consonants might be ignored or only partially experienced.

2. So, we want to feel sensation at the point of contact whenever we produce the sustainable consonant found in the middle and ends of words as well. Lessac described this concept as enjoying/including the **'Playable Opportunities'**[19], and so he assigned an orchestral musical instrument for each GA English consonant sound.

3. However, since not all students of English are familiar with the musical instruments found in a Western-Style orchestra, in this book, we will refer to this 'playing' as creating **'Sustainable Opportunities'** for held and lengthened consonants such as N, L, M, NG, F, V, S, Z, TH, SH, and ZH; and **'Tapped Opportunities'** for unsustainable or short, tapped consonants such as B, D, G, P, T, K, CH, DG, DZ, and TS.

4. So, to remind yourself to create a lengthened, rich, and clear N sound, place a *double-underline* and sustain the N sound in the following places:

   - Before Another Consonant: co<u>n</u>sonant, Su<u>n</u>day
   - Before a pause or punctuation: When I talked to Joh<u>n</u>, he was do<u>n</u>e.

5. But we *don't need* to mark the N at the word-initial positions (at the beginning of words) or before a vowel sound (even if it's in the following word) because we typically do not ignore or forget them in these positions.

   Examples: nice, no, new, initial, innate, enable, when I, then all, in order

6. Remember: if you *feel* it, your listeners will ***hear*** it!

For the Sustainable Consonant Exploration, explore with the following progression:

a. Hum on the double-underlined N sound for about 4 to 5 seconds in length,

b. Repeat the word, and this time, shorten the hum to about 2-3 seconds in length.

c. Now repeat one more time, at a general conversational speed of about 1-2 seconds in length.

---

[19] *The Use and Training of the Human Voice: A Bio-dynamic Approach to Vocal Life 3rd Edition* by Arthur Lessac McGraw-Hill Higher Education Publishing ©1997 p.73

Ex[20].1   In the following words, explore the N consonant by *double-underlining* the N spelling and sustaining the N sound in 'playable or sustainable opportunities' (before another consonant and before a pause or punctuation). The first 5 words are marked for you.

N[en], men, pen, in, pin, fun, sun, won, done, noon, moon, under, stand, one, ten, seven, nine, eleven, thirteen, hundred, thousand, million, billion, fine, line, mine, sign, shine, find, kind, bind, behind, grind, print, supine, brain, drain, train, main, mainly, maintain, maintenance, crane, plan, down, town, downtown, found, sound, round, around, resound, profound, mission, expression, impression, nation, education, clarification, addition

The Silent N

1. The final N in the following words is not pronounced.

   Autumn [ˈɔtəm]
   Column [ˈkɒləm]
   Condemn [kənˈdɛm]

2. However, the same final N is pronounced before the adjectival suffixes.

   Autumnal [ɔˈtʌmnəl]
   columnar [kəˈlʌmnɚ]
   condemnation [kɒndɛmˈneɪʃən]

Notes: ....

....

....

....

....

....

---

[20] 'Ex.' will stand for 'Exploration' or 'Experiment' not 'Exercise' throughout this text. We encourage you to engage with the curiosity of exploring and experimenting and not with the rote drill of exercise.

Ex. 2   Explore the N sound in the following sentences by *double-underlining* the N spelling and sustaining the N sound in the sustainable opportunity. The first two sentences are marked for you.

- Can you pronounce the word "pronunciation" clearly?

- Nine women attended a luncheon/[21] in the Triple Nine Restaurant downtown.

- Japan and Taiwan, along with Korea and Mainland China, are Far East Asian countries.

- Online collaboration sounds convenient for the scientists working in various locations.

- It is only nine in the evening. The Seven-Eleven stores should still be open.

- When I was seven, eight, or nine, I used to be frightened of thunderstorms.

- Martin sustained his N sounds when he said, 'One hundred.'

Notes: ....

....

....

....

....

....

....

....

....

....

....

---

[21] This symbol / indicates a pause for emphasis or for breath.

Ex. 3　　　　Explore the N sound in the following songs by paying attention to the Sustainable Opportunities (before a dissimilar consonant, before a pause or punctuation). *Double-Underline* the N̲.

Remember:

- Keep your lips slightly parted when making the N sound. When you close your lips, you are making a different consonant---the M sound.

- You do not need to sustain the N sound before a vowel, but you still want to feel the slight buzzy vibration the N creates on your gum ridge.

O My Darlin' Clementine

In a cavern, in a canyon,
Excavating for a mine
Dwelt a miner forty niner,
And his daughter Clementine.

O my darlin', O my darlin'
O my darlin' Clementine.
You are lost and gone forever
Dreadful sorry, Clementine.

(Percy Montrose, 1884)[22]

Amazing Grace

Amazing grace, how sweet the sound
That saved a wretch like me.
I once was lost, but now am found,
Was blind but now I see.[23]

(Lyrics by John Newton, 1772, Melody William Walker 1835)

---

[22] "O My Darling, Clementine" is a popular American Western folk ballad that is most often attributed to performers like Percy Montrose and Barker Bradford. Its origins, however, lie in an 1863 tune by H.S. Thompson called "Down By the River Liv'd a Maiden." Like "Clementine," the song is a mock-serious ode to the narrator's deceased lover, who drowned after she stubbed her toe and fell in the river.

[23] "Amazing Grace" https://en.wikipedia.org/wiki/Amazing_Grace a hymn published in 1779 with words written in 1772 by English Anglican clergyman and poet John Newton (1725–1807). It is an immensely popular hymn, particularly in the United States, where it is used for both religious and secular purposes.

When the Saints Go Marching in

O when the saints-- go marching in
O when the saints-- go marching in
O how I want to be in that number,
When the saints go marching in.[24]

(African American Spiritual)

Notes: ....

....

....

....

....

....

....

....

....

....

....

....

....

....

....

....

---

[24] "When the Saints Go Marching In", often referred to as simply "The Saints", is an African American spiritual. Though it originated as a hymn, it is often played by jazz bands. This song was famously recorded on May 13, 1938, by Louis Armstrong and his orchestra.
https://en.wikipedia.org/wiki/When_the_Saints_Go_Marching_In

The M [m] as in *Mom*

The M is a *sustainable voiced consonant* created between gently closed lips.

To create the M Consonant:

1. Gently close your lips together without pressing tightly or hiding your lips.

2. Keep some space between the upper and lower side teeth and rest the relaxed tongue on the floor of the oral cavity.

3. A gentle vibration will be created at the point of contact, where the lips meet *(M~~~)*, and the vibration will travel through your lips, nasal bone, and forehead. This is your M consonant.

Useful tips:

• Gently hum and stop, and again hum and stop to appreciate the vibration from the M sound (M~~~~, M~~~~).

• Actively seek the vibrations of the M and move to the next sound or word *only* when you are sure to have felt as much of the vibrations as you can.

• **Reminder: explore these three variations of sustaining the M:**

   a. By humming on the *double-underlined* M sound for a 4 - 5 seconds length,

   b. Then repeat the M in the word, this time for a shorter time (2-3 seconds length)

   c. Then repeat the word again, this time for a typical conversational speed (1- 2 second length).

   d. Remember: if you *feel* it, people will *hear* it!

Notes: ....

....

....

....

....

Ex. 1   Explore the M sound in the Sustainable Opportunities (before another consonant and before a pause or punctuation) by *double-underlining* the M and sustaining the sound. The first two lines are marked for you.

Feel free to mark the N we have just learned to explore as a Sustainable Opportunity as well.

come, from, am, time, lime, name, game, fame, same, him, some, sometimes, somewhere, Sam, somehow, someone, something, problem, team, seem, seam, drum, become, atom, autumn, them, alarm, became, anthem, compliment, complain, condemn, crumb, farm, harm, film, freedom, income, minimum, palm, momentum, perfume, poem, sum, supreme, Tom, Pam, Cambodia, Vietnam, addendum, improve, embarrass, amphitheater

Ex. 2   Explore the M consonant by double-underlining and lengthening that sound where there are sustainable opportunities (before another consonant and before a pause or punctuation). The first four lines are marked for you.

- Tom's job is matching names to the picture from time to time.

- Dom and Sam have the same last name!

- Pam Cunningham, somehow, will overcome some of her problems someday.

- Birmingham's about 30 minutes away from Pelham.

- Ramsey said he will do his homework at his home sometime this weekend.

- Sometimes, the mail to the University of Birmingham, England comes to the University of Alabama at Birmingham, USA. Isn't that something?

- James says sometime in the past, somehow, he dreamed the same dream that he had dreamed before, and in that dream, he frantically tried to solve the same math problems as before.

Ex. 3	Explore the M consonant in the following *dialogue* (by *double-underlining* and sustaining the M on Sustainable Opportunities). Mark the N we have explored so far as well. The first two exchanges of dialogue are marked for you.

Minami: Yong-nam, do you know how to make kimuchi?

Yong-nam: You mean kimchi?

Minami: Yeah, kimchi. I decided to learn how to make kimchi because I heard that it was famous as an excellent source of fermented food. So, I searched out the recipe from the Internet and tried to make it with my Korean roommate, but it did not turn out to be as yummy as your mother's kimchi that you brought from your home. I wonder if you really know the secret of authentic home-made kimchi.

Yong-nam: Hmm....The secret of making authentic home-made kimchi.

Minami: Any problem?

Yong-nam: Yeah, kind of. The problem is that I only know how to *eat* kimchi, not sure how to *make* it. I saw my mom making kimchi, but never paid close attention to how she did it exactly.

Minami: That *is* the problem. I am crazy about your mom's kimchi but don't know how to make it. I sometimes buy kimchi from the stores, but somehow, it is not the same.

Yong-nam: True. Moms make food with love for their family but the main purpose of stores making them is to make money. Stores can't compete with moms when it comes to the home-made quality.

Minami: You are right. I'd like to be able to make kimchi as wholesome and as delicious as your mom's someday.

Yong-nam: I am looking forward to tasting your home-made kimchi someday. Meanwhile, let me see if I can call home sometime this weekend and get the recipe from my mom for her famous kimchi.

Minami: Awesome! I am looking forward to your mom's special kimchi recipe.

Ex. 4

Explore the M in the following story by *double-underlining* and sustaining it where there are Sustainable opportunities. You can mark the N consonant that we have learned as well. The first sentence is marked for you.

Visiting Museums at Birmingham

Last Sunday, Min and Kim from New Hampshire came to visit us in Birmingham. After picking them up from the airport and having lunch at a Vietnamese rice-noodle restaurant in downtown Birmingham, my husband and I took them to the Birmingham Museum of Art and the nearby Martin Luther King Memorial Museum. To our surprise, we were able to visit the Martin Luther King Memorial Museum without paying the entrance fee because the museum does not charge an entrance fee on Sundays. Min and Kim both said the exhibitions at both museums were awesome. In the evening, they wanted to go to the Galleria Mall to walk off their heavy lunch meals and look around the stores. This was no problem. My husband Jim and I were happy to spend time with them. Min's husband, Kim, bought a golf T-shirt there. He said that he bought the same brand of shirt at the same department chain in another city when he visited last time. We all agreed to take Min and Kim to the Oak Mountain Golf Course in Pelham near Birmingham tomorrow morning. So, I made an appointment for a 7 a.m. tee-time.

Notes: ....
....
....
....
....
....
....
....
....

The L [l] as in *Lily*

The L consonant is a voiced sustainable sound. It does not have any voiceless counterpart in GA English.

To create the L Consonant:

1. Open your mouth gently so that there is enough space for your tongue to move freely.

2. Lightly touch the upper gum ridge (alveolar ridge) with the tip of your tongue. The sides of your tongue will feel slightly firm. (See page 24 for illustration)

3. Then, *hum (L~~~)* as you maintain this tongue-gum ridge contact point and feel the vibration. This is your L consonant.

Useful tips:

- Another option: First, create the [n] sound and then detach the side rims of the tongue blade leaving just the tongue tip on the gum ridge.

- For a clear L consonant, tongue-gum ridge contact point is crucial.

- Like the N consonant, you can see the underside of your tongue in the mirror when making the L consonant.

- The L consonant involves only the tongue tip and upper gum ridge—no tongue blade

- Lips are not rounded, but remain neutral, soft, and cushiony to the touch.

- Feel the L vibration on the gum ridge, moving up into the nasal bone and forehead.

Note: Some language speakers tend to round their lips and produce a [w] or [u] sound when they intend to create the L consonant. For example: 'cold' may sound like 'code' and 'culture' may sound like 'cow-ture' which don't sound like the GA English words they mean to convey.

Notes:...

....

....

....

Ex. 1   By singing the following song, explore the location of your upper gum ridge (alveolar ridge or hard palate behind the upper front teeth) and tongue tip contact point, and the movements of your tongue for the L sound. If you are not familiar with the song, visit the website in the footnote below to hear it.

Deck the Halls

Deck the ha<u>ll</u>s with boughs of holly, fa-la-la-la-la, la-la-la-la
'Tis the season to be jolly, fa-la-la-la-la, la-la-la-la
Do<u>n</u> we now our gay appare<u>l</u>, fa-la-la, la-la-la, la-la-la
Tro<u>ll</u> the ancient Yu<u>l</u>etide carol, fa-la-la-la-la, la-la-la-la.

(Thomas Oliphant, 1862)[25]

Reminder: explore these three variations of sustaining the L:

1. By humming on the *double-underlined* L sound for a 4 - 5 seconds length,

2. Then repeat the L in the word, this time for a shorter time (2-3 seconds length)

3. Repeat again, this time for a typical conversational speed (1- 2 second length).

4. Remember: if you *feel* it, people will *hear* it!

Ex. 2   In the next several experiments, explore the L sound by double-underlining the spelling of the L and sustaining the sound in sustainable positions (before another consonant and before a pause or punctuation). The first line is marked for you.

coo<u>l</u>, poo<u>l</u>, too<u>l</u>, schoo<u>l</u>, mu<u>l</u>e, molecu<u>l</u>e,
coal, mole, hole, sole, toll, whole, control,
all, ball, call, fall, hall, mall, tall, Paul,
bell, fell, gel, smell, sell, tell, well, yell,
bill, chill, fill, mill, pill, still, hill, will, grill, April,
heel, kneel, seal, steel, conceal, feel, meal, peel, reveal, wheel,
beautiful, careful, colorful, thankful, grateful, bulb, film, overwhelm

---

25 * https://www.liveabout.com/deck-the-halls-traditional-1322574 Jones, J. & Oliphant, T, *Welsh Melodies*, Vol. 2, 1862 Deck the Halls. August 8, 2021

Schwa [ə] Sound before the Final Syllable /-al/ Spelling—the syllabic L [!]

In the spellings /bl/, /pl/ and in some words where a consonant before the L is silent, the L functions as a *syllabic L*—which means it will be pronounced as [əl], by adding an unstressed schwa [ə] sound, which is a *neutral vowel*. A syllabic consonant is a consonant that can form an entire syllable on its own, without any vowel spelling. So *'bubble'* will be felt and sounded as *'bubbəl'*. All words in this next section will be pronounced with the [əl].

bubble, trouble, rubble, marble, warble, cobble, double, foible, liable, people, triple, principle, castle*, wrestle*, hassle, muscle

Silent T

Ex. 3   Continue to feel the syllabic L in these sentences—underline where it is playable or sustainable (meaning before another consonant made in a different place or at a pause). The first sentence is marked for you. Feel free to mark the N and M too.

- The Hubble telescope cobbled together vivid pictures of the galaxies of distant planets.

- We had no trouble making bubbles for the baby's bath.

- Double trouble is what you are, Mr. Stubble!

- The castle has been reduced to rubble since the earthquake.

- That government of the people, by the people, for the people, shall not perish from the earth.

Notes: ....

....

....

....

....

....

....

Ex. 4   In the following words and sentences, explore the final /-al/ syllable by moving quickly from the consonant directly before the /-al/ to the L and through it. Again, there will be a very short schwa [ə] sound. The first several words are marked in italics for that final syllable.

abdomin*al*, addition*al*, anatomic*al*, biblic*al*, chemic*al*, clinic*al*, congression*al*, critic*al*, educ*al*, emotion*al*, fin*al*, function*al*, geologic*al*, geographic*al*, government*al*, hypothetic*al*, institution*al*, international, interpersonal, intestinal, journal, judicial, longitudinal, metal, national, neurological, occupational, original, organizational, physical, professional, recreational, statistical, rational, spinal, sectional, theoretical, traditional, vital, vocational

- The anatomical dissection of a butterfly is an additional and final task for this class.

- Phil complained of abdominal pain after his chemical lab session.

- I am taking International Studies, Interpersonal Relations, Occupational Therapy, and Professional Horticulture classes this semester.

- Yuan goes through an annual physical check-up at the National Health Center.

- Jackie will be more functional and vital by April; however, she could use an additional month to improve her physical condition.

- We have been experiencing various physical, geographical, and environmental changes.

- Various rules of linguistic and phonological characteristics of each language affect the phenomena of pronunciation for English language learners in the academic and professional communities.

Notes: ....

....

....

....

....

Ex. 5   Explore the L sound on the following words and sentences by *double underlining* and sustaining the sounds on the Sustainable opportunities. The first line is marked for you.

elf, golf, gulf, child, wild, bold, cold, hold, fold, gold, mold, sold, told, involve, grilled, guild, called, help, health, fulfill, dealt, adult, result, default, difficult, smiled, illness, enrollment, himself, wholesome.

- Miss Pelf, a golf maniac, played golf in a tournament at the Gulf Shores Golf Course.

- The child smiled while watching his dad grilling wild Alaskan salmon.

- It is not so difficult to figure out the default bold feature.

- The class enrollment will start soon in the Philadelphia school system.

Notes:...
....
....
....
....
....
....
....
....
....
....
....
....

Ex. 6   Explore the L consonant in *word-initial positions* and *before vowels*. Remember, we do not sustain the sound on the word initial positions or anywhere within a word before a vowel, so we do *not* have to underline it.

lab, lap, land, lamp, last, lady, late, lately, lead, later, leg, let, lens, less, left, length, lender, legitimate, lit, list, limit, lily, live, light, likely, line, lively, liberty, legal, lot, love, long, lose, loan

Feel and pronounce the L *without* marking or sustaining before a vowel

Alex, Billy, belly, belief, biology, college, close, clean, clear, clarity, clinic, California, civilize, declare, delete, delegate, delicious, delirium, delivery, excellent, elevator, electronic, Italy, include, intelligent, usually, family, felony, Florida, galaxy, glorious, hilarious, melody, Molly, molecule, molecular, nullify, nationalize, knowledge, polarity, popular, plastic, relief, relationship, selection, specialist, yellow, telephone, village

- College is for knowledge.

- Yellow is Sally's favorite color.

- Haley got a telephone call from Italy.

- Sally and Malley are in line to buy tickets for the movie 'The Sky Line'.

- Larry will travel to California, Louisiana, Alabama, and Florida this fall.

- Hillary specializes in polarity and molarities in a molecular biology lab.

- Paul left early because he had to go to his ophthalmologist.

- Melody Marlene, a language learner, intelligently included clarity.

Notes: ....
....
....

The Silent L

The L spellings in the following examples are silent (not pronounced).

- cou*l*d, shou*l*d, wou*l*d

- ha*l*f, beha*l*f, ca*l*f

- ba*l*k, ca*l*k (cau*l*k), ta*l*k, wa*l*k, fo*l*k, Po*l*k, yo*l*k, Wa*l*ker, Fau*l*kner, Linco*l*n

- ca*l*m, pa*l*m, psa*l*m

- sa*l*mon, a*l*mond

The Consonant L pronounced as [ɹ]

In this word, the /l/ spelling is pronounced as R.

- co*l*onel [kəɾnəl]

The L Blends

The pronunciation of the L consonant combined with another consonant at the beginning of a syllable or word is called L-blend.

To pronounce the L-blend, proceed from the first consonant to the L and to the vowel sound without stopping between the first and second consonants of the blend.

blow, blend, bless, blind, blood, blur, clay, claim, clean, clan, glean, glow, flood, glad, glass, glaze, play, plain, slay, slow, slide, slurp, sloppy, slope, slime

Notes: ....
....
....
....
....
....
....

Ex. 7   Explore the *silent* L in the following sentences. It will be *italicized*. The voiced L consonant will have a *double underline* if it is in the playable position (before a differently placed consonant or a punctuation mark).

- Ca*l*m down, Co*l*onel Fau*l*kner, just wa*l*k and ta*l*k for ha*l*f an hour, we will be at our final destination--The Wa*l*ker Fo*l*k Village.

- I wou*l*d if I cou*l*d, but I am not at all sure whether I shou*l*d.

- I wou*l*d like to have baked sa*l*mon with slivered a*l*monds, please.

- Dates, coconuts, and pa*l*m oil are all from different breeds of pa*l*m trees.

- Psa*l*m 23 is one of the most beautiful psa*l*ms.

- On beha*l*f of Mr. McClain, Coach Wa*l*ker declared the ha*l*f-time of the game.

Ex. 8   Explore the L consonant in the following by sustaining the L on Sustainable Opportunities. We added M and N too.

Health Services Administration

Health Services Administration is a large academic field, focusing either on strategies or health services research, which involve the strategies of the health care organizations, including organizational behavior. But the Health Services Administration mainly deals with health care organizations such as nursing homes, hospitals, and many other healthcare facilities.

Adapted from Ferhat Zengul, Health Services Administration, University of Alabama at Birmingham

Notes: ....

....

....

....

....

42

Ex. 9   In the following *dialogue*, explore the L sound by *double-underlining* the sustainable <u>L</u> before another consonant, pause, or punctuation. See if you can find the <u>one</u> silent L and mark it with a *single underline*. The first 3 lines are marked for you.

Yue: What is your major?

Ben: My major is medica<u>l</u> sociology.

Yue: What is medica<u>l</u> sociology, and what do you actually study in that discipline?

Ben: Medical sociology was established as a specialized field in the United States during the 1940s. It is concerned with social causes and consequences of health and illness, and with the application of sociological theory and research methods to the study related to health and the health care system.

Yue: I see. What areas are included in medical sociology?

Ben: The major areas of medical sociology include the social facets of health and diseases, the social behavior of health care personnel and their clients, the social functions of health organizations and institutions, the social patterns of health services, and the relationship of health care delivery systems to other systems such as economy and politics.

Yue: For such studies, what assumptions take place in medical sociology?

Ben: Medical sociology assumes that social factors, such as socioeconomic status, gender, ethnicity, lifestyles, and high-risk behavior, play a critical role in determining or influencing the health of individuals, groups, and larger societies. Social factors also are important in influencing the way societies organize their resources in order to cope with health hazards and deliver medical care to the population at large.

Yue: What sort of job opportunities would the graduates of medical sociology find?

Ben: Since Medical Sociology has an applied focus with relevance for policy and health service delivery at the community, regional, societal, and global levels, graduates from medical sociology hold teaching positions not only in sociology departments, but also in public health, medical, and nursing schools. In addition, they are employed as researchers in public and private health agencies and in health-related industries such as insurance, and hospital management companies. I love teaching as well as research, so I would like to apply for teaching positions in universities in the future.

Yue: Thank you for sharing this information with me, and I wish you the best in your professional endeavor.

(Adapted from an essay by Yue Cao, Graduate Student, Department of Sociology, University of Alabama at Birmingham)

Ex. 10   In the following story, explore the L, M and N sounds by *double-underlining* and sustaining the sounds when they are Sustainable Opportunities (before another consonant, pause or punctuation). Watch out for the Silent L sounds, which are *italicized*. Half of the first paragraph has been marked for you.

I met confidence on a Golf Course

For golfers, "good weather" means good weather to play golf. This winter, the New Year's holidays were as warm as April in Birmingham, Alabama. Of course, I was not about to miss this golden opportunity. So, today my husband and I drove to the Oak Mountain State Park golf course near Birmingham. Here, we can play a nine-hole course for ten dollars during the week, which is not bad at all for occasional exercise. By the time we arrived at the pro-shop, the parking lot was crowded with the patrons' cars, and the first tee was also crowded with golfers waiting for their turns. Four teams were in front of us. My husband and I were teamed up with a father and his teenage son who were waiting for their turn in a golf cart. But I usually wa*l*k with my golf bag on my shoulders so I can pinch a few pennies as well as add to my exercise routine.

The marshal advised the golfers not to go onto the driving range as there was no way he cou*l*d estimate how quickly the games before us wou*l*d proceed. He said we might have to wait for roughly 45 minutes to an hour before we cou*l*d hit our first ball. So, I killed some time by warming up with one of the longest clubs for about 10 minutes, but even then, many people were still waiting before we could start. Then I began to pay attention to some of the waiting golfers because people-watching is fun for me. This southern city of Birmingham has become internationally known in recent years for its golfing. There were all kinds of people from all over the world here today. However, compared with other times, there were more female golfers today. One of the teams before us included four middle-aged ladies, and one of them caught my eye. Because of the unusually warm weather, she was wearing only a short sleeve T-shirt and shorts. Interestingly, one of her legs was made of a shiny metal bar. On her feet she had socks and shoes.

She and her team members did not choose to ride carts but to wa*l*k. And they didn't have any pull-carts. This meant that they would carry their own golf bags on their shoulders. Watching these ladies ta*l*king to each other waiting for their turn, I silently applauded this special lady for playing golf and dressing like any other person on a warm, sunny day.

After a while, I lost sight of that team. But I kept on applauding her for her courage, freedom, and confidence.

Carryover into real life:

Today and for the next few days, choose a block of time (15-20 minutes) during the day or evening to focus on feeling the consonants that we have covered and include them in conversations with family, friends, and co-workers.

Notes:..

....

....

....

....

....

....

....

....

....

....

....

....

....

....

....

....

....

....

....

The NG [ŋ] as in *Sing*

The NG [ŋ] is a sustainable nasal sound. In the English language, the NG does not occur in the word-initial positions.

To create the NG Consonant:

1. Inhale as if you are going to yawn, feel that generous opening inside your mouth (oral cavity)

2. Rest your tongue on the bottom of the oral cavity while the tip contacts the lower front teeth.

3. Raise the back of the tongue[26] to contact the location gently but firmly on the hard palate where it joins the soft palate. *Hum* while keeping your tongue in this position *(NG~~~)*. This is your NG sound.

Useful tips:

*   This sound is made in the same place where G [g] and K [k] are made.

*   Feel the NG vibrations in the nose, through the head and where the tongue touches the roof of the mouth. Experiment with removing and replacing the tongue in this position to feel the vibrations. This will sound like NG-AH-NG-AH.

*   Remember, if you can *feel* it, people can *hear* it.

Ex. 1   Create a rich and vibrant NG sound (without adding a [g] sound at the end) in the following words by *double-underlining* and sustaining the NG sound. The first line is marked for you.

sing, song, sang, long, lung, king, ring, zing, ping, pong, bang, ding, dong, wing, young, making, running, mixing, putting, going, singing, banging, explaining, learning, mimicking, bringing.

---

[26] Again, refer to the illustrations pgs. 23-24 in this text for clarification.

Ex. 2   Create a rich and vibrant NG sound in the following songs (by *double-underlining* and sustaining the NG, and by doing the same for consonants we have explored so far). The first two lines are marked for you.

Ding Dong Merrily on High

Ding dong merrily on high,
In heav'n the bells are ringing:

Ding dong! verily the sky
Is riv'n with angels singing. ('angels' contains an N followed by the DG sound)
Gloria, Hosanna in excelsis.

(George Ratcliffe Woodward, 1924)[27]

I'm Gonna Sing When the Spirit Says Sing

I'm gonna sing when the Spirit says sing,
I'm gonna sing when the Spirit says sing,
I'm gonna sing when the Spirit says sing,
And obey the spirit of the Lord.

(Traditional African American Spiritual)[28]

Notes: ....

....

....

....

....

....

....

[27] https://en.wikipedia.org/wiki/Ding_Dong_Merrily_on_High
[28] https://www.stantons.com/scores/C/M/9/5/2/0/cfn-cm9520.pdf

Dialogue: **When is there a G[g] consonant after NG[ŋ]?**

Ming: Do you say 'sing.er' or 'sing.ger' And do you say 'fing.er' or 'fing.ger'?

Jonghee: Whether 'to add or not to add' a [g] sound after the NG is the question, isn't it?

Ming: Yes. That is an issue, at least for me.

Jonghee: Let me explain with a few examples. First, let's look at the word 'singer.' It is made of the verb 'sing' and the suffix 'er,' right?

Ming: Right.

Jonghee: The verb 'sing' ends with the NG sound and is an actual word with a meaning we recognize. In this case, the English language does not add a [g] after NG.

Let's look at another example. The verb 'ringing' comes from an actual word 'ring' and adds the suffix 'ing' And here, again, no extra [g] before 'ing' because the 'ing' has a meaning in common with 'ring'. If you ring a bell, you are 'ringing the bell'.

Ming: That's clear to me.

Jonghee: Now let's look at a different example. The word 'English' has an NG sound in the middle of the word. However, the syllable 'Eng' is not an actual word in English that we know of. So, in this case, the [g] sound is added after the NG sound before the syllable 'lish.'

Ming: Let me see if I can repeat this in my own words. The 'Eng' part of 'English' is not a real English word. So, we add the [g] sound after the NG before completing the word. Right?

Jonghee: Right! Now let's look at the word 'single'. This word is not a combination of the word 'sing' and the suffix 'le' because 'sing' is a word in English, but when you add the 'le', that 'le' does NOT have a meaning in common with the 'sing'; it creates something new, which has nothing to do with singing—so an extra [g] sound is added after the NG.

Ming: Ah, now I've got it for sure.

Jonghee: So, let's remember this. The simple guideline on the extra [g] sound is that if the portion of the word that contains the medial NG sound has **no meaning** on its own as related to the entire word, add the extra [g] sound.

Ming:	Then, let me see if I can explain the case of the word 'singing'. Since 'sing' is an actual word in the English language, and the suffix 'ing' is added to it—and has a meaning in common with it, I should not add the extra [g] sound after the "sing" portion. Right?
Jonghee:	Well done!
Ming:	Now, let me see if I could think of some examples of both cases, WITH or WITHOUT an extra [g] sound after the NG [ŋ] sound.

- Without an added [g]: singer, ringer, singing, ringing, bringing

- With an added [g]: Eng(g)lish, fing(g)er, bong(g)o, ang(g)le, dang(g)le, jing(g)le, ming(g)le, ang(g)er, hung(g)er, hung(g)ry

Jonghee:	Excellent. The ability to distinguish the pronunciation of the NG sound with or without the extra [g] following it makes a big difference in how clear your speech is.

The NG consonant is created when the /N/ meets the /K/

Ming:	Now, I have another question. I see that the word 'sink' or 'think' is spelled with the N, but I hear people pronouncing the N portion as NG. Which way should it be? —N before K as N or as NG?
Jonghee:	The answer to your question is to pronounce the N before a K as an NG.
	The reason for this is that we tend to think ahead, preparing for the next sound as we are speaking. So, when we are articulating the N sound, we are thinking ahead for the K sound, which is pronounced where the soft palate (on the roof of the mouth at the upper back) joins the hard palate with the back of the tongue. So the nasal consonant N is pronounced as the nasal NG on the soft palate instead of the upper gum ridge.
Ming:	Because my First language does not differentiate the N from NG, I would like to learn how to produce the English NG consonant, so that I can feel the difference.
Jonghee:	Well, try the following words with just the N sound. Perhaps you may feel that it is more difficult to move from the N to the K. Now, repeat the same words pronouncing the spelling of the N as our new NG [ŋ] sound. You will feel the presence and the richness of the NG [ŋ] before moving forward to the next sound. And it may even be easier to move forward. Now read the 'ink, link, and sink' with the N pronounced as an N.

Ming:	in-k, kin-k, lin-k.

Jonghee: And now explore with the N pronounced as NG.

Ming: ingk, kingk, lingk.

Jonghee: Which way seemed more economical to you?

Ming: The NG way.

Jonghee: Can you tell me why?

Ming: It took some effort to change the position of my tongue from the N placement to the K position in my mouth.

Jonghee: Why do you feel it is less economical when your tongue goes from the N to K in this case? And more economical to go from NG to K?

Ming: I am not quite sure, but I feel that it's easier and smoother to make the K sound after the NG.

Jonghee: That's because the NG and the K are made in the same place—the back of the tongue placed where the hard and soft palate meet. It is easier to move from one consonant or sound to the next when the second is made in the same place as the first sound. Now let's try to pronounce the N as an NG in the following words.

Ink, kink, link, mink, pink, rink, sink, think, wink, zinc, bank, tank, sank, thank, yank, crank, frank, dunk, chunk, conquer

Ex. 3   Explore the NG [ŋ] sound in the following sentences by *double-underlining* and sustaining the sound on the Sustainable Opportunities (before another consonant, a pause or punctuation).

For the purposes of identification, we will use this **symbol: [ŋ]** for the **N spelling** of the consonant **blend NG.**

- The singer sang a long happy song/ in the concert.

- The husband of the English queen/ is not the king of England.

- I think the kitchen sink is leaking.

- The singer's parents were thankful that their son was a singer, not a sinner at this event.

Ex. 4   Explore the sustainable opportunities of the NG sound in the following story. Watch for the opportunities to pronounce the extra [g] sound as well. Mark the consonant sounds we have learned so far. The first two sentences are marked for you.

Sun-Young's Most Exciting Summer Travel Plan

Sun-Young is going to sing in a Kingston Symphony Orchestra Chorus in the upcoming spring concert during her university's spring break. Before joining this group, she was passing by a bulletin board at the Music Building of her university and happened to notice a flier announcing the upcoming Spring Concert of the Kingston Symphony Orchestra Chorus, and it was looking for singers. So, by emailing the chorus manager, Sun-Young found out that she had to prepare the song "When the Saints Go Marching In" for her audition. To prepare, Sun-Young had to search through many versions of the same song in different songbooks to find the right key for her voice range. None of the versions in the collections she found matched her range. So, she decided to do some additional searching by visiting her university library and by exploring on YouTube. After testing several options, Sun-Young finally chose one version that seemed right and used it for her audition. The audition went well and one of the judges informed Sun-Young that she had a beautiful voice, and that he would be sending the results of the audition by next Wednesday via email.

Of course, she passed her audition and will be attending weekly rehearsals every Monday from now on until the concert. She is very excited and looking forward to her first rehearsal. And what's more, she now is thinking about joining her University Choral Society, which will be traveling to Europe this summer singing recitals with European choral societies. Sun-Young is looking forward to a most exciting summer!

Notes:...

....

....

....

....

51

Ex. 5　　　　Explore the sustainable opportunities of the NG sound in the following story. Watch for the opportunities to pronounce the extra [g] sound as well as the N spelling pronounced as NG—using the symbol [ŋ] And mark all the consonant sounds we have learned so far. The first paragraph is marked for you.

Learning English Pronunciation

I started learning English in my country when I was thirteen. Even though I have been learning and using English for over ten years, I am having difficulty pronouncing English so that it is easy for Americans to understand. That is because, unlike my First Language, the English alphabet letters can be pronounced in so many different ways instead of just one sound for one letter. For example, I learned that there are about ten ways to pronounce the letter A, and about the same number of ways to pronounce the letter E. And what is more, some sounds are identified by more than one alphabet letter. Oh my!

I also found out that the consonant NG can be pronounced in two ways. When we add a suffix to a word like 'sing', such as sing-*er* or sing-*ing*, we don't add an extra [g] after the NG. But we add a [g] sound after the syllable that contains the NG when the last part of the word has no meaning in common with 'sing', as in 'sing-*gle*', or the syllable with the NG is not a word in English, such as 'Eng-*lish*'.

But I still don't understand why we add an extra [g] after the NG in words that are adjectives such as 'long(g)er' 'long(g)est,' 'strong(g)er,' strong(g) est, 'young(g)er, and 'young(g)est.' Whoever created the English spellings, I wish they had made up their minds or thought ahead of time before they came up with such a rule that will just confuse learners in the centuries to come.

Notes: ....

....

....

....

....

The V [v] as in *Viva*

The V consonant is a sustainable consonant. It is a voiced version of the F [f] consonant.

To create the V[v] consonant:

1. Place the lower edge of the upper front teeth close to the inside moist part of the lower lip so that they gently touch–but air can still escape.

2. Gently exhale the air through the gap between the teeth and the lip as in *(F~~~~)*.

3. Then add a voice by *humming* (creating vibration) to create the *(V~~~)* sound. You will feel it vibrating between your lower lip and upper front teeth as well as vibrating upward into the nose and forehead.

Useful tips:

• If you feel as if your [v] consonant is not evenly and smoothly flowing but sputtering, it might be because the pressure between your lip and the teeth is too strong. Give a little more space and less pressure between the lower lip and the upper front teeth, which might assist smoother flow of the [v] consonant on your lower lip.

• For a more confident and richer [v] consonant, pretend that you are playing with a toy car with a small child, creating the motor sound using the rich "*V~~~~~*" consonant vibration, holding the car in your hand and moving your 'car' back and forth. The action will give you a familiar behavioral approach, which can help the quality of the sound.

Ex. 1   Explore the V consonant in the Sustainable Opportunities by *double-underlining* the spelling and sustaining the sound before another consonant sound and before a pause or punctuation. The first line is marked for you.

love, give, live, have, five, dive, drive, gave, save, grave, nerve, improve, lively, behave, conceive, receive, deceive, believe, approve, positive, tentative, naïve, prove, twelve, valve, involve

Reminder:

Include the other 'sustainable' consonants we have explored so far in our training.

Ex. 2   Explore the *past-tense* verbs that end with the V consonant followed by /-ed/ by *double-underlining* the spelling and sustaining the sound. The first line is marked for you.

loved, lived, gloved, involved, proved, improved, received, believed, delved, conceived, approved, saved, paved, shaved, behaved, dived, revived, resolved

Ex. 3   Explore the V consonant in the word-initial positions and medial positions before a vowel. The V in the beginning of the word and before a vowel is not sustained, and thus, need not be underlined.

very, velvet, victory, vivid, Vivien, visit, viola, vision, village, viscose, Victoria, Victor, virus, violin, vibrate, volatile, volume, volleyball, eleven, never, relatives, paving, clover, David, Travis, Beverly, Denver

Ex. 4   Explore the V consonant in the following sentences by *double-underlining* the spelling and sustaining the sound. Apply the same to other sustainable consonants we have already learned. The first two sentences are marked for you.

- Vivian Reeve's phone number has five fives in it.

- Dave saved a hundred and twelve dollars and five cents in five weeks.

- Beverly Voss was involved in a nerve-racking accident but behaved calmly, which saved her, and the other person involved.

- Is it true that if two negatives make one positive, I can be a positive person when I am doubly negative?

- The executive tentatively approved the improved version of the previously submitted plan for developing a new valve system.

- Vicky lives at Vine Boulevard near Victoria's Vineyard.

Notes: ....
....
....

54

Ex. 5   Explore the V consonant in the following story—*double-underline* the [v] in all sustainable opportunities. Include the previously learned consonants as well. The first two sentences are marked for you.

Vivian and I visited the University Center on the last Wednesday of November to observe the English Pronunciation and Accent workshop class. We have[29] to observe five language classes. However, the instructor of this class invited us to join her class instead of just observing. This was a treat for us since we had not had any opportunities to receive any formal pronunciation lessons, either as speakers of the English language, or as future English teachers. This lack of opportunity served to make me feel unconvinced about teaching English pronunciation to my future students. The most impressive thing about this class was the way the instructor presented 'How to Create the English V Consonant" by inviting her adult students to imagine that they were playing with a toy car, showing it to a little 2-year-old child. When the students pronounced the [v] sound as the imaginary 'running-motor' sound of the car, it was much easier to create the sound with a more rich and vibrant sound quality--even the shyest person in the room, like me, created the most vibrant and focused sound. This class gave me a new insight and motivation as to how to involve my own future students.

Notes: ....

....

....

....

....

....

....

....

....

---

[29] V pronounced as F in the following case: to be required, compelled, or under obligation (followed by infinitival to, with or without a main verb):*I have to leave now.* https://www.dictionary.com/browse/have 12/27/2023.

The F [f] as in *Fluff*

The F is a sustainable, voiceless sound created at the point of contact between the upper front teeth and the lower lip. It is the voiceless version of the V consonant.

To create the F Consonant:

1. With your lips close together but not touching, let the lower edges of the upper front teeth barely touch the moist part of the inside lower lip. This is the point of contact for the F sound.

2. Gently allow air to seep out through the small space between the edge of the upper front teeth and the moist part of the lower lip. *(F~~~~)*. This is your F sound.

Useful tips:

*   Explore the optimum pressure needed between the teeth and lip by exploring various distances for a smooth, continuous, unrestricted flow of sound.

*   Lips are soft and relaxed, and face is neutrally relaxed.

*   Keeping constant even pressure between the teeth and lower lip is the key for the smoothly flowing F consonant.

*   You should feel no more effort than a pleasurable exhale.

*   Feel the warm air flow from the F sound on your palm or the back of the hand.

*   Feel the F sound by saying 'huff' or 'fun.'

Notes: ....

....

....

....

....

....

....

....

Ex. 1   Explore the F consonant by *double-underlining* and sustaining the sound in the Sustainable Opportunities on the following words. *Note: the [f] sound can be spelled as f, ff, gh, or ph.* The first line is marked.

if, life, half, leaf, surf, cuff, giraffe, off, Jeff,

fifty, fifth, fifteen, gift, sift, lift, drift, left, loft,

soft, after, African, safety, conflict, refrigerator, muffler,

face, fun, five, fall, fence, fellow, follow, fantasy, fence, fencing

enough, cough, graph, laugh, rough, tough, lymph,

Joseph, photograph, Rudolph, triumph, endorphin,

photography, philosophy, physiology, photosensitivity

For your information:

Notice how the */gh/* spelling can be pronounced as [p], [f], or silent (not pronounced):

- **gh** [p] hiccough
- **gh** [f] cough, rough
- **gh (silent)** dough, though, brought, taught, thought, through

Ex. 2   In the following, all three are included. See if you can determine the P pronunciation and the silent version. The F sound has been *underlined* for you.

Happy Rudolph's Happy Doughy Project

Yesterday, Rudolph taught his class how to make bread dough.
First, he bought some flour, yeast, salt, and sugar from the store and brought them to class today. As he demonstrated dough-making to his class, a sudden gust of tough hiccoughs erupted out of nowhere and a series of rough-- and tough coughs followed. Rudolph managed to finish his doughy project successfully, though! After the hiccoughs and coughs, Rudolph felt relieved and had a new level of energy. He wondered whether the muscular activities from those hiccoughs and coughs, though they took a relatively short time, could've formed some endorphins in his body! Happy Rudolph-- and happy doughy project!

Ex. 3   Explore the F consonant at the beginning of a word and before a vowel. You do *not* need to underline or sustain the F sound in this exploration.

fan, for, four, fore, five, find, fun, fund, fill, full, fulfill, film, fuse, five, fire, fair, fare, flag, form, force, free, fuel, fever, female, fighter, forty, field, food, first, father, family, fourteen, football, financial, factor, offer, effort, affect, effect, efficient, offensive, difficult, defend, benefit, coffee, safari, significant, solidify, exemplify, dignify, affiliate, beautiful, graceful, confront, confuse, profuse, reform, perfect, professor, traffic elephant, phone, phrase, Phillip, physical, physics, physiology, philosophy, morphology, metamorphosis, philanthropic, atmosphere, ophthalmology

Ex. 4   Explore the F consonant in the following poem.

Jeff Freddy is a Feather-light Fellow

Jeff Freddy is a feather-light fellow, and the feather-light fellow is Jeff.
On February 15, 1555, Jeff took a flying safety test:
Jeff flew fast, and Jeff flew far; Jeff flew high and Jeff flew low.
Jeff huffed and Jeff puffed; Jeff coughed and Jeff laughed.
Jeff finished the flying test safely with a fine score.
He felt fantastic and he felt free.
Jeff Freddy is a feather-light fine fellow with a fine flying score.

Ex. 5   Explore the F consonant in the following sentences by *double- underlining* and sustaining the sound. The first two sentences are marked for you.

•   Yes, we feel safe when flying with Jeff.

•   Phillip laughed softly to himself /after he coughed rough coughs for the fifth time.

•   "That's enough coughing," Rudolph said to himself. "Enough's enough!"

•   The graph-maker's left shirt cuff is left with rough fringes after enough use over half the century in his graph-making business.

•   The new employees' benefit fair informed Buffy that one of the fringe benefits would be two fifteen-minute coffee breaks! Buffy doesn't drink coffee, though!

Ex. 6	Explore the F consonant in the following *dialogue*.

Fay: Hi, I am Fay. How may I help you?

Ralph: Hello, I am Ralph Endolph. My family and I moved here to Fairfield, Florida a few days ago along with my wife, Flora; and I need a Florida driver's license.

Fay: All right. Please fill this form out for me.

Ralph: (Filling out the form) Hey Flora, what is our new address here in Florida?

Flora: Hmm... our address in Florida? Let me look at our folder here. I found it. It is 4454 First Street, Fairfield, Florida.

Ralph: Right. Now I need my phone number.

Flora: Here is your phone number. You know your office number, right?

Ralph: Definitely! I finished filling out my form. When you finish your form, we will take these to the officer at the front desk!

Notes: ....

....

....

....

....

....

....

....

....

....

....

....

| Ex. 7 | Explore the F consonant in the following *dialogue* by *double-underlining* the F consonant before another consonant and before a pause or punctuation. |

Genetically Modified Food and Grass-fed Beef

Joseph:	I, myself, am a little hungry. Do we have any food stuff to feed your hungry friend—meaning me, Joseph?
Sophie:	Well, would you prefer some non-GMO, non-fried, organic Veggie chips?
Joseph:	Non-GMO, non-fried Veggie Chips. Sophie, what is GMO? Is it a rip-off?
Sophie:	No. GMO means 'Genetically Modified food.' And there's proof that this food does not include genetically modified food stuff.
Joseph:	Genetically modified food? Would you mind transferring this gift of knowledge to your uninformed friend?
Sophie:	Well, some large farming companies in this country produce crops by modifying genes in the plants so they can fight off insecticides better.
Joseph:	So, what's wrong with that? Farmers need to produce better crops for their financial gain, right?
Sophie:	Right. But the problem is, after farmers spray stronger insecticides, the chemicals go into the farm products such as corns or soybeans, and when farmers feed those products to the farm animals for beef, the chemicals go into the cows, and then the chemicals from those insecticides will finally get into our bodies and affect us negatively.
Joseph:	Talk about a load of mischief! What else do I need to know about GMO?
Sophie:	I find that, in this country, GMO food is not required to be labeled. As you noticed, at least this food is labeled as "non-GMO." So, you can look for such a tipoff label. Another way to distinguish GMO from Non-GMO food is that when you go to the grocery store, you will find most fruits have small stickers on them. And the GMO food is labeled with 5-digit numbers; and non-GMO food is labeled with 4-digits.
Joseph:	And what else should I do to know more about GMO foodstuff?
Sophie:	Well, some people prefer grass-fed beef instead of corn or soy-fed beef. However, we are not sure what grass-fed beef farmers really feed their farm animals.

Joseph:	Hmm… you mean that soybeans might be filled with chemicals from insecticides?
Sophie:	Possibly. And if they are produced as GMO in this country, and are fed to the so-called grass-fed cows, then how can this be considered 'healthy'?
Joseph:	I am confused and a little afraid.
Sophie:	I can believe it. You just need to be better informed about the food stuff you put into your body and how to keep yourself– and the environment safe. That's what I am trying to do.
Joseph:	What a relief!

Carryover into Real Life:

Today and for the next few days, carry over into your conversations—all the Consonants we have covered so far. Choose a 15–20-minute block of time to include them in a conversation held with a friend, a family member, at dinner, on the phone or reading a bedtime story to your child. Be creative.

Notes: ....

....

....

....

....

....

....

....

....

....

....

....

The Z [z] as in *Zebra* or *Jazz*

The [z] is a voiced, sustainable consonant. It is the voiced version of the [s].

To create the Z [z] Consonant

With lips soft, let the tongue blade approach the upper front teeth leaving a very narrow space between the upper gum ridge and the front teeth. Add voice (humming) and what will be created is a fuzzy vibration of *(Z~~~~)*, which will be felt on the upper gum ridge and possibly the back of your upper front teeth. The sides of the tongue will touch the inside of the molars because the upper and lower teeth are positioned close together, but not touching each other. This is your [z] consonant.

Remember: when you can *feel* it, your listeners can *hear* it.

Useful tips:

- The key to creating the optimal [z] consonant is to keep a consistent space between the tongue and gum ridge.

- A consistently smooth Z sounds like the buzzing of a bee.

- Upper and lower side teeth do not touch each other but are in close proximity.

More useful Tips:

- The final [z] sound can be spelled with the spelling /s/ or /z/.

- The /s/ spelling after a voiceless consonant is pronounced as [s].

- The /s/ spelling after voiced sounds (vowels and voiced consonants) is pronounced as [z].

Notes: ....

....

....

....

....

Ex. 1   Explore the Z consonant in the following words by *double-underlining* the spelling and sustaining the Z sound in all the Sustainable Opportunities (before another consonant and before a pause or punctuation). The first few words are marked for you.

The /z/ spelling pronounced as [z] in word-final positions

Liz, Jazz, prize, breeze, generalize, memorize, ionize, ironize, internalize, jeopardize, realize, nationalize, neutralize, naturalize, organize, oxidize, specialize, vitalize

The /s/ spelling pronounced as [z] in word-final positions

is, was, has, his, use, does, wise, these, those, please, poise, James, because, surprise, hers, ours, yours, theirs, themselves, things, days, lies, prices, toes, stars, moms, princes, princesses, approves, confirms, systems, delays, Thursdays, names, games, bears, objectives, reaches, establishes, washes, successes, achieves, receives, recovers.

Ex. 2   Explore the [z] sound in the word initial and **word-medial** positions before a vowel. Remember, you do *not* have to sustain the [z] before a vowel sound or in the word-initial positions. There are also S spellings that are pronounced as a [z]. They will be *italicized* for you.

Z [zi], zoo, zone, zebra, zip, zap, Zack, Zahra, zenith, zipper, zeal, Brazil, New Zealand, Swaziland, lazy, Suzy, razor, blazer, dazzle, frazzle, gazelle, magazine, horizon, daisy, busy, easy, present, position, result, resolve, reason, resort, Roosevelt, Missouri, wisdom

Notes: ....

....

....

....

....

....

Ex. 3   Explore the [z] sound in the following sentences by *double-underlining* the /z/ spelling and sustaining the [z] sound before another consonant and before a pause or punctuation. The first two sentences are marked for you. The Z sound as a final consonant has been underlined, and the S is *italicized* when it is pronounced as a Z.

- Last Thur*s*day, Zahra, Zack, and Jame*s* went to the zoo and saw zebra*s*, chimpanzee*s*, and Chihuahua*s*.

- The*se* day*s*, Zane carefully pay*s* attention to the price*s* of grocery item*s* when she goe*s* to the store*s* because it seem*s* the price*s* go up every time she turn*s* around.

- I have traveled to many countries but haven't been to such countries as Brazil, New Zealand, and Swaziland yet.

- The global recession is evidenced in this country as even some large brand-name stores closed their venues because of poor activities.

Ex. 4   Explore the [Z] sound in the following *dialogue* with /s/ spelling by *double-underlining* the /s/ spelling but feeling it as a [z] sound. Underline regardless of where the /s/ spelling is positioned within the word.

Zed: Wow! There are many more [z] sounds in the English language than I ever knew. I am amazed. I like the feeling of the Z. Can you give me a few words to practice with?

Susie: Sure: How about *yours, his, theirs?*

Zed: Oh great! And would these also be included—*ours, hers, John's, clothes, chairs?*

Susie: Ah, you are finding that the possessive and the plural words use that Z sound!

Zed: Yes, I think I am getting it. I just have to remember that—plurals and possessives!

Susie: For now, this is enough to remember, Zed.

Zed: Thanks, it'll be fun looking for more words like *logs, frogs, and hogs!*

Susie: Cheers to you!

Explore the [z] sound in the following story. Notice how many S spellings are pronounced as a [z]. These have been *italicized* for you, so just feel them along the way. Remember, the [z] before a vowel is not sustained.

I met confidence on a Golf Course

For golfer*s*, 'good weather' mean*s* good weather to play golf. This winter, the New Year'*s* holiday*s* were a*s* warm a*s* April in Birmingham, Alabama. Of course, I wa*s* not about to miss the*s*e golden opportunitie*s*. So, today, my hu*s*band and I drove to the golf course at Oak Mountain State Park near Birmingham. Here, we can play a nine-hole course for ten dollar*s* during the week, which i*s* not bad at all for occasional exerci*s*e. By the time we arrived at the pro-shop, the parking lot was crowded with the patron*s*' car*s*, and the first tee wa*s* also crowded with golfer*s* waiting for their turn*s*. Four team*s* were in front of us. My hu*s*band and I were teamed up with a father and hi*s* teenage son who were waiting for their turn in a golf cart. But I usually walk with my golf bag on my shoulder*s* so I can pinch a few pennie*s* as well as add to my exercise routine.

The marshal advi*s*ed the golfer*s* not to go onto the driving range a*s* there wa*s* no way he could estimate how quickly the game*s* before us would proceed. He said we might have to wait for roughly 45 minutes to an hour before we could hit our first ball. So, I killed some time by warming up with one of the longest club*s* for about 10 minutes, but even then, many people were still waiting before we could start. Then I began to pay attention to some of the waiting golfer*s* becau*s*e people-watching i*s* fun for me. This southern city of Birmingham ha*s* become internationally known in recent year*s* for its golfing. There were all kind*s* of people from all over the world here today. However, compared with other time*s*, there were more female golfer*s* today. One of the team*s* before us included four middle-aged ladie*s*, and one of them caught my eye. Because of the unusually warm weather, she was wearing only a short sleeve T-shirt and shorts. Interestingly, one of her leg*s* was made of a shiny metal bar. Both feet had socks and shoe*s*.

She and her team member*s* did not choose to ride carts but to walk. And they didn't have any pull-carts. This meant that they would carry their own golf bag*s* on their shoulder*s*. Watching the*s*e ladie*s* talking to each other while waiting for their turn, I silently applauded this special lady for playing golf and dressing like any other person on a warm, sunny day. After a while, I lost sight of that team. But I kept on applauding her for her courage, freedom, and confidence.

The S [s] as in *Sister*

The S consonant is a voiceless, sustainable sound, which is produced as a result of exhaling the breath across the space between the tongue blade and upper gum ridge with the tongue tip facing the upper front teeth. It is the voiceless counterpart to the Z.

To create the S Consonant:

1. With soft lips and the upper and lower side-teeth (molars) close to each other without biting or clenching, let the tongue blade gently approach the back of the upper gum ridge (post alveolar) without actually touching it, and then gently exhale the air through the opening (aperture) between the blade and the gum ridge. The sides of the tongue will touch the upper molars on either side, but the tip of the tongue is suspended. The sound resembles the sound of air escaping gently through a needle sized hole from a full-blown balloon. This is your S[s] sound.

Useful tips:

- When you hold your palm or back of your hand near your mouth as you play the S consonant, the steady escape of air should gently warm your hand.

- *The GA American English S consonant ideally should be quiet, higher-pitched, and sharp in quality* (the tongue pressure will slightly increase if you think 'higher in pitch'. This is desirable).

For your information:

The spelling /s/ in the word-final positions can be pronounced as [s] after a voiceless consonant; but as [z] after a vowel or voiced consonant. Also, the Z sound is used for the possessive such as: hers, his, theirs, Joe's, Mary's etc. and for the plural of many words in English.

For Example: After a voiceless sound: books[s], looks[s], desks[s], tops [s]
              After a voiced sound: fingers[z], toes[z], names[z], nouns[z]

Sunny: Our fingers [z] have names [z] such as [z] thumb, index finger, middle finger, ring finger, and pinky. However, we don't seem to have names [z] for our toes [z].

Sandy: That's true! It looks [s] like the English language is kind of strange. And why do we have to add an S-suffix after nouns [z] to express plurals such as "books [s]" and "desks [s]"? Why not other spellings? [z]

Ex. 1   Explore the S consonant at the end of the following words or before a consonant by *double-underlining* the spelling. The first two lines are marked for you. *Note: The [s] sound can be spelled with the S, C, or X.*

S[es], this, bus, pass, gas, bass, mass, moss, hiss, bless, lips, tips, works, suspense, useful, base, mouse, basis, emphasis, best, past, task, guest, boast, roast, mass, moist, almost, mister, mistletoe, poster, plastic, dialysis, Christmas, atmosphere, whistle, wrestle, hustle, bustle, peaceful, question acid, nice, mice, once, twice, force, dance, entrance, clearance, capacity, place, practice, process, precipitation, reception, receipt, concentration, excellent (ks), explore (ks), except (ks), exception (ks), explain (ks), excuse (ks)

Ex. 2   Try sustaining the S at the beginning of a word before moving to the vowel, then shorten the S duration by repeating the same word before moving to the next word.

say, salt, salad, salary, sample, sandwich, set, send, sell, seven, scene, senior, scenario, seminar, sequence, senator, selfish, sensitive, six, silly, sing, sign, sigh, size, so, song, some, soon, sofa, solo, sold, solar, sound, sonata, sun, summer, system, Sunday

C, CD, CEO, cell, city, cent, center, celery, cider, citizen, cement, certain, certify, cervix, cellular, century, censor, census, centennial, centimeter, centrifuge, ceramic, ceremony, celebrate, Celsius, cease, ceiling, cerebral, sunny, sandy, decide, salad, Sunday, soy, sauce, balsamic, salami, sesame, seeds, sign, Sandy, sunset, grocery, wholesome, same

Ex. 3   Now feel your S consonant in this following passage:

Sunny Sandy decided to make a spring green salad for Sunday brunch. She bought a package of garden greens, soy sauce, balsamic vinegar, salami, sesame seeds, and sesame oil. This Sunday happened to be nice and sunny without a sign of clouds. Sunny Sandy's friend, Susan, showed up as early as six or seven in the morning to take Sunny Sandy hiking at Sunset Hill and then to the grocery store. The salad Sunny Sandy and Susan made together was so delicious and wholesome at the same time. *(Adapted after Yuko Tsuruta, Department of Dermatology, University of Alabama at Birmingham)*

Epenthesis

'Epenthesis' is defined as the addition of a vowel or consonant at the beginning of a word or between sounds.[30] Some first language speakers add an extra vowel sound such as [e] or [i] before words that start with the S when it occurs before another consonant in English: for example, '*e*Study' or '*e*speak' or '*i*Study' or '*i*speak'.

A strategy to eliminate this epenthesis, if this is the case for you, is to sustain the S at the beginning of the words and then proceed to the next consonant, such as 'S~~~~tudy' or 'S~~~~peak', without adding an extra vowel before the S + consonant sound.

Ex. 4   Explore the S consonant before another consonant (S-blends) without adding any vowel sound before it. Move smoothly from the S to the next consonant.

The sp-blends
spa, spot, span, speed, spend, speak, spoke, spoken, spank, spoon, spelling, spider, spray, sprain, spring, sponge, split, spooky, spool, splendid, specific, spectrum

The st-blends
stack, star, start, step, stop, student, study, store, story, stay, stone, stray, strain, street, strong, structure, statement, steam, steak, stock, stare, staircase, stimulate.

The sk-blends
skin, ski, skate, skill, skull, skirt, sky, squeak, scheme, school, scope, scooter, square, scramble, sclera, scoop, sculpture, sclerosis, skeleton, schizophrenia

Other s-blends
small, smart, smear, smell, snare, snail, sneaker, sneeze, snow, sweat, sweet, swim, swallow, slide, slow, slope, sleep, slept, slip, slump, slot

---

[30] Richards, Jack C. and Schmidt, Richard. <u>Longman Dictionary of Language Teaching & Applied Linguistics</u>, Pearson Education Limited, 4th Edition, 2010, p. 199.

The S as SH [ʃ]

Sometimes the S becomes the SH consonant when the S spelling is followed by a 'u' as in the following words:

- sugar—S + u------------------shugar [ʃʊgɚ]

- sure—S + u -------------------sh.ure [ʃʊɚ]

- issue: S + Yu------------------- i.shyu [ɪʃju] or i.shu [ɪʃu]

- tissue: S + Yu------------------ ti.shyu [tɪʃju] or ti.shu [tɪʃu]

Ex. 5   Explore the [s] sound in the following *dialogue*. Look out for that SH pronunciation.

Summer Semester in Spain

Sam: So, you decided to spend a semester in Spain in the summer?

Sarah: Yes. Indeed.

Sam: When did you say you're leaving?

Sarah: Ha! No pressure! On the sixth of this month.

Sam: When will the new semester start over there?

Sarah: On the sixteenth of May.

Sam: I see. So, are you going to have some time to settle down over there before the semester starts?

Sarah: Sure, that's not going to be an issue. I've been assured of that.

Sam: Of course, you must be excited about the trip.

Sarah: Yes and no. I am excited to explore the exotic places on my own, but at the same time, since this is my first time to go abroad by myself, I am somewhat scared, too.

Sam: I can understand that. But I am sure you're going to be fine.

Sarah: I think so, too. It's funny, but once in a while, the little child inside of me says 'I am scared' and wants a tissue, and then, in the next moment, my grown-up inside assures me that 'I should be all right'.

Sam: Have fun in Spain. I sure will miss you in the summer semester. Post some pictures on your blog and send lots of pictures and videos via your phone! That's your insurance that it really happened!

Sarah: I sure will. Thanks. See you when I get back.

Ex. 6   Explore the quiet, sharp in quality S consonant in the following story.

Mark the *S when it is located before another consonant* with a double underline. The first two paragraphs are marked for you. An S before a vowel is not marked, but still should be felt and created quietly and softly!

*If you see the words with /s/ spelling that are *italicized*, that means they are pronounced as [z]. You will find many words that end with an S in the plural are pronounced as [z].

Oh my, I DID it again!

Have you ever forgotten to serve a portion of food to your dinner guests and only discovered it after the party is over? It has happened a few times in my life.

One Sunday, my daughter Naomi called and asked me if I would cook Arabic food for her friends. I told her I was happy to do so. So, my husband and I bought two different packages of organic chicken parts: breasts, drumsticks, thighs, and wings, minced garlic, and a bag of lemons for "Grilled Lebanese Garlic Chicken" for the Saturday cooking class. We bought another set of chicken parts for Saturday dinner after the cooking class because the chicken for the Saturday dinner needed to be marinated longer for that perfect taste. This means, the chicken that will be marinated during the cooking class would not be quite as tasty as those that are marinated overnight. We bought the following items in addition to the chicken parts:

-    Italian flat celery, red Italian bell tomatoes, purple onions, and a bag of cracked wheat for 'Tabouli', the Mediterranean cracked wheat salad

-    A couple of bottles of Apple Cider, Ginger Ale, and oranges and apples to make Jeddah champagne

70

- Basmati rice, purple onions, pine nuts, and Garam masala spice for Saudi rice

- Arabic dates and pistachio-covered Turkish delight sweets for dessert

- Pita bread and Hummus for the chickpea dip

On Friday, I marinated the chicken parts, with crushed lemon juice, minced garlic, powdered ginger, salt, and black pepper to grill on Saturday. On Saturday morning, I took all the food materials out to the kitchen counter, making sure that I did not forget anything. Naomi came on time, for a change. She brought two of her friends—Sandra, and James. We were to make Lebanese garlic chicken, Saudi rice, Tabouli, and Jeddah Champagne. We were not going to make hummus this time because I preferred the store-bought version over my home-made version. Now for the cooking class: First, the chicken parts were washed, patted dry, and marinated with crushed fresh lemons, minced garlic, salt, black pepper, and ginger powder. For Tabouli, after a cup of cracked wheat was soaked in water for an hour and the water was drained out; James, with his skillful hand, chopped tomatoes and parsley, and put them into the salad bowl along with the cracked wheat and fresh-squeezed lemon juice and some olive oil. Sandra diced the purple onions and added them to the Tabouli Salad bowl.

When those ingredients were mixed all together, a tantalizing, tangy, Christmas-light colored 'tabouli' salad was created. Everyone was amazed at how easy, pretty, and healthy Tabouli salad looked. When I let everyone taste a small portion, they went "Humm…" while they were chewing the Tabouli.

While my husband and James were grilling the marinated chicken parts, I cooked a couple of cups of basmati rice in the rice cooker and made fried rice by adding cooked basmati rice to the fried chopped purple onions in the shallow pool of olive oil in the frying pan, where eventually a tablespoon of Garam Masala powder, roasted pine nuts, and some salt and pepper were added to perfect the dish.

Now everything was completed, and we were hungry just from smelling all those different foods. I wanted to make sure that everything we had prepared was placed on the table. Since we did not have many items to serve, I was confident that everything was taken to our dining area.

The chicken was grilled into perfectly juicy golden-brown pieces. Naomi quickly mixed the apple cider and ginger ale into the punch bowl, along with a diced red apple into the punch bowl to make Jeddah Champagne and set it on top of the buffet table in our dining room.

After my husband blessed the food, everyone started attacking and devouring it as if they had starved themselves for weeks. They were awed by the taste sensations that they had never tried before. But very soon, their exclamations were replaced by silence. They used their mouths for only one function—digging into their bowls to feed themselves!

After dinner, we retired to the living room where oak logs were burning in the fireplace. While everyone was enjoying Turkish delights and Arabic dates for dessert, I casually got up and went into the kitchen to put away some leftover food. When I opened the refrigerator, guess what!? I discovered the appetizer– hummus and pita bread waiting to be served to my guests! Oh my! I did it again.

I told the folks in the living room what had happened. Naomi comforted me, "We didn't miss them, Mom." So, I made sure that everyone took the leftover food from their cooking class home for another meal. It was a very successful cooking class and dinner in spite of my "I did it again" episode.

Notes: ....

....

....

....

....

....

....

....

....

....

....

....

TH Consonants [θ] as in *Thank* and TH [ð] as in *They*

The TH sounds are both sustainable. The [ð] is voiced, and [θ] is voiceless.

The Voiceless TH [θ] as in *Thank*

This sound is the whispered version of the voiced TH [ð]. It is the sound of air flowing between the contact points of the upper and lower front teeth and the tongue tip.

To Create the Voiceless TH [θ] Consonant

1. Allow just enough space for the tip of the tongue to gently slide through between the upper and lower front teeth. The tongue will be lightly resting on the edges of the bottom front teeth, so that it is easy to allow a gentle breath stream to escape around it. You will see the tongue. This consonant is made through friction rather than pressing the upper and lower front teeth into the tongue.

2. Explore slightly different tongue positions (a little farther forward or back) to see where you get the most seamless, even, free-flowing breath stream *(TH~~~~)*. This is your Voiceless TH sound.

Useful Tips:

• Play this sound lightly and softly without forcing any air at all.

• You will often be moving so efficiently and smoothly in speech that a minimal amount of tongue is exposed.

• For acquiring the sound, hum it where you feel the most concentrated quality.

Notes: ....

....

....

....

....

....

....

Ex. 1   Explore the voiceless TH [θ] consonant by *double-underlining* the spelling and sustaining the sound for 2 to 3 seconds in the sustainable opportunities (before another consonant and at the end of each word) in the following word list. The first line is marked for you.

math, birth, earth, death, teeth, tooth, forth, fourth, mouth, width, breadth, cloth, month, north, south, warmth, health, faith, Keith, Heath, Smith, Judith, Duluth, Meredith, fifth, sixth, seventh, eighth, ninth, tenth, eleventh, twelfth, thirteenth, fourteenth, fifteenth, sixteenth, twentieth, thirtieth, fortieth, fiftieth, sixtieth, seventieth, eightieth, ninetieth, hundredth, millionth, billionth, trillionth

Ex. 2   Explore the TH [θ] consonant at the word-initial positions and before a vowel. You do *not* have to underline or sustain but be mindful of the voiceless TH [θ] consonant.

thank, think, thing, three, third, thirty, thirteen, thousand, thought, thief, thrift, thrill, thread, Thursday, thunder, thermometer, Thornton, theology, therapy, mathematics, athlete, Nathan, Ithaca, author, empathy, sympathy, Matthew, Martha, Anthony, Cynthia, Bethany, Gaither, thumbtack, Northampton, orthodontist, ophthalmology, enthusiastic, anesthesia

For your information:

The /th/ is silent (not pronounced) in the word "is*th*mus [ismǝs]

Notes: ....

....

....

....

....

....

....

....

Ex. 3   Explore the TH [θ] consonant in the following sentences.

• Thank you, thank you, and again, thank you very much.

• The fourth day of the month of July is the birthday of the United States.

• To get a job is one thing; to maintain a job is another thing; but to be thirsty for a job is quite a sympathetic and empathetic situation.

• The earthquake and tsunami from the South and North threatened other countries.

• Thurmont Thermal Thermometer produces thirty-three thousand thermometers a month.

• Nathan Gaither, Martha Smith, Matthew Ithaca, Cynthia Thornton, and Bethany Thorndike showed their sympathy to the victims of the earthquake through their donations.

• The thought of dividing an apple into one-seventh, three-thirteenth, or eleven-hundredth sections is theoretically possible in math but practically, not worth much.

• On her 30th birthday, Martha Smith thought she was the healthiest, wealthiest, and most beautiful young lady that she knew.

Notes:..
....
....
....
....
....
....
....
....
....

Ex. 4	Explore the TH [θ] consonant in the following *dialogue*

Theodore: I am sorry; I can't come to the meeting next Thursday. I have a physical therapy appointment.

Garth: I see. What happened, Theo?

Theodore: Well, three months ago, I was involved in a traffic accident, and was diagnosed with whiplash. So, Garth, my neck and shoulders were injured. But I am thankful I did not get hurt seriously. Next Thursday will be my third session with the therapist.

Garth: Next Thursday is April 13th. I will make a note. By the way, what is whiplash?

Theodore: You get whiplash when your head is suddenly and quickly thrown backward and forward. It can cause injury to your muscles, ligaments, back-bone, or nerves in your neck.

Garth: Sounds terrible. Does it cause fever as well?

Theodore: No. When I was taken to the emergency room, a nurse put a thermometer in my mouth to check my temperature, but it was normal.

Garth: Thankfully! Take care of your health and see you next Thursday.

Theodore: I thought I told you! I can't come next Thursday, Garth!

Garth: Oh my. You are right, Theo. You said you couldn't come next Thursday. What was I thinking? Maybe I wasn't thinking at all!

Notes: ....

....

....

....

....

....

....

....

The voiced TH [ð] as in *They*

This consonant is the voiced version of the voiceless TH [θ].

To Create the Voiced TH [ð] Consonant

1. Position the contact points of the teeth and tongue tip just as for the voiceless TH

2. While the teeth and tongue tip are in position, protruding slightly from between the upper and lower front teeth—create a gentle hum to feel the consonant's vibration (*TH~~~*).

3. Feel the vibration at the teeth and the tongue tip contact point.

Useful tips:

- Because there is vibration along the whole front rim of your tongue, you are producing it with good quality if you feel gentle vibration on your lips and surrounding locations.

- Explore the different qualities of sound that happen when you place the tongue in different positions—sliding forward or back a little, allowing more or less of the tongue tip to be visible. In what position do you feel the most buzz or vibration?

- If the sound is not smooth, reduce the pressure of your teeth on your tongue a little more.

Ex. 1   Explore the Voiced TH [ð] consonant by sustaining the *double-underlined* TH portion in the sustainable opportunities in the following words and expressions.

* The TH[ð] before a vowel needs not to be underlined or sustained but be mindful of feeling it.

bathe, soothe, smooth, clothe, breathe,

the, this, that, these, those, they, their, then, them,

nevertheless, withdraw, rhythm,

and the, and then, in the, on the, send them, but that, put those

Notes: ....

....

Ex. 2   Explore the Voiced TH [ð] consonant by sustaining the *underlined* TH portion in the sustainable opportunities.

- The new mother is learning to ba<u>the</u> her baby in the bathtub.

- Open the window and brea<u>the</u> nice, fresh air.

- But the main reasons for this and that and these and those incidents are unknown to them.

- Put those in this box, and then put these in that box.

Ex. 3   Explore the Voiced TH [ð] consonant in the following passage.

I don't know who invented the TH sounds. It is awkward to speak with the tongue sticking out of my mouth. As if one is not enough, the English language uses two of them. Why in the world do human beings have to have those funny sounds in their languages? Don't they feel any discomfort using them? They are difficult to produce, pronounce and for me to listen to when others use them in their speech.

The most difficult word for me is "Health." As a student of "Public Health," when I say the word "health," people don't understand, and they think I am saying "hell" because the TH sound at the end of that word is barely heard to my listeners, and they think that I am saying "Public Hell."

And then I say, "Why bother to make and use the sounds such as those if they are so hard to produce and to be understood?" I can communicate just fine without those funny TH sounds in my own language. I can express all my thoughts without using those sounds, but I don't know why the English language has to have those sounds? I just don't get it.

Who knows, maybe, the creators of the English alphabet letters and pronunciations ran out of symbols and sounds and instead, created a joke by adding the TH sounds!

And guess who has to suffer trying to learn them? But if I want to have the option of being understood by my American friends, I will need them in my speech...so I will do my best with them!

Notes: ....

....

....

Ex. 4   Explore the difference between the voiceless and voiced TH consonants in the following words.

voiceless [θ]

bath   [bæθ]

breath   [brɛθ]

cloth   [klɔθ]

birth   [bərθ]

earth   [ɝθ]

voiced [ð]

bathe   [beɪð]

breathe [brɪð]

clothe   [kloʊð]

soothe   [suð]

smooth [smuð]

Notes: ....

....

....

....

....

....

....

....

....

....

....

....

....

....

....

....

The SH [ʃ] as in *Shush*

The SH is a sustainable consonant. It is the voiceless version of the ZH [ʒ] sound.

To create the SH Consonant

1. Begin by rounding your lips forward as if you are beginning to whistle.

2. The tongue is in a similar position as the S Consonant made with the rounded lips; it slides back slightly as the lips are rounded. The tongue is curled close to the surface of the hard palate right behind the position where the N would be placed. The sides of the tongue hug the inside of the upper molars. The tip is not touching the upper gum ridge but is very close to it. The front teeth are close to each other without touching each other.

3. Now, gently blow air into the gap between the gum ridge and tongue blade with pursed and rounded lips. The action is similar to 'shushing' a child. *(SH~~~~)*. This is your SH [ʃ] consonant.

This sound can be spelled /sh/, /ch/, /sch/ and as the first sound of the syllables /-tion/, /-cion/, /-ssion/.

Ex. 1   The SH consonant in the word-initial position is not sustained and thus not underlined here.

/sh/   she, shy, shoe, ship, shop, show, shown, shot, shark, shake, shave, shall, sharp, should, short, share, shore, shadow, shallow, shaggy, sheik, shell, sheep, sheet, sheath, sheriff, shine, shimmer, shivery, shoulder, shrink, shroud, shunt, shuttle, Shamrock, Shelby, Sheila, Shekel, Shakespeare, Sherlock, Sheba, Shem

/sch/   schwa, Schwab, Schwartz, Schmidt, Schubert, Schweitzer, Schilling

/ch/   chandelier, chaperone, charade, chute, chateau, chauffeur, chauvinism, Chicago, Charlene, Charlotte, Cheryl, Chevron, Chevrolet

Notes: ....

....

Ex. 2   Explore the SH [ʃ] sound in the following words by *double-underlining* the spelling and sustaining the sound in the sustainable opportunities (before another consonant and before a pause or punctuation). If the SH is followed by a vowel in the spelling (unless it is silent) there will be no underlines, but just sustain it long enough to feel its presence.

/sh/   a<u>sh</u>, ca<u>sh</u>, di<u>sh</u>, fi<u>sh</u>, hu<u>sh</u>, pu<u>sh</u>, wa<u>sh</u>, wi<u>sh</u>, ru<u>sh</u>, bru<u>sh</u>, fini<u>sh</u>, flash, English, British, shoe, shop, shirt, sheet, shall, ship, shell, shelf, sheep, sheet, shake, shame, share, shave, shore, shampoo, shimmer, Sherman, shaggy, shepherd

/ch/   Charlotte, Champaign, Chevron, Chevrolet, Chicago, chandelier, charade, chute, brochure, machine, Michigan, champagne

/su/   sugar, sure, insurance

/ssu/   pressure, issue, tissue

/ssion/ admission, confession, commission, permission, profession

/ce/   ocean

/ci/   physician, clinician, gracious, spacious, suspicious, associate, appreciate, facial, special, crucial, beneficial, efficient, deficiency, sufficient

/ti/   patient, patience, action, nation, examination, exception, evolution, creation, construction, contribution, distribution, differentiation, graduation, partial, preparation, pronunciation, spatial, injection

Notes: ....

....

....

....

....

....

....

81

Ex. 3   Explore the SH [ʃ] sound in the following sentences by *double-underlining* the spelling and sustaining the sound in the sustainable opportunities. Do not underline or sustain before a vowel sound.

- Sherry Shaddock needs to shop for sugar, bed sheets, and a pair of shoes.

- Sheena Sheehan showed sufficient patience in learning to fish.

- Shane Shady showed the importance of uniform distribution of pressure in designing ships.

- Cash, shirt, and shoes are required to shop at the Chateau Lake shopping center.

- Milk shakes and Danish croissants are Charline's favorites in Chicago Deli.

- Auditory contamination as well as visual contamination is our national concern.

- Sherry is in a rush to finish her preparation for the National competition.

- I wish I could go to an ocean beach and relax in the sunshine.

- Scientists wonder about the public's views on the tissue issue as tissue rights have potential controversy in social and scientific research.

Notes: ....
....
....
....
....
....
....
....
....
....

Ex. 4	Explore the SH [ʃ] sound in the following dialogue by paying attention to your lip-opening and feeling the tongue tip near the upper gum ridge.

Dialogue: **Insurance Assurance—get a good policy!**

Shane: Yesterday, I received an advertisement flier from Schmidt's insurance company. It was for a 20-year term life insurance. What exactly is term life insurance?

Josh: Term life insurance means you are only covered for the designated years in the policy. Which means, your family members or designated beneficiary will be reimbursed if you die within 20 years, in the case of a 20-year term insurance policy.

Shane: Gosh, are you joking? I can hand cash over every month for 20 years and if I stay in good health and do NOT die, I lose all the money I've put in?

Josh: No joke—unless your policy states otherwise. It's important not to rush things when you search for insurance. You want to get the right kind.

Shane: OK, I'm ashamed to say I didn't read the fine print, now I know not to rush. What other options are there?

Josh: No problem, I can show you. There is "conventional life insurance." This policy will surely cover your family at the time of your death no matter how long you stay boyishly young.

Shane: Don't make me blush! I intend to! But let me ask you, why don't people enroll in conventional life insurance instead of term insurance?

Josh: It's all about the cash, Shane. The monthly payment for conventional life insurance is a lot more than the term insurance costs.

Shane: But one may lose a stash of cash from the term insurance policy in the end.

Josh: I guess we can't have sugar and spice and everything nice, huh?

Shane: I wish I weren't between a rock and a hard place. But at least one thing I know for sure is that my family will get some protection from the insurance policy that I receive through my workplace.

Notes: ....

....

....

The ZH [ʒ] as in <u>U<u>s</u>ually</u> or <u>Gara<u>g</u>e</u>

The ZH is a sustainable consonant. It is the voiced version of the SH sound.

To create the ZH [ʒ] consonant

The simplest way to make the ZH [ʒ] consonant is by adding vocal vibration to the SH [ʃ] consonant.

1. Begin by rounding your lips forward as if you are beginning to whistle.

2. The tongue slides back slightly as the lips are rounded. The tongue is curled close to the surface of the hard palate right behind the position where the N would be placed. The sides of the tongue hug the inside of the upper molars; this is the contact point. The tip is not touching the upper gum ridge but is very close to it. The front teeth are close to each other without touching each other.

3. Then, add voice while feeling your contact point *(ZH~~~)*. This is your ZH sound.

Ex. 1   Explore the relationship between your tongue blade, gum ridge, and lip-pursing of the ZH [ʒ] consonant in the following words. The ZH sound is *italicized* for you in each word to identify it. Notice the different spellings for this sound: *si, su, zu, ti, g*

Asia, usual, casual, visual, leisure, measure, pleasure, seizure, version, vision, envision, division, revision, occasion, conversion, convulsion, immersion, equation, garage, mirage, genre

Notes: ....

....

....

....

....

....

....

....

Ex. 2   Explore the ZH [ʒ] consonant in the following expressions. It will be *italicized* as it is followed by a vowel in these words.

- the Divi*s*ion of Vi*s*ion Sciences

- u*s*ually ca*s*ual occa*s*ions

- mea*s*ure the vi*s*ual conver*s*ion.

- immer*s*ion in language learning.

- A plea*s*ure to meet a trea*s*ure in life.

- lei*s*urely strolling on the beach with an unu*s*ually plea*s*urable friend.

- David is a future vi*s*ionary scientist with an unu*s*ual vision.

- I wonder who invented the televi*s*ion!

- The suffix '-*t*ion' in 'equa*t*ion' can be pronounced as either '*zh*ion [ʒən]' or 'shion [ʃən].

Ex. 3   Explore the ZH [ʒ] sound in the following passage. The ZH followed by a vowel is italicized. It is *Double underlined* where the ZH is in a playable position–before another consonant or before a pause or punctuation.

*J*acques Colla*g*e needed a massa*g*e badly, so while in Baton Rou*g*e, he luckily found the Mira*g*e Massa*g*e Center. He parked in the building's spacious gara*g*e/ and entered through a bei*g*e door into a restful a*z*ure blue office that vi*s*ually was very peaceful and lu*x*urious. The floor was covered with a beautiful Per*s*ian rug, and the staff members were welcoming and seemed to take great plea*s*ure in their vocation. He knew he had made the right deci*s*ion to come here. He was treated to the best massa*g*e/ in his life. What a trea*s*ure to find the Mira*g*e Massa*g*e Center!

(Nancy Krebs, Lessac Master Teacher, 2023)

Notes: ....

....

....

85

The H [h] as in *Hat*

The H is a voiceless, sustainable consonant. There is no voiced counterpart for this sound in GA American English.

To create the H consonant:

1. Allow your jaw to float down and forward slightly as you open your mouth to inhale.

2. Gently breathe the air out of the open mouth as if whispering "AH", keeping your tongue flat on the floor of the oral cavity, without force or pressure. *(H ~~~)*

3. This is your H sound. It is simply a whispered sigh.

Useful tips:

• If the space between the tongue and the arch of the soft palate is too close, you might produce the KH sound instead.

• So, keep your throat comfortably relaxed and open to create the H consonant.

• Since the [h] consonant before a vowel is not sustained and the /h/ spelling in word-final position, as in *hah*, or *rah*, is not pronounced, the [h] consonant is not usually sustained in speech. Even if it is sustained, no one will or can hear it easily.

• For this consonant, no contact or friction (rubbing) is created between the tongue and throat—just uninterrupted whispered sigh-like air flow "h-h-h".

Ex. 1   In the following words, explore the H consonant with a whispered, open-throated "sigh" feel.

he, her, has, have, ham, hat, how, hard, hand, half, home, holy, hose, huge, handle, happy, habit, hammer, healthy, heavy, hedge, human, humor, hurry, hound, humidity, hospital, hostility, hamburger, Hamilton, Harriet, Humphrey, holiday, helicopter, foothills, behalf, behave, inhibit, forehead, rehabilitate, farmhand, beehive

Notes: ....
....

86

Ex. 2   The H is sometimes *not pronounced* or *silent* in certain spellings. Here the Silent H is marked in *italics*.

*h*our, *h*onor, ha*h*, ra*h*, hig*h*, boug*h*, doug*h*, thoug*h*, yea*h*, eig*h*t, mig*h*t, sig*h*t, tig*h*t, exhaust, ex*h*ibit, Vaug*h*n, caug*h*t, oug*h*t, boug*h*t, broug*h*t, naug*h*t, soug*h*t, taug*h*t

Ex. 3   In the following sentences, explore the H consonant. Be on the lookout for the *silent H*, which are italicized for you.

- He came home from the hospital half an hour ago, at eig*h*t o'clock.

- Hurriedly, he handed his hat to his hat holder.

- Harriet Humphrey gave half of her wealth to a foreign humanitarian organization on behalf of her hometown, Harrisburg.

- Humor is free medicine for a happy and healthy human life.

- Happy Harriet hardly had to do any homework for her home-economics class.

- Helen hurled her too-tig*h*t headband from her head--it was hurting her.

- How about volunteering for half a day at the Habitat for Humanity work site?

Notes: ....
....
....
....
....
....
....
....
....

Ex. 4　　　　　In the following *dialogue*, explore the H sound. Watch for the *Silent H*.

Dialogue: Half a Day with Habitat for Humanity

Hannah:　　　Hi, Harriet, do you have any plans for this Saturday morning?

Harriet:　　　Nothing special. How about you?

Hannah:　　　How about coming with me for half a day to work for Habitat for Humanity?

Harriet:　　　Habitat for Humanity?

Hannah:　　　It's a charity organization that builds houses for low-income people.

Harriet:　　　Honestly, I'm horrible at construction. How can I help over there?

Hannah:　　　There are professionals who do the serious jobs and keep us out of harm's way. Happily, there are plenty of things we can do to help.

Harriet:　　　Do you have more information that I should know about volunteering at the Habitat for Humanity construction site?

Hannah:　　　One Habitat worker, Henry Harvey, told me that we have to wear a "hard hat."

Harriet:　　　Hard hat? Oh, you mean the round yellow plastic safety hat?

Hannah:　　　Yeah, Henry says we have to wear those hats.

Harriet:　　　Cool. Can't you just see me happily hanging out with my yellow hat and hammer? By the way, wasn't Habitat for Humanity founded by Jimmy Carter?

Hannah:　　　The Habitat homepage says that the Habitat was founded by Millard and Linda Fuller, but Jimmy Carter and his wife are humanitarians who helped make it known internationally.

Harriet:　　　I see. How did you hear about Habitat and find out about the schedule for this weekend?

Hannah:　　　Hey, it's my first time, too. I haphazardly saw the advertisement flyer in Hill University Hall, and it happens that this Saturday is a half-day event I can attend.

Harriet:　　　Count me in! When, where, and what time do we meet to go help?

Hannah:	At half-past 7 at Hill University Hall. That's the hour most Habitat meetings start. A healthy breakfast will be served.
Harriet:	Terrific! Sounds like a good day to do a good deed and make someone happy. Let's remember sunscreen, sunglasses, and lots of H2O! Hey, let's ask Herbert and Harry if they want to join us.
Hannah:	Sounds like you have a heart for helping! Habitat will be thrilled if more helpers show up. A great idea!
Harriet:	Thank you for inviting me to help Habitat for Humanity.
Harriet:	It was my honor!
Ex. 5	In this story, explore the H sound.

Hal Hastings was a hotshot headhunter from Halethorpe who had a knack for finding the best ranch hands anywhere. He had a hunch that the ranch hands he was hoping to find had a habit of hiding out in beer halls. He started out haunting tollhouses, and cat houses, with no luck; but then happily came upon the best hideaway for ranch hands ever…the Hopping Hills Beer Hall in the foothills of Mt. Holyoke outside of Hollywood. He hit a homerun there by finding a heck of a lot of high-quality ranch hands, offering hundreds of dollars to each hopeful hand and promising them a horse as well. They all agreed to hotfoot it back to Halethorpe for a heck of a good job, high-stepping horses and hopefully, happy lives. Hooray for Hal!

(Nancy Krebs, Lessac Master Teacher 2022)

Notes: ....

....

....

....

....

....

....

The R [ɹ] as in *Rare*

The R is a sustainable, voiced sound. (The retroflex R)

To create the R Consonant:

1. Allow the sides of your tongue to touch or 'hug' the inside of your upper side teeth (molars). The tip of your tongue is suspended between top and bottom near the front, curled slightly backward and up toward the hard palate. The entire tongue feels pulled back somewhat, retracted.

2. Form your lips to be slightly rounded and forward as if you were going to create an SH; they should be soft, and cushiony to the touch.

3. Add voice. It may sound to you as if you are growling like a lion or dog, or imitating the sound of a running car engine *(R~~~~ R~~~~~ R~~~~~)*. This is your R sound. The IPA symbol for this sound is [ɹ].

Ex. 1   In the following words, explore the R consonant.

R	[ɑɹ]	are	[ɑɹ]	art	[ɑɹt]
car	[kɑɹ]	far	[fɑɹ]	card	[kɑɹd]
dark	[dɑɹk]	mark	[mɑɹk]	park	[pɑɹk]
orb	[ɔɹb]	fork	[fɔɹk]	course	[kɔɹs]
rest	[ɹɛst]	sort	[sɔɹt]	order	[ɔɹdəɹ]
run	[ɹʌn]	dorm	[dɔɹm]	portion	[pɔɹʃən]
fort	[fɔɹm]	form	[fɔɹm]	sports	[spɔɹts]
morn	[mɔɹn]	port	[pɔɹt]	torn	[tɔɹn]
crew	[kɹu]	north	[nɔɹθ]	source	[sɔɹs]

Notes: ....

....

....

....

....

....

Ex. 2   Explore the R consonant with an SH-like lip-opening plus retroflexed tongue (in the word-initial positions; R-Blends; and before an unstressed vowel. (To pronounce R-blends, proceed quickly from the first consonant to the R and to the vowel without adding any other sound.)

1. In the word-initial positions

rain, rare, run, race, radio, ratio, rigor, role, route, reform, region, release, rhythm, rectangle

2. In the R-Blends (a Consonant + R)

brave, bread, creature, brain, cry, dry, drain, drug, gray, fry, frame, Grace, great, grant, gravity, green graduate, approach, contract, concrete, decrease, increase, library, pray, spray, premature, prepare, present, priority, project, program, protest, spectrum, trace, tractor, train, traffic, tradition, treaty, trend, triangle, sprain, spread, street, structure, electronics

3. In an unstressed syllable

better, lecturer, reader, professor, runner, speaker, waiter, manufacturer, altar, confirmation, simpler

Notes: ....
....
....
....
....
....
....
....

Ex. 3   Explore the R sound in the following sentences.

- I am ready already.

- Are you ready already? I am ready already, too!

- Grace parked her car in the garage.

- Mr. Parker, the star player, hit four home runs already.

- Ronny Remer and Larry Royer are running in the presidential race.

- Respiration is a combination of inspiration and expiration.

- Teachers often inspire confidence in their students through their professional expertise and kind gestures.

- I realize that even trees in the yard recognize their own territories.

- The traffic lights in some countries are working only as street decorators.

- To organize your work, first, prioritize your work according to urgency or importance.

- Greg prepared his presentation for his graduate program.

- Brad sprained his right ankle and rushed to the emergency room.

Notes: ....

....

....

....

....

....

....

....

....

....

Ex. 4   Explore the R consonant in the following song.

A Useful tip:

The following song includes both the R and L sounds. If the GA English L and R sounds are not included in your first language, the following tips might help you to distinguish one from another.

- The L: The contact point is between the tongue tip and gum ridge.

- The R: Has a slightly backward-raised (retro-flexed) tongue tip which doesn't touch the gum ridge and the lips slightly forward like your SH sound.

Now, feel the difference between the L and R consonants and have fun distinguishing them in this song.

Row, Row, Row Your Boat[31]

Row, row, row your boat

Gently down the stream

Merrily, merrily, merrily, merrily

Life is but a dream.

(Traditional English Nursery Rhyme)

Notes: ....

....

....

....

....

....

....

....

....

....

---

[31]https://www.classicfm.com/discover-music/row-row-row-your-boat-lyrics-history-nursery-rhyme/

Ex. 5   Explore the R consonant in the following passage.

What's the Story?

Sunday morning, on my way to church, I came to the intersection of Green Springs Avenue and Green Springs Highway. The traffic light was red, so of course, I stopped. The traffic light cycle in the intersection went through its normal course except I did not get a green light. I waited through the second cycle. And again, no green light. All the traffic was stopped at the intersection. I was becoming antsy and frustrated. When I saw that there were no other cars coming from either direction on Green Springs Highway, which lay horizontally before my eyes, I proceeded through the red light toward the entry lane to Interstate 65. But guess what!? Before I reached the freeway entrance, a policeman had his lights on and was following me. Uh-oh! I pulled over to the side of the entry lane. The first words out of the policeman's mouth were "What's the story?" I said, "I ran it, Officer." Then I continued, "I waited for two full cycles of stop lights before I ran it". He asked me to show him my driver's license, car registration, and proof of insurance. When he realized who I was, he simply told me, "Mr. Maddox, just wait for the light next time. Get on out of here." I said, "Bye." Boy was I relieved!

(Adapted from a story by Harry Shadix, Birmingham, Alabama, USA)

Carry over into real life: Once again, choose times during each day to focus on including Consonant awareness in conversations (15–20-minute blocks of time) with a friend, family member, work situation, on the phone etc.

Notes: ....

....

....

....

....

....

....

....

The W [w] as in *Wow*

The W is a vowel-like, voiced consonant when it begins a syllable or a word and functions as a vowel or diphthong when it is within or ends a syllable or word.

To create the W[w] Consonant

1. With your lips, create the smallest possible open circle with the lips parted without pressing (pursing) or creating unnecessary tension.

2. Involve facial muscles by feeling an inner sense of beginning to yawn (creating some space inside the oral cavity) with this small lip opening.

3. Hum with this facial posture and feel the gentlest sensation on the bottom lip just where the inside lip gets wet *(W~~~~)*. You will also feel vibrations in the surrounding areas of your lips and front of the face.

Useful tips:

- When sustaining this sound, it does begin to sound like the Lip-Rounding Vowel #1[32], so appreciate those similarities.

- The W spelling is considered a consonant in the word-initial or syllable-initial position as in *word, was, wayward,* and in word-medial position, *power, lower, flower,* but functions as part of a diphthong in the word-final positions, such as when the first word ends with the [u], [oʊ], [aʊ] sounds: do-w-it, flow-w-on, now-w-engage

- The W consonant also occurs between the vowels when the first vowel ends with the [u] sound, for example: go-w-ing; do-w-ing

Notes: ....

....

....

....

....

....

---

[32] This Vowel will be introduced in the next chapter, but it is the sound of the Long OO as in 'shoe'.

The W-insertion for the Vowel-to-Vowel Linking

The W consonant will be used for **vowel-to-vowel linking** when the first word ends with a vowel or diphthong [u], [oʊ], [aʊ], and the second word begins with another vowel. It also can be found between syllables containing vowels as in these examples. The -w- indicates the W connecting the two words or syllables.

- you-w-are
- no-w-entry
- go-w-along
- go-w-on
- co-w-workers
- who-w-opened

now-w-is the time

go-w-in

go-w-away

co-w-operate

to-w-exercise

who-w-is it?

Ex. 1   Explore the W-Insertion in the Vowel-to-Vowel linking opportunities. The first two sentences are marked with the W connective.

- Who-w-is the winner?

- You-w-are the winner.

- Now is the time. Yes, now is the time for us to ask ourselves these questions—"who are we, and where are we?"

- You two are ready to go on with your project—go ahead!

- Who opened the window already?

- Please go away and take some time to calm down.

Ex. 2   Explore the /w/ sound in the following sentences.

- Mr. Woodward would no longer go-w-into the woods to gather wormwood.

- I have to study now because I can find no-w-excuse not to.

- Go-w-ing through Homewood Street, Mrs. Woodruff had a fall but had no-w-injury.

- Where can I find a wonderful one like that?

- The show was really wonderful.

- What made you think you were not the one?

Ex. 3   Compare the B, V, and W sounds in the following words and sentences.

[B]	[V]	[W]
bet	vet	wet
best	vest	west
berry	very	weary
bow	vow	wow
ban	van	Wan

- I bet the vet got very wet in the rain.

- Mr. West was wearing his best vest that he bought at the Western Mall on the weekend.

- I was quite weary having to pick so many berries from very early in the morning to very late in the winter evening.

- Wow, have you seen Mr. Vower wearing that beautiful and wonderful tie today?

- Wan told me he was banned from driving his father's work van.

Notes: ....

....

....

....

....

....

....

....

....

....

....

Y [y] as in *Yay*

Y is a *Consonant* in the *beginning* of a word or syllable, as in <u>Y</u>ay! And Y can also be a *Vowel* at the end of a word, as in *Ya<u>y</u>*!

When a word contains a Y, it can be pronounced several different ways:

1. as the vowel-like, voiced consonant [j] as in <u>y</u>es

2. as a vowel [ɪ] as in c<u>y</u>st

3. as a vowel [i] as in ver<u>y</u>

4. as the final vowel in the diphthong (compound vowel) [ai] as in sk<u>y</u> or [ɔi] as in bo<u>y</u>

5. as schwa [ə] in word-medial positions as in *anal<u>y</u>sis*

To create the Y consonant [j] as in 'yes', found in word-initial position:

1. The front part of your tongue urges forward and up (see illustration p. 19), close to the roof (ceiling) of your mouth near the gum ridge.

2. The tip of the tongue will be anchored to the bottom of your lower front teeth. The sides of your tongue will be spread so that you feel them cushioned between your upper and lower molars (side teeth).

3. Your lips will be loose, cushiony to the touch and somewhat forward, as if you are going to shush a child (Shhhh). Hum into this position and you will create a Y *(Y~~~~)*.

Reminder:

The Y-spelling functions as a consonant when it initiates either a word or a syllable—but functions as a vowel when it is within a syllable or ends a word.

Ex. 1   Explore the Y-spelling pronounced as [j] consonant in the Word-Initial Positions

yes, yeah, yard, year, yellow, you, young, yearn, yield, yonder, yeast, yesterday, Yale, Yemen, yardarm, yolk, yippee

Ex. 2   Explore the Y sound between two connecting vowels *within* a word.

li-y-on   bi-y-ology   antibi-y-otics
sci-y-ence   pi-y-ano   re-y-ality
annoy-y-ance   see-y-ing   be-y-ing
vi-y-olin   say-y-ing   physi-y-ology

Ex. 3   Explore the Y-linking opportunities, as mentioned in Ex. 2, *between* words.

be-y-inside   every-y-year   the-y-alternative
the-y-answer   the re-y-ality-y-is   Osprey-y-is
Osprey-y-Island   the-y-island,   completely-y-isolated
carry-y-everything   supply-y-of   be-y-able
the-y-other   the-y-only   we-y-ate
only-y-at   they-y-ate   the-y-end
we-y-asked   any-y-oysters   they-y-import

Ex. 4   Explore the Y-spelling pronounced as Open [ɪ] vowel in the Word-Medial Positions

cyst, mystery, typical, symptom, physical, analytical, synthesize, oxygen

Ex. 5   Explore the Y-spelling pronounced as Closed [i] vowel (Major Vowel) in the Word-Final Positions or in the final vowels of diphthongs (compound vowels).

boy, toy, joy, soy, very, away, gray, annoy, spray, ready, every, energy, story, history, mystery, empathy, sympathy, baggy, remedy, lawyer, analogy, eulogy, currency, typically, geometry, taxonomy, positivity, negativity, gravity, mobility

Ex. 6   Explore the Y as the diphthong (compound vowel) [ai] in the Word-Medial or Final Positions

by, cry, my, cycle, sky, rye, type, hyper, hypo, analyze, multiply, glycogen, cytosis, psychosis, psychology, phenotype, genotype, glycolysis, aldehyde

Ex. 7   Explore the Y as Schwa [ə] in the Word-Medial Positions

analysis   [əˈnæləsɪs]   catalysis   [kəˈtæləsɪs]
dialysis   [daɪˈæləsɪs]   electrolysis   [ilekˈtrɒləsɪs]
hydrolysis   [haɪˈdrɑləsɪs]   glycolysis   [glaɪˈkɑləsɪs]

Ex. 8   Explore the different Y sounds in the following sentences.

- The-y-answer to the question is "every-y-year."

- Be-y-ing a bi-y-ology student taking an anatomy lab class, Julie had difficulty-y-eating meat.

- Yes, you yearned to work in the yard when you were young.

- Yesterday, Mr. Young made a batch of yeast dough that yielded three loaves of bread.

- Yumi is learning pi-y-ano instead of vi-y-olin.

- My garden yielded a bumper crop last year; however, this year is a different story.

- Every boy does not have to have every toy that he is see-y-ing in the toy store.

- Soy sauce sure looks different from soybeans.

- American doctors are stingy when it comes to prescribing antibi-y-otics.

Notes: ....
....
....
....
....
....

| Ex. 9 | Explore many different Y sounds in the following dialogue. |

Dialogue: Year or Ear; Yeast or East

| Yuri: | When I say the word 'year' as in the 'year 2021,' or 'yeast' as in 'yeast bread,' people say I am saying 'ear' for 'year'; and 'east' for 'yeast.' I can hear when other people say them clearly, but I don't seem to know how to pronounce them myself. |

| Yeji: | Believe me, I had the same challenge with pronouncing those words, too, but now I can say them easily. |

| Yuri: | Really? How? I am still having problems with those words. |

| Yeji: | Honestly, I had the same kind of experience! I wasn't used to the pronunciation of the /y/ because I don't have that sound in my language! But I learned it in my English pronunciation class. |

| Yuri: | So, tell me what you learned. I cannot wait to hear it. |

| Yeji: | Simple. First, I say 'Yes' and 'You' by elongating the first sound—yyy**yes**, yyy**yes**, yyy**yes**; and then, yyy**you**, yyy**you**, yyy**you**. As you know, the first sound in both words is the English Y consonant. Funny enough, even though the Y is not in my language, the first sound I make in those words are pronounced as Y. Yet, for some reason I didn't use or feel them as a Y when I said 'year' and 'yeast' because.... perhaps, I was just more used to saying those words as 'ear' and 'east.' You know what they say, you have to have awareness! And now that I'm aware of it, I want to feel the Y! It makes those words so much clearer and more easily understood. |

| Yuri: | That makes sense. |

| Yeji: | I also learned another way to feel the Y sound which might help. It is at the end of the word in 'every.'—**every**yyy, **every**yyy, **every**yyy. Then I connect the word "**every**yyy" into a word that starts with a /y/--"**every**yyy year", "**every**yyy year", "**every**yy year" and I feel the organic connection between the final 'Y' in 'every' and the initial 'Y' consonant in 'year.' |

| Yuri: | Go on. I'm following you. It makes sense to me. (tries it) "**every**yyy year" |

| Yeji: | You got it. Now do the same thing, but with just a tiny adjustment. This time, I will say the word 'every' to myself and then just say 'year' out loud. (thinks '**every**yyyy' and says) 'year'. (pause for thinking everyyyy again) 'year'. |

Yuri: Wow! So, really, just by thinking 'every' in your mind and saying 'year' makes your Y sound so clear and natural! Fascinating! I'm going to remember the 'Every' tip.

(Adapted from a dialogue submitted by Crystal Robbins, Lessac Master Teacher, Associate Adjunct Professor Theatre Department, Santa Monica College, Instructor UCLA Extension)

Notes: ....

....

....

....

....

....

....

....

....

....

....

....

....

....

....

....

....

....

....

The Tapped (Unsustainable) Consonants

'Tappable' is a spring away action (like the tapping of a drum) by the tongue, lips or other articulatory organ. See pages 14-15 to refresh your memory.

The B [b] as in *Bob*

The B consonant is an unsustainable consonant. It is the voiced version of the P consonant.

To create the B Consonant:

1. Let the lips lightly touch each other, as if getting ready to create an M.

2. Add just a little pressure, then quickly and lightly spring apart the lips from each other while producing a short hum, a momentary vibration of the vocal folds *(B-B-B)*

3. To keep the consonant short in length, do not add a vowel after it *(B-B-B, not Buh-buh-buh)*. This is your B consonant.

Ex. 1   Explore the B consonant found in various positions in the following words. There will be a *single underline* when it is placed at the end of a word, or before a dissimilar consonant to remind you to feel the spring away action.

be, big, baby, back, been, beach, become, beauty, bench, business, bump, blue, brain, brown, bring, bribe, broad

table, stable, double, rubber, tuber, problem, Elizabeth, abdomen, sublime, subject, substance, subtract, subtropical, probably

cab, dab, lab, grab, cob, job, mob, sob, dub, rub, tub, sub, Deb, club, probe, microbe, superb, disturb, suburb, absorb

Notes: ....

....

....

....

....

Ex. 2   Explore the B consonant in the following sentences. *Single Underlines* are marked for you. You provide the last sentence's *underline*.

- Ro<u>b</u> had a blueberry muffin and a super<u>b</u> slice of banana nut bread for breakfast.

- The spider's beautiful co<u>b</u>we<u>b</u> wasn't distur<u>b</u>ed by the shru<u>b</u>…in the subur<u>b</u>s.

- Bob Buren's boss Ben Bugle gra<u>bb</u>ed Bob's shoulder and praised, "Bo<u>b</u>! Super<u>b</u> job in the la<u>b</u>!"

- Jacob Dobb, the DeKalb County Sheriff, swore that he did not bribe the mob's boss in the cab.

Ex. 3   Explore the B consonant in the following nursery rhyme. <u>*Single-underline*</u> the B before a punctuation or another consonant.

Rub a Dub Dub

Rub-a-du<u>b</u>-du<u>b</u>,
Three men in a tu<u>b</u>,
And who do you think they be?
The butcher, the baker, the candlestick-maker,
All put out to sea.[33]

(Children's Nursery Rhyme)

Notes: ....
....
....
....
....
....

---

[33] https://allnurseryrhymes.com/rub-a-dub-dub/ "Rub-a-dub-dub" is a Traditional nursery rhyme dating back to the late 18th century England. Accessed August 1, 2021.

Ex.4	Explore the B consonant in the following *dialogue*.

A Backyard Barbecue in the Suburb

Bob:	Hey, Deb, has the mob shown up yet?
Deb:	No, Bob. Not yet. I don't think anyone will show up exactly on time.
Bob:	That's a relief. But guess what? I am still stuck in my lab having a hard time with my stubborn lab job. I have to submit this lab report soon but I'm still wrestling with it now. I am way behind on my deadline.
Deb:	That's too bad. Hey! Billy, Bob, and Brenda Cobb just drove in.
Bob:	Great! In that case, would you please go to Busy Bees grocery in our suburb and buy the following items?
Deb:	Ok. Let me grab a pen. I am ready. Shoot.
Bob:	A package of beef patties for burgers, chicken breast, a bottle of BB's Barbecue Sauce, a few boxes of Home-Brewed bottled beer, a loaf of banana nut bread, blueberry muffins, butter, baby broccoli and a head of Boston lettuce.
Deb:	Bravo, you're making me hungry. I will grab all these at the Busy Bees and Barron's Bakery and will go ahead and put the meat on the grill. So, go ahead and finish your job and hurry back home.
Bob:	Thanks. See you soon.

The Silent B

Ex. 5	The /b/ spelling marked in *italics* in the following words are ***silent*** (not pronounced).

bom*b*, clim*b*, crum*b*, dum*b*, lam*b*, lim*b*, num*b*, thum*b*, wom*b*, plum*b*er, catacom*b*, de*b*t, dou*b*t, su*b*tle

Notes: ....

....

....

Ex. 6   Explore the *Silent B* in the following words and sentences

- Have you ever clim*b*ed the Himalayas or Mt. Everest?

- To fry the most delicious lam*b* cutlets, the cook coated the lam*b* meat with bread crum*b*s.

- The plum*b*er felt his thum*b* go num*b* after rubbing out the strange substance from the surface of a pipe.

- The baby in the mother's wom*b* is called a fetus; but when the same baby has been delivered from the wom*b*, it is called an infant.

- Bob sent a su*b*tle message to his wife, Debby, stating that he is finally de*b*t free from his student loan. But the message was so su*b*tle, Debby dou*b*ted her husband's de*b*t-free declaration.

Carry over into real life: Now you have the 'tappable' consonants to include in your everyday conversations. Choose a 15-minute block of time to just focus on what we have covered so far. If you forget, don't criticize yourself—just recognizing that you didn't include a B, or an N is positive feedback! It means that your *awareness* is growing.

Notes:..

....

....

....

....

....

....

....

....

....

....

The P [p] as in *Pop*

The P is an unsustainable consonant. It is the voiceless version of B.

To Create the P Consonant:

1. Close your lips together as if you are getting ready to form an M consonant.

2. Build a slight pressure as you did with the B consonant

3. Then spring apart your lips with a light presence of air without vocal vibration *(P-P-P-P)*.

   (Hint: if you allow vibration to take place, a voiced sound—you will be creating the B)

Ex. 1   Now explore the P sound in the word-initial positions in the following words.

pay, pen, pin, park, part, people, Peter, pipe, pick, pilot, police, policy, particular, polite, poise, pulse, purpose, pickle, patter, pencil, political, pump, power, paste, periscope, painless

Ex. 2   Explore the P sound in the word-medial positions before a stressed syllable.

com**pare**, com**pete**, com**plete**, com**put**er, de**port**, ex**port**, im**port**, im**press**, **pi**pette, post**pone**, pre**pare**, re**peat**, re**ply**, re**sponse**, re**port**, re**pul**sive, sup**port**

Ex. 3   Explore the P sound in these word-medial positions.

piper, pepper, paper, happy, campus, principle, discipline, sample, couple, triple, example, maple

Ex. 4   Explore the P sound after the S.

*Sp*ain, *sp*am, *sp*are, *sp*ecial, *sp*eed, *sp*irit, *sp*iral, *sp*lit, *sp*lendid, *sp*inach, *sp*onge, *sp*orts, *sp*ectacular, *sp*read, *sp*y, e*sp*ecially, ex*p*eriment, ex*p*lain, ex*p*lore, in*sp*ection, in*sp*ire

Ex. 5   Explore the P sound before another consonant.

You will feel it as a separate spring away action before the consonant that follows.

apt, adapt, baptize, captain, caption, concept, deception, disrupt, interrupt, MapQuest, option, optimum, optimistic, perhaps, perception, popcorn, Popsicle, popstar, pop-tart, prompt, reception, redemption, reptile, apnea, dyspnea

Ex. 6   Explore the P sound in the word-final positions. The first few words are marked for you.

cap, clap, gap, lap, map, nap, Pap, rap, sap, trap, ape, cape, grape, tape, shape, escape, sharp, dip, hip, lip, rip, tip, ship, slip, ripe, type, jeep, keep, sheep, sleep, cop, hop, mop, pop, sop, top, stop, amp, bump, jump, pump, stump, coop, hoop, cope, hope, pope, rope, scope, soap, soup

Notes: ....
....
....
....
....
....
....
....
....
....
....
....
....

Ex. 7   Explore the P sounds in the following expressions and sentences. *Single underline* the P before another consonant that is created differently than the P and before punctuation or a pause. The first two sentences are marked.

- A sheep-shaped ship; a ship-shaped sheep

- Where did Pip hide the Tip Top Famous Pizza coupons?

- Do you prefer using MapQuest or Google Maps?

- Your prompt reply is appreciated greatly.

- Would you rather purchase a top-priced laptop computer or desktop computer?

- The pop star's popular snacks are popcorn, pop-tarts, and popsicles.

- Pop your lips with a puff of gently pressurized air for the aspirated "P" sound.

- President Hopkins postponed her campaign trip because of sleep deprivation.

- The popular princess wore a pretty purple dress for the reception.

- The bishop rehearsed "The Prayer Song" to perform on 'Parents' Night.'

- Writing about personal experience is one way to prevent plagiarism.

Ex. 8   Explore the P sound in the following tongue twister.

Peter Piper

Peter Piper Picked a Peck of Pickled Peppers;
A Peck of Pickled Peppers Peter Piper Picked.
If Peter Piper Picked a Peck of Pickled Peppers,
Where's the Peck of Pickled Peppers Peter Piper Picked?[34]

(Nursery Rhyme)

---

[34] http://www.sweetrhymes.com/nursery-rhymes/peter-piper-picked-a-peck-of-pickled-peppers/
https://allnurseryrhymes.com/peter-piper/ July 30, 2021

Ex. 9   Explore the P sounds in the following story.

I usually park my car at the parking deck and then try to walk across the University Parkway to go to the Public Health building. This can be particularly dangerous during rush hour. Patrick Plamp told me that he saw a pretty bad traffic accident yesterday as he was waiting for the traffic light to change in that very spot where I use the pedestrian crossing directly in front of the Public Health building.

Patrick told me that it was about 3:00 pm, so the traffic was getting pretty heavy. He said that there was a pedestrian crossing University Parkway, and a Prius was turning right onto Interloop. Probably the driver was typing on his cellphone. He just stepped on the gas and plowed right into the young female pedestrian who was walking properly in the pedestrian crosswalk.

This sort of problem has reportedly become a profoundly serious one at our university. There are large numbers of pedestrians walking from sun-up to sundown around the campus, but drivers do not pay enough attention to them. They only look out for other vehicles. The campus police told us that people have even been killed while crossing streets in and around our campus.

Patrick told me that this pedestrian was not injured seriously because the driver of the SUV was not speeding. Even though she was plowed down by the Prius, no serious injury was perpetrated. Patrick said that the pedestrian was obviously shaken,but she was able to stand up on her own when the police and ambulance arrived at the scene. And, fortunately, the Emergency room of the University hospital was on the same street just a few blocks away from the scene on Interloop. She was *plumb lucky!

*The b in plumb is silent

Notes: ....

....

....

....

....

The D [d] as in *Dad*

The D is an unsustainable consonant. It is the voiced version of the T consonant.

To create the D Consonant:

1. Place your tongue on the upper gum ridge, and then lightly spring away

2. Simultaneously hum, *(D-D-D-D)* which will give you a brief voiced bounce.

3. Try not to add any unnecessary extra vowel sound at the end of the vibration. It should sound more like D-D-D, rather than Duh-Duh-Duh

4. You should be able to see a small portion of lower front teeth in the mirror.

Ex. 1   Explore the D consonant in the word-initial positions in the following words.

dad, deal, divine, deadly, definite, design, decimal, degree, define, delicate, delicious, different, dynamic, drastic, domestic, daffodils

Ex. 2   Explore the D consonant in the word-final positions in the following.

dad, add, pad, glad, mad, sad, odd, God, old, bed, red, seed, need, bid, did, aid, acid, code, mode, bread, breed, method, period, subside, trade, attitude, proud, ground, found, sound, mound, provide, proceed, greed, grade, trend

Ex. 3   Explore the D consonant in the word-medial positions before a "stressed vowel."

academic, indeed, induce, reduce, deduce, introduce, introduction, redeem, condense, condition, addition, rendition, mundane, address, Abdullah, identify

Ex. 4   Explore the D when it occurs between two vowels, the second of which is unstressed.

daddy, added, Addison, Canada, Canadian, study, student, order, odor, radio, radius, radical, radiant, radiator, radiation, resident, irradiation, madder, maddest, meddle, middle, Middleton, muddy, muddiest, sadder, saddest

Ex. 5   Explore the D consonant in the following sentences. *Single underline the D when it appears before a different consonant or before a pause or punctuation. The first sentence is marked for you.*

- Dylan's da<u>d</u> really di<u>d</u> reduce his debt through stock tra<u>d</u>e.

- Brad Ford found his grade points went up considerably during this grading period.

- Dr. Dodi Dobson opened his door and greeted all the dignitaries with delight.

- It seemed as if Reed had ordered a lot of notepads the other day, but I could only find one of them.

- I did my homework on the pages I should have done.

Notes: ....
....
....
....
....
....
....
....
....
....
....

The Blended D with L

When the spelling is DL, there is no vowel in between the two consonants. The tongue remains in the D position and the L simply stays there on the gum ridge, but just the tip remains—you will feel a firming of the sides of the tongue as you transition from the D to the L. It will feel like moving from an N to an L (N~~L).

Ex. 6   Explore this combination in these words:

noo*dl*e, pe*ddl*e, pu*ddl*e, poo*dl*e, pe*dal*, me*dal*, id*l*e, me*ddl*ing, cra*dl*ing, kin*dl*y, frien*dl*y

Ex. 7   Explore the DL combination in these sentences:

• Don't me*ddl*e with my noo*dl*es.

• The pe*dal*s of the bike were difficult to pe*dal*.

• I stepped in the pu*ddl*e while cra*dl*ing my me*dal*s.

• The kin*dl*y, frien*dl*y doctor helped me grea*tl*y. (TL blend)

Notes: ....

....

....

....

....

....

....

....

....

....

....

Pronunciation of the '-ed' endings of the Past-tense Verbs:

1. **The '-ed' is pronounced as [d] after a voiced consonant[35].**

    When the /ed/ sound follows a voiced consonant in past tense verbs or passive verbs, the /e/ is silent and the *–ed* suffix is pronounced as [d]. Feel the brief vibration of your vocal folds by putting one hand on your throat where your larynx is.

open*ed*---------open*d*	learn*ed*----------learn*d*
listen*ed*--------listen*d*	show*ed*----------show*d*
lov*ed*-----------lov*d*	clean*ed*----------clean*d*
bugg*ed*---------bug*d*	realiz*ed*----------realiz*d*
acknowledg*ed*—acknowledg*d*	show*ed*-----------show*d*

*   Nancy remember*ed* she had open*ed* her birthday present already.

*   Mother cann*ed* and stor*ed* a lot of vegetables each year.

*   Dad open*ed* his wallet and show*ed* his driver's license to the officer.

*   Mosquitoes bugg*ed* me at summer camp.

*   Maddox clean*ed* his desk and realiz*ed* he had fun while doing it.

Notes: ....

....

....

....

....

....

....

....

....

....

---

[35] *Voiced consonants: b, g, j, l, m, n, ng, r, v, z, zh*

2. **The '-ed' is pronounced as [t] after a voiceless consonant[36], even though it is spelled with a D.**

When the /ed/ sound follows a voiceless consonant in past tense verbs or passive verbs, the /e/ is silent and the **–ed** suffix is pronounced as [t].

worked----------work*t*   searched---------search*t*
popp*ed*----------pop*t*   kick*ed*-----------kick*t*
wash*ed*---------wash*t*   notic*ed*----------notis*t*
knock*ed*------knock*t*   cuff*ed*-----------cuff*t*

- I work*ed* way too many hours last night and I feel like a zombie right now.

- We notic*ed* that the youth leader unpack*ed* and popp*ed* more popcorn.

- Jack knock*ed* on the door and ask*ed* if he could come in.

- Christopher search*ed* and found the answers to his own questions.

- The goalkeeper kick*ed* another ball toward the center of the field.

- I wash*ed* my clothes and notic*ed* my cuff*ed* pants were torn.

Notes: ....

....

....

....

....

....

....

....

....

....

---

[36] *Voiceless Consonants: f, k, p, s, ch, sh, ts*

3. The '-ed' is pronounced as [id] after a D or T.

started----------startid	ended-------------endid
mounted---------mountid	sounded-----------soundid
wanted------------wantid	needed------------needid
rented-------------rentid	awarded-----------awardid
expected--------expectid	experimented-----experimentid

- Our company start*ed* to build a new office building because it was need*ed*.

- They mount*ed* a huge clock on the wall.

- The construction end*ed* earlier than we expect*ed*.

- Jared applaud*ed* his co-worker, praising his success.

- We rent*ed* a tent just in time for my daughter's birthday party.

- Edison experiment*ed* all day and night to create his inventions.

Ex. 9	The '-ed' in 'Naked' and 'Learn*ed*' in this *dialogue*.
Sun:	In our classes, we learned to pronounce the /-ed/ ending as a [d] at the end of a verb that contains a voiced consonant before it. Then why do we pronounce the /-ed/ in the word "naked" as [id] instead of [t]? The K is not voiced!
Jonghee:	Yes, [neɪ.kt] instead of [neɪ.kɪd]! A good question. I see that you've been paying attention to the pronunciation of /-ed/ endings. In the case of 'naked,' you assume that 'naked' is the past tense of the verb 'nake.' However, the word 'nake' is not found in the English dictionary, and thus 'naked' is not the past tense of 'nake.' 'Naked' is an adjective and is pronounced as [neɪkɪd].
Sun:	Oh, I see. I have another question about the /-ed/ sound. What about the past tense of 'learn'? I heard someone saying [lɝnɪd] instead of [lɝnd].
Jonghee:	Another good question. The word 'learned' can be used as the past-tense verb, where you move directly to the D from the N, but it can also be used as an <u>adjective</u>, meaning 'educated,' pronounced as [lɝnɪd] with that extra syllable.
Sun	Oh, my! English is so complicated!
Jonghee:	It can be, but it gets easier with time.

The T [t] as in *Tot*

To create the T consonant

1. Open your mouth so that the lips rest slightly apart.

2. Lightly tap the gum ridge with the tongue blade to produce a spring away action with the slightest release of air. *(T-T-T-T)*

3. Experience this tapping without adding vocal vibration. This is your T consonant.

Useful tips:

- Your lips remain in a neutral orientation, not pursed or urged forward.

- Try to avoid creating any sort of vowel sound at the end of the T. (T-T-T, rather than Tuh-Tuh-Tuh)

- You can feel the slightest release of air coming out of your mouth when you put your palm close to your mouth.

- /T/ is a short consonant, so it does not sustain even if you try to make it longer.

Notes: ....

....

....

....

....

....

....

....

....

....

....

Exploring the T consonant in the Word-Initial Positions (at the beginning of the words).

Ex. 1   In the following words and sentences, explore the T consonant in the word-initial positions before a stressed syllable.

tan, table, take, tell, team, test, tie, tickle, Tina, teach, telephone, temperature, terrify, told, too, two, Toby, Tom, tomato, town, traffic, travel, trouble

- Today, Tom told Toby that he experienced a terrifying tornado in Texas for the first time in his life.

- What time is it in Tel Aviv right now?

- It's twenty minutes to two in the afternoon. We have plenty of time.

- Is that right? It's for the ten-o'clock television news in Tuscaloosa.

- What is the time difference between Taipei and Tucson?

- Tim timed his Ted talk today to fit into the time limit.

- Teresa travels around the town to teach at two different training facilities each day.

Notes: ....
....
....
....
....
....
....
....
....

Exploring the T consonant in the Word-medial Positions (in the middle of the word).

Ex. 2   Explore the T sound before an unstressed vowel in the word-medial position in the following words and sentences.

water, meter, forty, eighty, ability, party, committee, chatting, cattle, Natalie, tomato, potato, brighter, reporter, charter, creator, computer, native, positive, creative, better, quality, bitter, sitting, putting, supporting

- Betty bought some butter to make some batter.

- For some reason, the moon looks brighter and prettier tonight.

- The meter man checked the water meter later in the afternoon yesterday.

- Natalie was cutting some tomatoes and potatoes for her party.

- Christy got up at eight o'clock and fried some green tomatoes and sliced potatoes for her breakfast.

- The quality control committee reported positively on our team's performance.

Exploring the T sound in the word-final positions (at the end of the words)

Ex. 3   In the following words and sentences, explore the /T/ sound in the word-final positions. *Single underline* them as you find them.

at, that, cat, sat, mat, pat, bit, bet, beat, cut, hit, heat, sent, rent, meet, quit, rate, date, debate, graduate, interstate, illustrate, illiterate, smart, repeat, internet

- I bet Pat and Brad spent hours and days on the test.

- That cat was found on the mat before Matt intended to sit on it.

- When you cut corners, you cut profits because our customers are very smart.

- At this rate, we will have to reset the date for the debate.

- Go straight 8 miles on Interstate 8, and then exit to the right.

How to pronounce the T sound at the end of a word before a TH, D, TS, CH that begins the next word:

1. Place your tongue tip on the back surface of the upper front teeth and

2. Keeping the tongue tip at this spot, continue to the TH consonant, which is created between the upper and lower front teeth. This movement is very quick, like a sliding action from the T to the TH or to a D, T, S, N, TS, DZH, CH, DG

that this	that tsetse fly	but John	fat chance
thought Don	won't throw	that seems	but now

Note: Some students of GA English tend to add an additional Schwa sound [ə] after the T sound before the TH consonant.

atə the	thatə the	butə the
notə the	butə then	butə not
notə that	justə that	putə the

A strategy:

To avoid an unnecessary schwa [ə] sound, simply keep your tongue tip on the upper gum ridge (ceiling of the oral cavity near the top front teeth) as you move to the TH as indicated above. After creating the TH, then allow your tongue tip to release into the vowel that will follow.

Ex. 4   In the following sentences, connect the T sound in the word-final position of the first word to the TH, D, T, CH, DZH sound in the next word. The first two sentences are marked for you.

- At the beginning, I could not create the /t/ sound, but now I can.

- Matt Durwood was in the meeting at that judicious time.

- My expert tutor demonstrated the /t/ consonant by asking us to 'Try it this way and that way,' and after following her way; I can create just the ideal T now.

- I went job-hunting for the first time today, but the result was not that dynamic.

Ex. 5   The /ed/-endings pronounced as the T consonant

The /-ed/ spelling of past-tense verbs is pronounced as a T consonant when the verb ends with a voiceless consonant such as f, k, p, s, ch, sh.

For example, a word such as *worked* would sound more like [wɜ-kt].

Explore the T consonant of the -ed-endings in the following words and sentences.

chop*ed*, cook*ed*, cramp*ed*, experienc*ed*, dump*ed*, kick*ed*, mapp*ed*, napp*ed*, popp*ed*, pump*ed*, slic*ed*, stopp*ed*, touch*ed*, walk*ed*, wash*ed*, work*ed*, clasp*ed*, lurch*ed*, inch*ed*, sash*ed*

- The chef napped before he chopped up the meat and vegetables.

- He kicked off his shoes and washed his hands.

- She would have liked a baked potato, but instead asked for French fries.

- The music stopped as he unlocked the door.

Notes: ....

....

....

....

....

....

....

....

....

....

....

The G [g] as in *Gag*

The G is an unsustainable consonant. It is the voiced version of the K.

To create the G[g] Consonant:

1. Allow your jaw to rest down as if to inhale through your mouth.

2. Raise the back of your tongue to gently touch where the soft and hard palates join in your mouth.

3. Let your tongue tip rest on the back of the lower front teeth.

4. Gently spring away (remove) your back tongue from the soft palate with a hint of vocal vibration *(G-G-G-G)*. This is your G sound.

Useful tips:

- You can see the front of your tongue in the mirror if you open your mouth.

- The slightest gentle and delicate pressure is felt on the back of the tongue against the ceiling where the soft and hard palate meet and then springs away from that location.

- There is no force applied or no deliberately added vowel sound (G-G-G rather than Guh-Guh-Guh).

Ex. 1   Explore the G[g] consonant in the *word or syllable initial positions* and *before a vowel*. You do not mark the G in the word-initial positions or before a vowel.

get, go, gate, gas, gap, gadget, goal, glad, glass, graph, grass, giggle, guard, guarantee, grant, grape, group, ground, gravity, rectangle, triangle, congress, argue, category, struggle, negative, configuration

Ex. 2   Explore the G[g] consonant in the word-final or syllable final positions by *single-underlining* and tapping the back of the tongue against the soft palate. The first 3 have been done for you.

bag, augment, beg, ignore, big, Craig, dog, egg, Doug, drug, fig, zigzag, fog, frog, gag, gig, hug, lag, leg, log, peg, pig, sag, tag, vague, vogue, league, fatigue, intrigue, analog, catalog, cognition, recognize, significant

Ex. 3   Explore the **added G [g] consonant after the NG [ŋ] in the medial position.** You will notice that the extra G sound does not show in the spelling. However, if you recall from your NG unit, the NG sound is spelled as an N in these words.

For your information:

As you proceed from the NG sound to the extra[g], you will realize that NG and G are both pronounced at the contact points of the back of the tongue and the back of the soft palate (on the back of the roof (or ceiling), which is where the hard and soft palate of the oral cavity meet.

anger	/ang.**ger**/	angry	/ang.**gry**/	English	/Eng.**g**lish/
finger	/fing.**ger**/	hunger	/hung.**ger**/	hungry	/hung.**gry**/
Hungary	/Hung.**gary**/	longer	/long.**ger**/	longest	/long.**gest**/
younger	/young.**ger**/	stronger	/strong.**ger**/	strongest	/strong.**gest**/

Ex. 4   Explore the Silent G consonant in the following words. The g/gh are not pronounced. The G is in the spelling but is silent. The silent g or gh is *italicized* below.

g*nat*, g*naw*, dou*gh*, thou*gh*, ei*gh*t, li*gh*t, ni*gh*t, ri*gh*t, brou*gh*t, tau*gh*t, thou*gh*t, thou*gh*.

Ex. 5   Explore the G [g] consonant in the following sentences by single-underlining and tapping the sound on the tap opportunities.

• When Doug zigs, Mag zags; and when Mag zags, Doug zigs.

• This morning's fog made Greg's far-sight vision vague.

• Fatigue from jet lag caused Gary to struggle to stay awake in the geography class.

• Meg recognized that the augmented experiment significantly changed the pigment.

• The big dog at the gate was Meg's.

• At the end of the league, Craig's legs finally gave out.

• I forgot that I left the water jug under the fig tree.

• Doug reported to his gastro-intestinal specialist that he sometimes experiences a gag reflex and gnawing pain in his gut.

Ex. 6   Explore the G [g] consonant in the following passage by *single-underlining* and tapping the <u>G</u> consonant on the tap opportunities.

Granny Greta's Farmhouse

Mag and Greg's family visited Granny Greta's farmhouse. When they arrived at the farm, Granny Greta and Uncle Craig and Cousin Doug came out to meet them. Granny Greta, Uncle Craig and Cousin Doug gave everyone a big hug. Not surprisingly, Granny's dogs, pigs, geese, ducks, and chickens also came out to the gate to meet them. On the front yard of Granny Greta's house, other dogs, pigs, and geese were playing hide-and-seek games with ground squirrels, frogs, toads, and grasshoppers. When the gang went into the living room, two of the cutest puppy dogs were having a tug of war with the ends of the living room rug. Granny Greta said those puppies also love to play tag with each other. After a while, Uncle Craig and Cousin Doug grilled juicy hamburgers while Granny Greta made the most delicious egg omelets with the fresh eggs from her chickens. She also served us a fresh green salad harvested from her garden. They were yummy.

After a great lunch, Mag and Doug's family had a short walk around Granny Greta's farm. When the family came back to Granny's house, Grandma Greta and Cousin Doug brought surprises to Mag and Greg—two lovely puppy dogs playing tug of war and gnawing on Granny Greta's living room rug! Mag and Greg were thrilled to bring those puppies home to let them play tag with each other, have a tug of war, and gnaw on their own rugs!

Notes: ....

....

....

....

....

....

....

....

The K [k] as in *Kick*

The K is an unsustainable consonant. It is the voiceless version of the G. The GA English [k] sound can be spelled with /k/, /c/, /ck/, /ch/, and /q/.

To create the K Consonant:

1. Allow your jaw to rest down as if to inhale through your mouth.

2. Raise the back of your tongue to gently touch the place where the soft and hard palates meet. This is the point of contact.

3. Let your tongue tip rest on the back of the lower front teeth.

4. Let the back of your tongue lightly spring away from the palate without any vocal vibration *(K-K-K-K)*. In GA, a K in initial and medial positions tends to have a slight aspiration (air) before the next sound.

Ex. 1   Explore the K consonant in the following words. Italicized consonants are pronounced as an S instead of K sound.

/k/	cook, book, took, hook, chalk, skip, skirt, skeleton.
/c/	cue, cat, cut, come, cook, case, cord, carry, cause, campus, caloric, con*c*ise, create, Mac, sac, basic, picnic, economic, domestic, Atlantic, electric, metric, fact, sect, object, reject, collect, correct, select, perfect, scare, scale, scarlet, practi*c*e, ac*c*ent, ac*c*ept, ac*c*ident, ac*c*elerate
/ck/	back, pack, Jack, tack, deck, neck, kick, pick, sick
/ch/	Christmas, chord, chemistry, stomach, technique, technicolor
/q/	quiz, queue (cue), queasy, queen, Quinn, qualm, quilt, quarter, quartet, quadruple, quintet, quintessential, unique, technique, Quaker
/x/ [ks]	ax, lax, tax, taxi, mix, fix, six, dixie, next, text, X-ray, exer*c*ise, ex*c*ellent
Silent /K/	know, knew, known, knowledge, knee, knob, knock, knight, Knute

Ex. 2   Explore the K consonant in the following expressions. Single underline the 'playable' opportunities.

- Kate ki<u>ck</u>ed her crazy habit of craving any kind of ca<u>k</u>e.

- While having a picnic in their backyard under a gigantic pecan tree, Mac and Dominique mimicked their favorite actors.

- Scarlet Quinn felt queasy in her stomach during the chemistry class.

- The measuring cup with the metric system works perfectly in my kitchen.

- The committee carefully selected the contestants for the technical support crew.

- I can accept the fact that I speak differently from the way some people do, but as long as I can be understood, I can communicate when I talk.

Ex. 3   Explore the /K/ consonant sounds in the following dialogue. It is italicized for you.

Dialogue: This Squeaky-Clean Feeling

Jack: I feel s*qu*ea*ky c*lean.

Kim: Did you ta*k*e a nice and s*qu*ea*ky-c*lean bath?

Jack: No, not really.

Kim: Then?

Jack: I just finished a chapter of my *c*ommittee report by *c*ommunicating ba*ck* and forth with my *c*olleague *Ch*ristina. The sense of a*cc*omplishment is as good as the feeling you get after ta*k*ing a nice, s*qu*ea*ky-c*lean bath.

Kim: I know what you mean. I know I will also have that s*qu*ea*ky-c*lean feeling when I finish my *c*ourse wor*k* and present the result of my research before the *c*ommittee members. I *c*annot wait for the day, and I *c*an't wait for that s*qu*ea*ky-c*lean feeling of su*cc*ess. Yea!

Ex. 4   Explore the /K/ consonant in the following passage.

Note: In words like 'e<u>x</u>periment' and 'e<u>x</u>ceptions' the /x/ is a K sound followed by an S (KS) There will be an * to identify these words for you.

Chemistry Lab 106

Welcome to Chemistry Lab 106. My name is Jack Clockson and I will be your instructor for this semester. As you might have already guessed, Chemistry 106 is your first level Chemistry class in this university.

What is chemistry? Chemistry is defined as a study of matter, and the changes that matter undergoes. The observation and interpretation of chemical change is essentially what chemistry is. How do we know when a chemical change has taken place? How do we know that a chemical reaction has actually occurred? Fortunately, nature provides some clues to let us know that a chemical change has occurred.

In today's *e<u>x</u>periment, you will create some reactions, and look for the clues that a reaction has occurred. This will require careful work and keen observation on your part. You must observe carefully and record your observations on the Data Sheet provided. You will work with many chemicals and formulas that are unfamiliar to you at this point. Don't be concerned about this. You will very soon learn the significance of these.

Now, I have an announcement. Beginning with the next class, make sure to keep all the safety rules that I handed out in the syllabus, including wearing safety goggles and closed-toe shoes always in the lab. The university is very strict about keeping these safety rules, and anyone who does not abide by them will be *e<u>x</u>cluded from participating in any *e<u>x</u>periments performed in our classes.

There will be no *e<u>x</u>ceptions. So, please bring your safety goggles and wear your tennis shoes instead of your summer sandals in the lab. Do you have any questions? If not, we will go through a safety quiz before we embark on our first *e<u>x</u>periment.

(Adapted from an essay by Jun Chen, Graduate Student, Department of Chemistry, University of Alabama at Birmingham.)

Notes:..

....

....

The DG (DZH) [dʒ] as in *Judge*

The DZH is an unsustainable voiced consonant and is the voiced version of the CH [tʃ].

To create the DZH (DG) [dʒ] Consonant

1. Place your tongue blade where the D is positioned on the upper gum ridge, the point of contact.

2. Experience a quick, bouncing release of the D and a gentle, short ZH sound together. Let the tongue tip slip downward, springing away from the gum ridge as you form a gently pursed *zhhh* with your lips.

3. The D sound will blend into the *zhhh* to form this blended short consonant combination *(DZH-DZH-DZH-DZH)*. This is your DZH Consonant.

Another Option for the DZH (DG) [dʒ] Consonant

As the spelling DG suggests:

Place your tongue blade at the D position and say the **name of the GA letter /g/** with the slight lip-pursing. (GEE)

The DZH[(DG)[dʒ] consonant can be spelled with the /j/, /g/, /dg/, /dj/, or /du/.

| Ex. 1 | Explore the DZH (DG) [dʒ] consonant in the following words on the **word-initial positions.** |

/j /   Jack, Jane, Jared, Jasmine, Jeff, Jennifer, John, Jordan, juice, jump, junior, jelly, jet, jean, jeep, jest, job, jock, joke, joy, joint, junk, journal, journey, judicial, jury, jurisdiction

/g/   gentle, gentlemen, general, gesture, germ, German, gist, giant, ginger, gymnastic, geography, giraffe, gigantic

Notes: ....

....

....

....

Ex. 2   For the following group of the words, explore the vocal vibration for the DZH [dʒ] sound on the **word-medial positions.**

/g/   agent, agitate, algebra, angel, biology, danger, digit, digest, emergency, energy, engineer, exaggerate, magic, merger, legislative, nitrogen, original, oxygen, register, religion, vegetable, Virginia

/dj/   adjust, adjective, adjourn.

/dg/   budget

/j/   majestic, major, sojourn, inject, subject, object, project, rejoice, enjoy, major

/du/   procedure, verdure, supersedure, ordure

Ex. 3   For the following group of the words, feel the vocal vibration for the DZH [dʒ] sound on the **word-final positions** but avoid adding any vowel sound after the DZH[dʒ].

/g/   age, large, stage, orange, George, sponge, average, beverage, bulge, cabbage, challenge, charge, college, diverge, drainage, emerge, engage, encourage, image, lunge, message, merge, package, plunge, purge, rage, range, salvage

/dg/   badge, bridge, Coolidge, dodge, edge, hedge, wedge, ledge, pledge, knowledge, acknowledge, judge, nudge, ridge

Notes: ....

....

....

....

....

....

....

Ex. 4   Explore the DZH (DG)[dʒ] sound in the following sentences by *single-underlining* and *tapping* the sound in the Tappable Opportunities (before another consonant; before a pause or punctuation). The first three lines are *marked* for you.

- George nudged Jacky to try a Jean jacket in the Jemison Jean store.

- The president pledged to make an adjustment in the budget for the new fiscal year.

- For the [d], [t], [tʃ], and [dʒ] sounds, our tongue blade briefly touches the gum ridge.

- The edge of the ledge was covered by a ridge of hedge.

- John Coolidge acknowledged college is for knowledge not for bridge parties.

- You misjudge your knowledge of marriage. It is actually huge.

Ex. 5   Explore DZH (DG) [dʒ] sound in the following poem.

"Judy jumped to the rock at the edge of the sludge.
She joked, "I'll just stand here and I will not budge!"
John Johnny, the generous magician who loved her,
trudged to the adjacent rock ledge to join her.
Judy gestured to him to adjust his condition
so their eyes could conjoin in juxtaposition.
He said, "I'll conjure up a ginormous jet
with jellybeans and fudge and a gerbil for a pet;
if you'll genuinely adjust your gestures to say:
"I'll join you, John Johnny, on that jet for a day!"
(Deborah A. Kinghorn, Lessac Master Teacher © 2022)

Notes: ....
....
....
....

The CH [tʃ] as in *Church*

The CH consonant is unsustainable. It is the voiceless version of DG (DZH) [dʒ].

To create the CH Consonant:

1. Place your tongue tip on the T contact point on the gum ridge.

2. Experience a quick, bouncing release of the T and a gentle, short SH sound together. Let the tongue tip slip downward, springing away from the gum ridge as you form a gently pursed *shhh* with your lips.

3. The T sound will blend into the *shhh* to form this blended short consonant combination (*TSH-TSH-TSH-TSH*). This is your CH consonant.

Useful tips:

• The most efficient CH consonant is quick, energetic, and tapped lightly without any breath or vocal vibrations added in.

• This consonant is often spelled with the C, CH, TCH, TI (as in '-tion' as in /question/, and TU (as in '-ture' as in /picture/).

Notes: ....

....

....

....

....

....

....

....

....

....

....

Ex. 1   Explore the CH consonant in the word-initial, medial, and final positions.

CH consonant in the Word-initial positions

chain, chair, chalk, chance, chaplain, Chad, Charles, chat, cheap, check, cheese, chest, chick, chew, chicken, chill, China, child, chin, chip, choice, chuck, chunk, church

CH consonant in the Word-medial positions

ketchup, kitchen, purchase, creature, preacher, orchard, Richard, lecture, denture, vulture, duchess, ratchet, butcher

CH consonant in the Word-final positions

watch, match, catch, batch, patch, rich, itch, hitch, beach, which, switch, march, reach, peach, coach, bench, clinch, punch, search, pitch

CH sound in the /-tion/ and /-tu-/ spellings

Ques*tion*, punc*tu*al, punc*tu*ate, cul*tu*re, ges*tu*re, na*tu*re, pic*tu*re, punc*tu*re, su*tu*re, tinc*tu*re, ves*tu*re, vul*tu*re

Notes: ....

....

....

....

....

....

....

....

Ex. 2   Explore the CH consonant in the following sentences. *Single underline* the CH sound before a dissimilar consonant.

- Chaney's family purchased a dining room set with pea<u>ch</u>-tone chairs.

- I use checks to pay bills and keep the copies of them in my checkbook.

- China is a large country with a rich culture that features fine Chinese cuisine.

- Last March, the children of Ms. Chin's church went to the zoo and watched cheetahs, chimpanzees, chipmunks, and Chihuahuas.

- Chocolate-covered cherries are Rich's favorite chewy treat.

- In the future, NASA might search for exotic creatures on other planets.

- Chapter 7 of the Chinese lecture is on Channel 6, but it might be changed to Channel 5.

- Chun ordered a chili dog, a cheeseburger, and some potato chips but forgot the ketchup.

- Mitch cooked on the porch under the torch light, as the light switch in his kitchen didn't work.

Notes: ....

....

....

....

....

....

....

....

....

....

Ex. 3	Explore the CH Sound in the following *dialogue*. Again, you can *single-underline* those places where the CH is positioned before another consonant or a pause/punctuation.

Chun: Charlie told me that there is a 'Yard sale' on Church Street and they also sell china. I searched for an answer, but I don't understand how people can just sell their yard by itself without selling their house as well. And if I choose to buy their yard, how can I move it to my yard; and in which part of my yard should I choose to put the yard I bought? And I also don't understand how American people can sell and buy my country China without China's permission.

Chuck: I guess Charlie didn't explain to you what 'yard sale' and 'china sale' mean. I can understand your confusion. 'Yard sale' doesn't mean that they choose to sell the ground in front of their house. It means they choose to sell things they don't want to keep, by displaying them in their yard and then watching for rich customers. And 'china sale' does not mean they want to sell your country, China. In this case, 'china' means porcelain dinner plates and bowls.

Chun: Then how come they call fine porcelain dinner sets 'china'?

Chuck   Perhaps western people named the fine porcelain plates and bowls as china because China was the first culture that produced them?

Chun: Oh, yes, that much is true!

Notes: ....

....

....

....

....

....

....

....

....

Ex. 4   Compare the sensations in the CH and SH sounds in the following words and sentences.

Remember: The CH consonant is short and light; "SH" is (sustainable) and smooth.

chair—share	catch—cash	choose—shoes
chose—shows	chain—Shane	batch—bash
witch—wish	Chai—shy	much—mush
match—mash	cherry—sherry	chin—shin
cheer—sheer	chime—shine	church—shirts

- *Ch*arlene doesn't want to share her shoes for a change. (*Ch*arlene uses the SH)

- Charles might want to exchange whiskey for sherry for an after-dinner change.

- Shane bought a gold chain for Jane.

- Dr. Cho chose to pay for the tickets to the Chinese New Year's Festival shows.

- To preach at the church today, Pastor Sherwin chose to wear a white dress shirt.

Notes:...

....

....

....

....

....

....

....

....

Feel the difference in the CH, SH, and S sounds in the following words and sentences.

Ch	Sh	S
chain	Shane	sane
China	shine	sign
Chai	shy	sigh
chin	shin	sin
chalk	shock	soccer
cheap	sheep	seep
cherry	Sherry	serenade
cheer	sheer	seer
choose	shoes	sues
chose	shows	sows
catch	cash	Cass
match	mash	mass
march	marsh	Mars
clutch	clash	class
switch	swish	Swiss

- Shane went insane after going through too many chain reactions when having to make unnecessary changes.

- Until this moment, Young-Shin did not recognize the distance between the chin and the shin in our bodies.

- Shane's sheep-skin shoes once were shiny and gorgeous; however, after water seeped through them in the rain, they looked old and cheap.

- Sherry and her sister Sarah surely love fresh, vine-ripened sweet cherries.

- As Martin Luther King, in his picturesque speech described his people's suffering as 'searing in the flames of withering injustice,' vast numbers of people sent him sheer cheers at Liberty Square.

- Chow's crop shows that when he sows the seeds too late in the season, they surely don't grow.

The DZ [dz] as in *Friends*

The DZ [dz] is an non-sustainable consonant blend. Even though the Z consonant is sustainable, the D consonant influences the entire DZ blend to be experienced as a short, percussive sound. It is the voiced version of TS consonant blend.

To create the DZ [dz] Consonant Blend:

1. Place your tongue tip on the upper gum ridge where you create the D consonant.

2. Quickly spring the tongue tip away while voicing the Z consonant. The sides of the tongue will remain close to the upper side molars.

3. You will hear the combined sounds of the DZ, *(DZ-DZ-DZ-DZ)* which is not the same feeling as the spring-away action of the D. The Z sound should be short rather than sustained.

Useful tips:

*   The DZ sound is usually spelled as /ds/ as in 'friends' or 'ads.'

Ex. 1   Explore the [dz] consonant blend in the following words. *Single underline* the appropriate spelling while pronouncing the [dz] consonant blend.

ads, adds, aids, attends, bends, birds, kid's, cards, crowds, dads, deeds, needs, hands, ends, bends, lends, blends, fields, finds, kinds, minds, holds, hundreds, husband's, rods, roads, seeds, sounds, grounds, thousands, electrodes, orchards, Richard's, commands, demands

Ex. 2   Explore the DZ sound in the following sentences. *Single underline* the DZ spelling and tap the [dz] sound briefly and lightly.

*   Jared said, 'I don't know how my kids send me different kinds of cards every Father's Day.'

*   In the Richard's Seeds Company, hundreds and thousands of customers demand hundreds and thousands of pounds of seeds every year.

*   The Chinese students' demands for English pronunciation classes are increasing because of the differences between the English and Chinese sounds.

*   Fred decided he needs to learn to feel the movements of his articulating system to pronounce English sounds.

The TS [ts] as in *Hats*

The TS [ts] is a non-sustainable consonant blend. Even though the S consonant is sustainable, the T consonant influences the entire TS blend to be experienced as a short, percussive sound.

The TS blend is the voiceless version of the DZ consonant blend.

To create the TS Consonant Blend:

1. Place your tongue tip on the upper gum ridge where you create the T consonant.

2. While the tongue is still on the T place, quickly slide the tongue tip away to create the S consonant.

3. You will hear the combined sounds of the TS, *(TS-TS-TS-TS)* which is not the same feeling as the spring-away action of the true T. The S sound should be short rather than sustained.

Ex. 1   Explore the TS sound in the following words by *single underlining* the spelling and tapping the sound briefly and lightly.

It's, its, that's, sits, pits, kits, gifts, mints, let's, pets, pests, sets, cents, tents, bats, cats, fats, hats, mats, acts, pants, shirts, grants, casts, pasts, adapts

what's, Watson, lots, spots, contracts, converts, concerts, pockets, profits, products, prospects, participates, mounts, boasts, unites, routes, doubts, promotes

limits, omits, instincts, indicates, invests, instructs, instruments estimates, resists, requests, rejects, physicists, debates, effects, exempts expects, experiments, environments, specialists, separates, students

courts, sorts, ports, sports, transports, charts, darts, parts, quarts, markets, imports, exports, meets, fleets, puts, commits, adjusts, penetrates, scientists, clients

Notes:...

....

Ex. 2   Explore the TS sound in the following sentences by *single underlining* the spelling and experiencing the blend briefly and lightly.

- That's the store called "Pat's Mats" that sells all sorts of mats.

- He is the scientist who debates the effects of new experiments on patients.

- The physicists discovered new sets of rules.

- The splints were given to the medical students as gifts.

- A hospital sign reads: "We'd like to thank our patients for their patience." (patience' is actually an N followed by an S sound effect, not the TS consonant blend. 'Audience' is another such word')

Ex. 3   Explore the TS sound in the following paragraph by *single underlining* the spelling (before a dissimilar consonant) and tapping the sound briefly and lightly. The first two sentences are marked for you.

Kate is one of the receptionists who works in a large university hospital. She usually wears dress shirts, pants, and shoes to work. She sits at a desk and accepts payments from the patients. Each of Kate's colleagues performs different sorts of tasks: one computes, and another either adapts or activates different policies and contracts; and still another person attracts the attention away from the other hard-working office saints.

Notes: ....

....

....

....

....

....

....

....

....

Ex. 4   Explore the TS in the following *dialogue*.

June: So, how is your weekend going?

Sandy: This weekend has been busy for me because I've had to sing in a few concerts to commemorate the 50th anniversary of the Civil Rights activist, Martin Luther King.

June: I also attended some other events, including taking my students to the Civil Rights Museum and judicial courts, as well as attending one of those concerts you mentioned.

Sandy: I saw all sorts of advertisements for the Martin Luther King Day activities around this campus. Don't you think it is great to learn that when even one person contributes parts of his life for his people, the history of human rights can be changed for the good of a great many.

June: True. Let's not forget, though, in all parts of the globe, lots of important contributions have been made by countless famous artists, scientists, philanthropists, and every day, ordinary people who also changed the world for the better.

Sandy: You are right. However, wouldn't it have been a lot better if human rights had been respected in all parts of the world from the beginning of time, without any mistreatment of others' rights in the first place by all inhabitants of our globe?

June: That's an absolute fact!

Carryover into everyday life: We have now concluded all the GA English Consonants. Choose times throughout the day to include as many as you can in your conversations, either on the phone, online, or in-person. We are now ready to learn about the Vowels/ Diphthongs found in GA English!

Notes: ....

....

....

....

....

....

Chapter 2

Sensing and Shaping GA English Vowels (The Music of the Vowels)[37]

[37] *The Use and Training of the Human Voice: A Bio-Dynamic Approach to Vocal Life 3rd Edition* by Arthur Lessac, McGraw-Hill Higher Education Publishing 1997, pg. 160

A *vowel* is a sound produced without blocking or obstructing the air flow from the lungs. The teeth, lips, or the tongue do not restrict the sound at all, as they do when the *consonants* are formed. The oral cavity is shaped to provide different vowel sounds. Vowels are always 'voiced', whereas consonants may be voiced or unvoiced. When the vowels are produced, a gentle hint of warmth can be detected when you put your hand close to your mouth. In English, the alphabet letters *A, E, I, O, U* and the *W* and *Y* in the word-final positions, represent vowel sounds. Sometimes the *y* within a syllable can be pronounced as a vowel depending on the spelling of the word—such as: id*y*llic or m*y*stery.

English vowels are changeable in their pronunciation depending upon where the speaker lives within the English-speaking world. For the purposes of this text, we will focus on those vowels and diphthongs found in General American English (GA)—used in social and professional circles.

Classification of American English Vowels

GA English vowels can be classified in many ways. Vowels have **quality and quantity.** They may be short or long. Vowels may be **classified** according to the position of the tongue, the place or point of articulation (front, middle and back of the oral cavity); they can be 'tense' or 'lax', and they can be determined by the shape and size of the lip-openings.

However, for the purposes of this book, we will focus on **sensing the movement of the facial muscles and the shapes and sizes of the lip openings to create the vowels and diphthongs.**

A. **The Structural Energy Vowels and Diphthongs[38] (Lip-Rounding Vowels)[39]**

   Lip-rounding vowels involve the movements of our facial muscles[40] with round or oval lip-openings. These Structural Energy vowels are the major or lax vowels: They are ideally formed giving more space between the upper and lower side teeth—creating a more open feel in the oral cavity.

   Experiment: inhale as if to begin a yawn—feel all that openness inside as well as the soft palate rising in the back—this is what is meant by 'yawn space'.

---

[38] Ibid, pp.160-161 and 164-167

[39] *Lip Rounding and Lip Relaxing* are terms that Ms. Shadix used when teaching at the University of Alabama, Birmingham, and found them helpful to her students.

[40] zygomatic and/or levator)   https://www.kenhub.com/en/library/anatomy/zygomaticus-major-muscle

There are 11 Structural Energy Vowels and Diphthongs in GA English

Lessac	IPA	Sample
#1	[u]	as in *food*
#21	[oʊ]	as in *old*
#3	[ɔ]	as in *awful*
#3y	[ɔɪ]	as in *boy*
#3n	[ɔɚ]	as in *more*
R	[ɚ]	as in *bird*
#4	[ɒ]	as in *fog*
#5	[ɑ]	as in *father*
#51	[aʊ]	as in *cow*
#6	[æ]	as in *add*
#6y	[aɪ]	as in *hide*

Neutral Vowels and Diphthongs (Lip-relaxing Vowels/Diphthongs)

B. Neutral Vowels[41]: These vowels involve minimal optimal movement of the facial muscle 'yawn' and a relaxed, neutral positioning of the lips.

Lessac	IPA	Sample
N1	[ʊ]	as in *took*
N2	[ɪ]	as in *tick*
N3	[ɛ]	as in *tech*
N4	[ʌ]	as in *tuck*

C. Neutral Diphthongs: These are blended vowels that always have as their second vowel the neutral schwa [ə] and are always words that end with an R spelling.

N1n	[ʊɚ]	as in *poor, tour, cure*
N2n	[ɪɚ]	as in *peer, pier, dear*
N3n	[ɛɚ]	as in *pare, pear, chair*
3n	[ɔɚ]	as in *shore, more, door*

---

[41] *The Use and Training of the Human Voice: A Bio-Dynamic Approach to Vocal Life 3rd Edition* by Arthur Lessac, Publisher McGraw-Hill Higher Education Publishing ©1997 pp 184-192

A. Lip-Rounding Vowels (The Lessac Structural Energy Vowels)[42]

- The concept of *Structure*[43] was created by Arthur Lessac to describe the shape, mold and size of the oral cavity to form specific vowels and diphthongs. These vowels/ diphthongs use the muscular activity of the levator and zygomatic muscles, a generous yet appropriate 'yawn space' within that cavity and a forward facial orientation to produce those vowel sounds.

- The 'lip rounding' refers to the shape of the lip-openings, which are either circular shape or oval.

- These vowels are identified by numbers—the lower the number, the smaller the lip opening. Two numbers or symbols will identify a 'diphthong'—a combination (blending) of two vowels, where there will be movement between those vowels.

Notes: ....

....

....

....

....

....

....

....

....

....

....

....

....

....

....

---

[42] You will also often see it written as NRG in *The Use and Training of the Human Voice: A Bio-Dynamic Approach to Vocal Life 3rd Edition* by Arthur Lessac, Publisher McGraw-Hill Higher Education Publishing ©1997. p. 273

[43] *The Use and Training of the Human Voice: A Bio-dynamic Approach to Vocal Life, 3rd Edition* ©1997 McGraw-Hill Higher Education Publishing, pp. 160-161

Lip-rounding Vowel #1 [u]
(The Lessac Structural Energy Vowel #1)

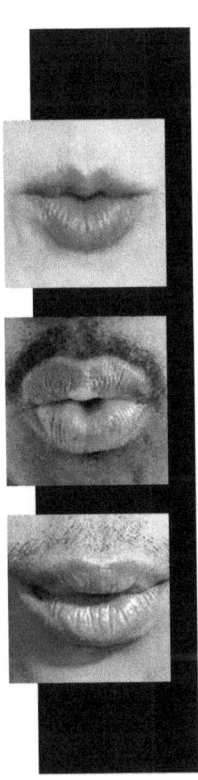

The long [u]

The Lip-rounding Vowel #1 (= The Structural Energy Vowel #1), the long [u:], one of the major vowels, is a single vowel sound and tends to be stressed in words. These photos are to be used as models[44]

To create this sound

1. Create a very small circle with your lips as if you are blowing out a candle. When you add voice —you will discover your [u:] #1 Structural Vowel.

2. This circle is slightly larger than the W consonant. You could fit the tip of your pinky finger into the size of this small opening.

Useful tips:

The photographs above are good models for the shape and size for the Vowel #1 lip-opening. As you pronounce the [u:], feel the gentle involvement of the cheek muscles moving forward to the lips. Check the movements of the muscles on your face by putting your palms flat against your cheeks.

- Your lips should always be soft to the touch.

- This sound is often spelled with /u/, /ue/, /ui/, /o/, /oo/, /ou/, /eu/, and /ew/.

---

[44] These are models for the size and shape of the lip openings that you will feel as you follow the instructions throughout this section. They are not for imitation, but as a reference for you. Aimee Blesing, Eric Berryman and Syaiful Ariffin are our models for these openings.

For your information:

- The sentences, words, stories, and dialogues in this book are designed for you to explore the movements of articulating organs (lips, tongue, palate, facial structure).

- Rely on *feeling* the movements of your articulating system, not *listening* to yourself.

Ex. 1   In the following words, explore the Structural Energy Vowel #1 [u].

/u/   super, dude, flute, lunar, rude, rumor, crucial, crude

/ue/   Sue, blue, true, pneumonia

/ui/   fruit, juice, suit, cruise, bruise

/o/   do, to, two, who, whose, whom, bosom, tomb

/oo/   too, coo, moo, boo, zoo, food, tool, fool, pool, moon, noon, loom, room, root, moose, oodles, noodle, poodle, raccoon, choose, broom, school, scooter, troop

/oe/   shoe

/ou/   soup, route, group, wound (injury)

/ew/   drew, crew, screw, chew, cashew, sewer

Notes:..
....
....
....
....
....
....
....

Ex. 2   In the following expressions, explore the Structural Energy Vowel #1 [u].

- Sue opened a shoe store on June 2nd, 2002.

- Who invented internet search engines such as Google or Yahoo?

- Hoon rides a scooter to his school, too.

- Abraham Lincoln said, "You can fool some of the people all of the time, and all of the people some of the time, but you cannot fool all of the people all of the time."

- However, a pool of people who fool other people are ruling those who they fool.

- Whose two blue shoes are you talking about?

- Do raccoons drink juice and chew their food in the zoo?

- June and Susan said that Moon Pies, which do not include any pieces of the moon, are the favorite snack food for their Girl Scout troop.

Ex. 3   Below is a list of words that contain the /y1/, meaning there is a short /y/ consonant linked to the #1 vowel when the word is spelled with: /ou/, /u/, /ue/, /eu/, /eau/, /ieu/, /ew/ or /iew/. Below are words that must use the /y1/, and others that optionally use the /y1/. Optional usage is indicated in italics.

Explore the combination of /y/ + vowel #1 =#y1 [ju] in the following words.

/you/   you

/u/   cupid, fuel, future, furious, cube, cubic, cute, huge, fume, fuse, mute, muse, music, volume, infuse, confuse, community, communicate, *attitude, latitude, duty, tulip, student, duplicate, tube, nutrient, nutrition, stupid*

/ue/   cue, argue, continue, value, venue, *avenue, revenue, Tuesday, due*

/eu/   euphonic, eulogy, *pseudo, pneumonia*

/eau/   beauty, beautiful

/ew/   Matthew, sinew, few, *dew, Jew, new, stew*

/iew/   view, review, preview, interview

147

Ex. 4   Explore the #y1 sound in the following sentences. Again, optional /y1/ is identified in *italics*. These words can also be pronounced with the #1.

- Matth*ew* M*u*se is studying N*u*trition Science at N*ew* York *U*niversity.

- As *u*niversities start their semesters, *u*niversity towns are getting crowded with n*ew* and old st*u*dents.

- A f*ew* countries got together and opened a h*u*ge n*ew* ven*ue* for exhibiting d*u*ty-free b*eau*ty products.

- J*u*ne D*u*ke will be a J*u*ne bride as she will marry in J*u*ne.

- The n*ew* graduate st*u*dents of the university comm*u*nity now incl*u*de international st*u*dents and scholars from 102 countries.

- We got a prev*iew* of the energy and enth*u*siasm of these st*u*dents during our very successful N*ew* St*u*dent Move-in Day.

- During the N*ew* St*u*dent Move-in Weekend, the n*ew* st*u*dents could enjoy movies, m*u*sic and other fun activities provided by the school.

Notes: ....
....
....
....
....
....
....
....
....
....
....
....
....

Ex. 5   Explore the vowel #1 and #y1 in the following story: they are underlined. Remember that the #y1 will only be spelled with a /u/, /ue/, /eu/, /ew/, /ieu/, and /iew/. Words that can use either #1or #y1 are *italicized*.

Oodles of Noodles

Many people like n<u>oo</u>dles. We don't even know wh<u>o</u> invented n<u>oo</u>dles. Today, instant n<u>oo</u>dles are popular among college st<u>u</u>dents because they are inexpensive, delicious, and good f<u>ue</u>l for the body.

If y<u>ou</u> want t<u>o</u> cook a package of ramen n<u>oo</u>dles for just yourself, y<u>ou</u> don't have t<u>o</u> worry about transferring them from the pot t<u>o</u> a bowl. Y<u>ou</u> could just cook them in a small pot and then eat them directly from the pot like a servant, or y<u>ou</u> may transfer the entire n<u>oo</u>dle s<u>ou</u>p int<u>o</u> a nice china bowl and eat them as if y<u>ou</u> were a king or queen.

By the way, d<u>o</u> kings and queens eat instant n<u>oo</u>dles, t<u>oo</u>? Maybe after their servants have gone t<u>o</u> bed, a junk-f<u>oo</u>d-hungry king or queen may sneak into the royal kitchen and fix one or tw<u>o</u> packages of n<u>oo</u>dles on their own, I suppose! I wonder what they really d<u>o</u> when they tr<u>u</u>ly want to eat some n<u>oo</u>dles.

Well, I went off track for a second. I just came back from the royal kitchen t<u>o</u> contin<u>ue</u> this story about n<u>oo</u>dles. So, here I go again. OK, I said, cooking ramen n<u>oo</u>dles for one person is no problem. However, when y<u>ou</u> cook <u>oo</u>dles of n<u>oo</u>dles in a large pot for several d<u>u</u>des, transferring the n<u>oo</u>dles into individual bowls can be a chore for a clumsy d<u>u</u>de like me.

In such a case, a ladle will work fine for the s<u>ou</u>p part of the n<u>oo</u>dles, but it is not very convenient for transferring long, slippery n<u>oo</u>dles because the lengthy n<u>oo</u>dles will not stay inside the ladle. The n<u>oo</u>dles will slip off the ladle and go wherever they want t<u>o</u> go except int<u>o</u> the bowl. It feels a little st<u>u</u>pid. So, instead of <u>u</u>sing a ladle alone, y<u>ou</u> might want t<u>o</u> invest in a small, inexpensive <u>u</u>tensil designed for transferring n<u>oo</u>dles from one place t<u>o</u> another, which could be the best gift for y<u>ou</u>, if y<u>ou</u> happen t<u>o</u> be a d<u>u</u>de who eats <u>oo</u>dles of n<u>oo</u>dles for survival.

The Lip-Rounding Vowel #2 [o]
(*The Structural Vowel #2)

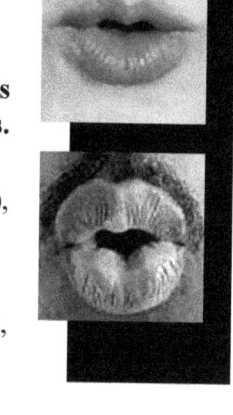

This is a pure vowel not found in most American English usage, but it is used here as a transition to the GA #21 Structural Diphthong

The English /o/ or [oʊ] equivalent is pronounced as [o] in other languages.

Italian: O (oh), sole (sun), mio (my), Roma, Milano, soprano, solo, sonata

Japanese: Osaka, Tokyo, Toyota, Hiroshima, Nagoya, Kobe

Korean: oee (cucumber), bom (spring); don (money); gom (bear); son (hand)

Spanish: taco, Mexico, Colombia, amigo

To create this sound:

1. Round your lips into a slightly larger circle than the #1 Structural Vowel, while adding voice. This is your #2 vowel.

For your information:

In GA English, When the phoneme [o] is spelled as /o/ in GA English, it can be pronounced in the following ways:

- It is often pronounced as the Structural Energy Vowel #21 [ou] as in 'so' [soʊ] and 'no' [noʊ];

- Or as the Structural Energy Vowel #4 [ɒ] as in 'God' [gɒd] or 'odd' [ɒd]. (But this will be a larger lip opening. See #4 later in this chapter.

Ex. 1   In the following story, explore the Structural Energy Vowel #2 [o].

Mr. Oh met his college friends for lunch in a Bulgogi (Korean barbecue) restaurant in the Gang-nam district of Seoul, Korea, and then flew to Osaka for a dinner meeting at a Kobe-style Japanese steak house. And then the next day, he visited the company's plants in Tokyo, Hiroshima, Nagoya, and Yokohama. He made sure that he got to visit a Toyota plant before he flew to Mexico City for a taco dinner with his amigos.

Notes: ....

....

....

....

....

....

....

....

....

....

....

....

....

....

....

....

....

The Lip-Rounding Vowel #21 [oʊ]*
(The Structural Vowel/Diphthong #21)

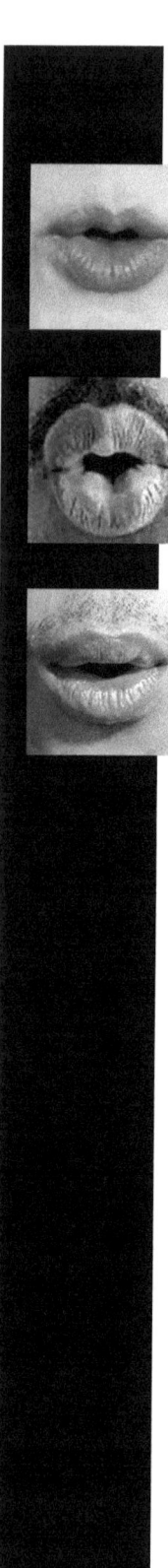
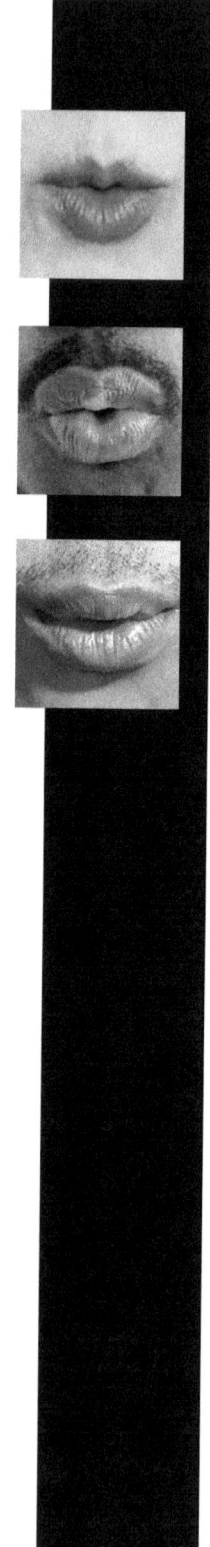

*The 'number 21' is read as 'two-one' rather than 'twenty-one'. It describes the muscle movement from the #2 lip opening to the #1 lip opening. The IPA symbol [oʊ] indicates a slight difference in the second sound. However, it is simpler to begin learning the sound with vowels you already know, such as the #2 and the #1. Doing so allows you to feel a continuation of the yawn space into that second sound, rather than collapsing the internal space. We therefore encourage *feeling* [ou], while we will *write* the standard symbol [oʊ] for IPA.

The Structural Vowel #21 is a blending of the [o] and [u].

To create this diphthong:

Begin by rounding your lips into the circular #2 Vowel.

Smoothly and gradually move to the smallest round lip opening, the #1 Vowel [u]. Maintain a spacious yawn size between your side teeth, even when moving to the #1 lip opening. Doing so encourages a tactile awareness of the forward cheek muscle movement.

The stress falls on the **[o]** part of the combination.

Note: The above photos can serve as a good model for the actual size of the lip-openings for the diphthong #21 [oʊ].

A Useful tip

The Structural Energy Vowel #21[oʊ] is often spelled with /o/, /ou/, /oa/, /oe/, or /ow/.

Ex. 1   In the following words, explore the shapes and sizes of the lip-openings for the Structural Energy Vowel #21[oʊ] by stressing the [o] part only. The second part of any diphthong is always shorter than the first.

/o/   oh, ok, old, open, ocean, odor, Olympic, go, no, so, audio, also, solo, micro, don't, focus, code, node, nose, pose, rose, those, home, bone, cone, phone, tone, zone, alone, chosen, hole, pole, stole, whole, gold, cold, fold, hold, sold, moment, quote, program, grocery, notion, post, won't

/ou/   dough, though, thorough

/oa/   oak, oat, boat, coat, load, road, toad, coal, goal, soak, roam, coach, poach, roach, broach, boast, roast, toast

/oe/   Joe, toe, Poe, roe, doe, foe, roe

/ow/   know, snow, bow, crow, low, mow, row, tow, grow, own, rainbow, tomorrow

Ex. 2   Explore the Lip-Rounding Vowel (The Structural Energy Vowel) #21[oʊ] in the following poem that has been translated into many languages.

Moses supposes his toeses are roses,

But Moses supposes erroneously;

For nobody's toeses are posies or roses,

As Moses supposes his toeses to be.

(1896, English Nonsense poem)[45]

Notes: ....

....

....

....

....

....

....

---

[45] https://www.mamalisa.com/?t=es&p=2482 Moses Supposes poem/English children's song

Ex. 3   Explore the Structural Energy Vowel #21 [oʊ] in the following sentences.
                     * Notice that the **[o]** part of the [oʊ] is the stressed part.

   • Why don't our toes have names?

   • Toby, watch your toes when you unload those boats.

   • The homemade fried green tomatoes at Edgar Poe's Cafe are already
     sold out.

   • Roasted sweet potatoes and white potatoes are Joe's favorite snack on
     the road.

   • Who knows when we can go home?

   • Focus on your nose bone to improve your vocal tone.

Ex. 4   Explore the Structural Energy Vowel #21 [oʊ] in the following *dialogues*.

                     Dialogue I

Sony: So, Tony, you've got a new smartphone.

Tony: I just discontinued my home phone and upgraded my cell phone to this
           one.

Sony: Oh. I like your phone so much.

Tony: It has so many cool features, including show-stopping dial tones.

Sony: Oh, I see. May I listen to a few of these dial tones?

Tony: Sure. Hold my phone. Let me phone you with your phone, and you can
           listen to the dial tones on my new phone.

Sony: Wow, it's so cool. By the way, do you want to go to my home for a roast
           beef dinner and some ice cream cones for dessert?

Tony: Going to your home is okay, but I don't know how to get to my home from
           your home.

Sony: Don't worry. I will show you how to get to my home.

Tony: OK, let's go then.

Dialogue II

Olga: My t<u>oe</u> hurts.

Omar: What about your t<u>oe</u>?

Olga: I said my t<u>oe</u> hurts.

Omar: <u>O</u>h, which one?

Olga: The one that ate r<u>oa</u>st beef.

Omar: The one that ate r<u>oa</u>st beef? I d<u>o</u>n't get it. What do you mean by that?

Olga: I mean the one that ate r<u>oa</u>st beef.

Omar: I still d<u>o</u>n't get it.

Olga: D<u>o</u>n't you kn<u>ow</u> the children's rhyme that g<u>oe</u>s like this? "This little piggy went to the market, this little piggy stayed h<u>o</u>me, this little piggy had r<u>oa</u>st beef, this little piggy had none, and this little piggy cried 'wee, wee, wee' all the way h<u>o</u>me."

Omar: <u>O</u>h, that's s<u>o</u> cute. S<u>o</u>, you are saying that your middle t<u>oe</u> is hurting. I didn't realize that our t<u>oe</u>s d<u>o</u>n't have names. Hmmmm.... I wonder why!

Notes: ....

....

....

....

....

....

....

....

....

....

The Lip-Rounding Vowel #3[ɔ]
(The Structural Energy Vowel # 3)

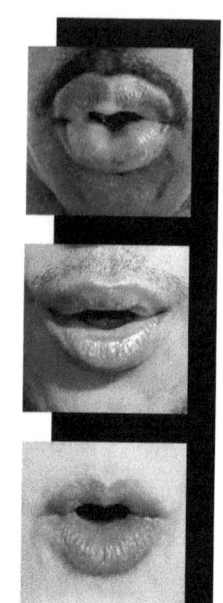

The Structural Energy Vowels #3 does not seem to exist in many languages, and thus, could be a new linguistic experience for you. Also, many GA speakers do not use this vowel, they may substitute the #4 or #5, which you will be introduced to later in this chapter.

To create the Structural Energy #3 Vowel:

1. Round your lips into a slightly larger circle than for the beginning of the #21 Diphthong.

2. Another way is to place your thumb (vertically positioned by letting your thumb nail face a corner of your mouth, palm facing down) inside your oral cavity just passing the lips, wrapping your lips around the inserted thumb tip and feel as if you are yawning inside.

3. Remove your thumb without changing the lip opening— and create the vowel that emerges from this lip-opening by adding voice. This is your Structural Vowel #3.

Useful tips:

- Remember lips are relaxed and feel soft.

- There is an awareness of space in the mouth overall—between your side teeth, especially.

- A gentle sensation of yawning will easily support this position without any jaw tension.

- This vowel is often spelled with /a/, /au/, /aw/, /o/, and /ou/, and is followed by a consonant, or /r/ + another consonant. In the case of /or/, if the syllable or word ends with an /r/ but with no following consonant, please see #3n.

156

| Ex. 1 | Explore the Structural Energy Vowel #3 in the following words by underlining the appropriate spelling and making a vertical thumb-size circle lip-opening. The first line of each spelling sample is marked for you. |

/a/   all, also, almost, always, already, ball, call, fall, hall, mall, small, tall, salt, scald, waltz, talk, stalk, walk

/au/   aught, audio, August, cause, pause, caught, taught, fault, haunt, naughty, Maureen, Paul, Austria, Australia, vault

/aw/   awe, awesome, jaw, law, raw, paw, drawn, lawn

/ou/   ought, bought, fought, sought, thought, brought *(occurs only when /ough/ is followed by /t/. If /ou/ is followed by /r/ and no other consonant, see #3n)*

/or/   dorm, normal, born, fortunate, corn, morning

| Ex. 2 | Explore the Structural Energy Vowel #3 in the following sentences by making your lip-opening into a thumb-size circle. |

- Dr. Chaucer taught small classes all day in the fall.

- Paul and Dawn always walk and talk in the hallways.

- Shawn ought to have called the lawn doctor prior to buying a lawn mower.

- Just the thought of eating raw fish induced lock jaw and nausea in Dawn.

- Yawn your way to the awesome structural energy vowels.

- The athletes fought a good fight in the Olympics and brought home awesome medals.

Notes: ....
....
....
....

The Lip-Rounding Vowel #3n [ɔɹ] *
(The Structural Energy Vowel #3n)

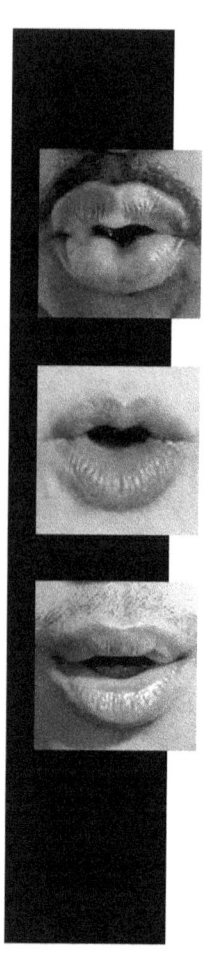

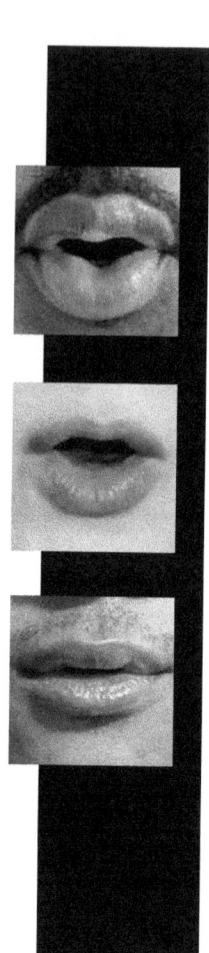

*Here, the /n/ represents the 'Neutral' vowel "Schwa [ə] + /r/, or [ɚ]. We understand that current IPA transcription would be [ɔɹ]. The use of [ɚ] here helps those speakers whose first language uses a tapped or rolled R.

To create the #3n Structural Energy Vowel:

1. First round your lips into your **#3[ɔ]** Structural Vowel feeling a generously full space (yawn) between the side teeth, creating the sound that accompanies this lip position.

2. Slide into the **[ɚ]** sound, which is the combination of the schwa[ə] + r sound, as in /more/, /door/ or /gore/; [mɔɚ], [dɔɚ], [gɔɚ]

3. *This sound is often spelled with /or/, /ar/, /oar/, /oor/ or /our/ and is always* followed by an R consonant. The /r/ is not followed by another consonant.

Notes: ....

....

....

....

....

....

....

....

....

....

Ex. 1   Explore the Structural Energy Diphthong #3n in the following words by beginning with a thumb-size lip-opening followed by the [ɚ] sound.

/or/   or, bore, core, more, pore, for, fore, more, score, shore, tore, store, wore, adore, before, explore

/oar/   oar, roar, soar

/oor/   door, floor

/our/   four, pour

/ar/   war

Ex. 2   Explore both Structural Energy Diphthong #3n [ɔɚ]   and #3 in the following sentences. Those words that contain the #3 Structural Vowel are italicized; #3n is underlined.

- Pour more, soar more, and score more.

- Hawthorn's four horses have hoarse voices.

- The door was not level with the floor.

- George Porter entertained his dorm mates more and more with his imitation of a lion's roar.

- This store will open before four in the morning.

- Go ahead and explore the resources for the core courses.

Notes: ....

....

....

....

....

....

....

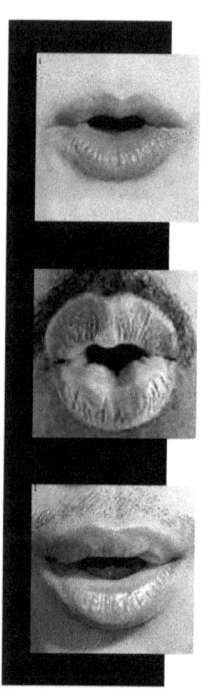

The Lip-Rounding Vowel #3y [ɔɪ]
(The Structural Energy Vowel/Diphthong #3y)

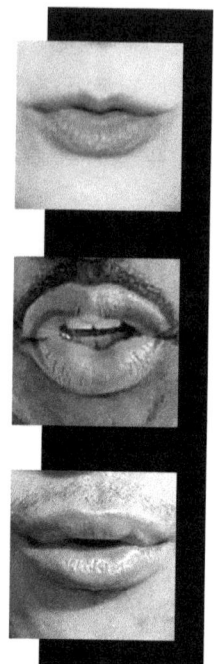

To create the #3y Structural Vowel:

1. Create your #3 lip opening.

2. Smoothly move (glide) to the /y/ sound, releasing the circular shape to a more neutral forward lip shape as you simultaneously create the sound.

3. The stress falls on the #3[ɔ] part. So it is pronounced stronger, longer and possibly higher in pitch than the /y/ or [ɪ] part: [ɔɪ]

This diphthong is often spelled with /oy/, /oi/, or /awy/ and /eu/ (as in Freud).

Ex. 1   Explore the Structural Energy Vowel #**3y** in the following words.

/oy/   boy, toy, joy, Roy, soy, troy, annoy, alloy, employ, envoy, Doyle, loyal, royal, foyer, oyster

/awy/   lawyer, Sawyer

/oi/   coin, join, joint, point, noise, poise, voice
oil, boil, coil, foil, soil, toil, hoist, moist, poison, goiter

/eu/   Freud, Freudian

Ex. 2   Explore the Structural Energy Vowel #3y in the following sentences.

- Joy and Joyce Freud are enjoying their new toys.

- Roy informed Troy that soy sauce may spoil the taste of the fresh oysters.

- The boys and their employer raised their voices to sing "Joy to the World."

- The noise subsided as the envoys entered the foyer to join the lawyers.

- The joint soil test in the oil field was successfully avoided.

- Troy demonstrated a Freudian slip as he accidently said "Detroit," the name of his hometown; when he meant to say "destroy."

The Lip-Rounding Vowel
R-Derivative: ℞ [ɝ]

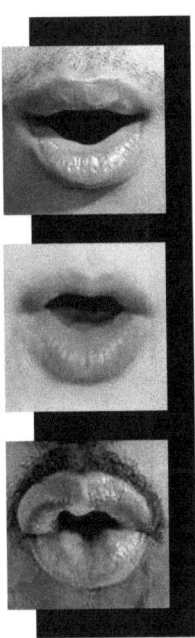

When the syllable [ɝ] is the 'only syllable' or a 'stressed syllable' in a word, it is pronounced as the Structural Energy Vowel ℞[46] which is pronounced as [ɝ] as in '*early*' with the same size and shape as the #3 Vowel. Its full name is the "R-derivative"[47]. You will find this vowel in both stressed and unstressed syllables.

To create the ℞ Structural Energy Vowel:

1. Create your circular lip opening of the #3 Structural Vowel with a full yawn space within your oral cavity.

2. Instead of voicing the #3 vowel, voice an /r/ sound. Because of the yawn space, the R only adds color to the vowel and is not fully an R consonant because there is no constriction, as there is with the consonant. This R *colored* vowel is your ℞ [ɝ] sound.

3. If the ℞ is located in an unstressed syllable, reduce the size of the yawn space within your oral cavity, but keep a sense of R *coloring*, rather than the constriction of the R consonant. For a deeper look at this, go to "Neutral Vowels—Unstressed ℞".

* This sound is often spelled with /er/, /ir/, /or/, /ur/, /our/, /ear/, or /yr/ with the same circular opening as found in the #3 Structural Vowel.

---

[46] The symbol ℞ was used by Arthur Lessac in his text *The Use and Training of the Human Voice* © 1997.

[47] This vowel is always attached to an /r/, which is often considered by phoneticians as a "vowel-like consonant". In conjunction with the feeling of openness in the oral cavity, the r loses its consonant quality of constriction, instead forming a new, unrestricted vowel sound, as commonly found in *word, heard, and bird*.

Ex. 1   Explore the Structural Vowel R̥ in the following words

  /er/ h<u>er</u>, B<u>er</u>t, nerve, serve, jersey, kernel, certain, person, verse

  /ir/ s<u>ir</u>, b<u>ir</u>d, birth, third, v<u>ir</u>tue, c<u>ir</u>cus, whirl, swirl, skirt, flirt, Kirk, squirrel, shirt

  /or/ w<u>or</u>d, work, worse, worm, world

  /ur/ n<u>ur</u>se, purse, curse, curve, burn, blur, b<u>ur</u>dock, curb, c<u>ur</u>tain, C<u>ur</u>tis, fur, f<u>ur</u>ther, p<u>ur</u>ple, tu<u>r</u>tle

  /our/ adj<u>our</u>n, soj<u>our</u>n

  /ear/ l<u>ear</u>n, heard, earn, earth, early

  /yr/ M<u>yr</u>na, M<u>yr</u>tle

Ex. 2   Explore the Structural Vowel R̥ in the following sentences. It has been <u>underlined</u> in the stressed syllables (using optimal yawn space). The unstressed R̥ is *italicized* to help you distinguish the two. The unstressed R̥ used a reduced yawn space.

- L<u>ear</u>n <u>ear</u>ly, <u>ear</u>n <u>ear</u>ly.

- Have you h<u>ear</u>d the story about the b<u>ir</u>th of the <u>ear</u>th?

- M<u>yr</u>na and M<u>yr</u>tle hu<u>rr</u>ied farth*er* to catch the f<u>ur</u>ry creat*ure*s f<u>ir</u>st.

- The n<u>ur</u>se did not have the n<u>er</u>ve to carry the baby squi<u>rr</u>el in her p<u>ur</u>se.

- S<u>ir</u>, I c<u>er</u>tainly h<u>ear</u>d the c<u>ur</u>tain call.

- C<u>ur</u>tis B<u>ur</u>ton's black tu<u>r</u>tle-neck T-s<u>hir</u>t and blue jeans f<u>ur</u>th*er* reminds me of a world-renowned computer fig*ure*, H<u>er</u>man B<u>ur</u>ton C<u>ur</u>tis.

- B<u>ur</u>bank l<u>ear</u>ned from the online news that too much smartphone use can cause Tu<u>r</u>tle-neck Syndrome which accompanies neck and should*er* pains.

- <u>Bir</u>mingham G<u>ir</u>ls Incorporation <u>ur</u>ges the local m<u>er</u>chants to donate their time and financial resources to this w<u>or</u>thy organization.

Ex. 3   Explore the Vowels #3, #3y, #3n, and Ɽ in the following *dialogue*.

Dialogue: Ordering food in a Restaurant

Waiter: Good m<u>o</u>rning, s<u>ir</u>. How many are you <u>all</u> together?

Guest: We need a table <u>for</u>[48] <u>four</u>, please.

Waiter: <u>All</u> right. A table <u>for</u> <u>four</u>. Come with me please. Is this table <u>all</u> right for you <u>all</u>?

Guest: Yeah, this will do for <u>all</u> of us.

Waiter: Would you like to <u>or</u>der something to drink f<u>ir</u>st?

Guest: <u>All</u> right. We would <u>all</u> like to have a glass of water each, and we are ready to <u>or</u>der. This young lady wants a sm<u>all</u> p<u>or</u>tion of chicken c<u>or</u>n soup, and she wants h<u>er</u> soup to be at a lukew<u>ar</u>m temperature. And this young lady would like to have a s<u>ir</u>l<u>oi</u>n steak. And for me, a grilled t<u>ur</u>key b<u>ur</u>ger and c<u>or</u>n on the cob with mustard s<u>au</u>ce.

Waiter: S<u>ir</u>, you are <u>or</u>dering from our lunch menu. A better ch<u>oi</u>ce is to look at our breakfast menu.

Guest: We had our breakfast at d<u>aw</u>n on the plane, and we are m<u>ore</u> than ready for our lunch. By the way, this is lunch time in our part of the w<u>or</u>ld.

Notes: ....

....

....

....

....

....

....

....

---

[48] Most of the time, prepositions, such as 'for' are not stressed in conversational speech. So, "for" in the dialogue can be pronounced as [fəɹ]. However, when it is stressed, it is pronounced as [fɔɹ].

The Lip-Rounding Vowel #4 [ɒ]
(The Structural Energy Vowel # 4)

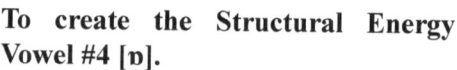

The Short (o)

Arthur Lessac demonstrating the Structural Energy Vowel #4 [ɒ] as in 'God.'

Resource: The Lessac Training and Research Institute

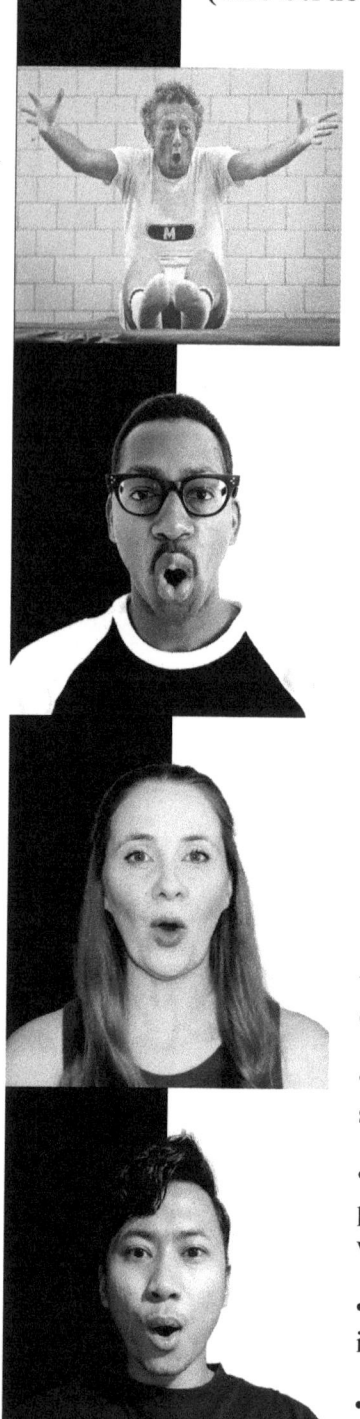

To create the Structural Energy Vowel #4 [ɒ].

1. Yawn as if you are going to create the round #3 vowel shape.

2. Shift the vertical length of the lip-opening into a slightly longer, more rectangular shape, with upper and lower lips facing slightly forward.

3. As you create this lip-opening and add voice, what sound emerges? This is your #4 vowel [ɒ].

Useful Tips:

• Speakers of second or third languages tend to pronounce the English spelling /o/ as the narrow or pure [o] as experienced in their own languages.

• However, in GA English, the alphabet spelling /o/ has several pronunciations.

• When the spelling /o/ is **"stressed"** and **"long,"** it is pronounced as the Vowel #**21** [oʊ], a combination of two vowels, the **stressed [o]** and the unstressed [ʊ].

• And when the spelling /o/ is **"stressed"** and **"shorter,"** it is pronounced as a single **vowel #4 [ɒ].**

• The above photos can be used as models for the actual lip-opening size of a person for the vowel #4.

• This sound is often spelled /a/ or /o/

- **Note: many GA speakers do not use this sound, but substitute either the #3 or #5 for example words in this section. There is great latitude in using this vowel.**

Ex. 1   Explore the Structural Energy Vowel #4 [ɒ] in the following words.

/a/   what, wand, wallet, waffle, watch, wash, quality, quantum

/o/   odd, ox, omelet, occupy, osmosis, oxygen, obligate, opposite, sonic, ionic, bionic, Bob, box, bond, bottom, bottle, bother, dock, clot, plot, slot, cop, copy, collar, copper, contact, contrast, constant, concentrate, confident, consequent, compromise, complicate, cost, economy, economic, silicon, accommodate, dollar, Donald, fox, fond, fossil, God, goggle, gotten, honk, hobby, holiday, hospital, lot, blot, mom, mop, mock, model, modify, molecule, homogenous, not, knot, knowledge, nodule, novel, nostril, pop, pot, spot, pond, pocket, posture, popular, positive, polymer, postulate, prodigal, respond, rob, rotten, prosper, tropical, approximate, sob, sod, sock, shop, Tom, top, stop, toddler, tolerate, volume, beyond, zombie, on, gone, golf, long, wrong, strong, tomorrow

Ex. 2   Explore the Structural Energy Vowel #4 [ɒ] in the following sentences.

- It's odd. My wallet is gone. I know I used it in the Waffle House.

- The cop stopped a popular pop-icon at the stop sign.

- Scott was concentrating on his pop quiz when he dropped his bottle of water.

- Finding a compromise between opposite options is not impossible.

- Contrary to popular belief, Vermont's economy is not so prosperous.

- With constant changes of schedules, Tom had to modify his living accommodation.

165

Ex. 3   Explore the Structural Energy Vowel #4 [ɒ] in the following *dialogue.*

Dialogue--Grocery Shopping

Don: Scott, where do you usually shop for your groceries?

Scott: I usually shop either at the One-Stop-Mart or sometimes Wholesale-Shop. com. What about you?

Don: Well, I also shop at One-Stop-Shop for my shopping, or sometimes Top Shop, Bronx, and the farmer's market. I have never thought about shopping for groceries online because I eat lots of fresh, unprocessed food including green salads, omelets, stir-fried spicy octopus, and braised oxtails.

Scott: You make me hungry and homesick with those food items. I am a poor student, and I constantly have to compromise and watch the condition of my wallet.

Don: The same here. I also have to constantly monitor my bank account. But I consider eating quality food as part of my obligation to my body. So, I sometimes also have to compromise my wallet for my appetite. But, at the same time, I often just listen to my body. Probably I have gone too far and am acting as if I was your mom. Or maybe I sound too philosophical.

Scott: Don't mock yourself too harshly. I do agree that we need to constantly care for ourselves. When we don't care for our bodies, our bodies won't care for us either. When that happens, our hard-earned degrees or professional achievements won't be of any use to us. But you say you have never shopped for groceries online?

Don: No, but I know Donna usually shops online. She says because she doesn't have a car, she has to modify her lifestyle, and shopping online is one of the options. She finds shopping online moderately cheaper than shopping in the grocery stores.

Scott: Really? But what about perishable goods?

Don: I'm not sure, but I know Donna is not terribly bothered about not eating fresh vegetables or unprocessed food, and she could do without fresh seafood or delicacies such as octopus or oxtails. The other day, Donna got a box of goods including milk, cereal, bottled water, and some cotton socks. I guess for the people who neither have a car nor have enough time, online shopping certainly can be an option. It can definitely save time and gas money, especially with economic conditions today.

Scott: I see your point. I have to be honest and say that it does take quite a lot of time for transportation to and from where I go to shop for groceries and home: shopping, loading and unloading the goods into and out of the car, and then stocking those items somewhere in the house. But shopping for groceries online is not going to be my option, because shopping in an actual shop cools my head off and moderately relieves my stress.

For your information:

As mentioned earlier, the American English spelling /o/ is rarely pronounced as the pure [o]. It can be pronounced either as the Structural Energy Vowel #21[ou] or #4 [ɒ]. However, at times, the /o/ can be reduced either to schwa [ə] or is silent.

Ex. 4   In the following, compare the pronunciations of the Structural Energy Vowels #21 [oʊ] and #4 [ɒ].

#21 [oʊ]	#4 [ɒ]	#21 [oʊ]	#4 [ɒ]
Tony ----------- Tom		robe ------------ Rob/Robert	
Lobe ----------- lob/lobby		role/roll -------- robbery	
Troll------------ trolley		tone ------------ tonsil	
probe----------- probably		own ------------ on	
owner ---------- honor		ode/owed ------- odd	
phone ---------- fond		postponed ------ pond	
holy ------------ holly		know/no -------- non	
go--------------- God		cone ------------ con	
stove ----------- stop		bone------------ bond	
toed ------------ Todd		soak ------------ sock	
coat------------- cot		grocery -------- groggy	
program -------- promise		dome ----------- Don	

Notes:..

....

....

....

....

Ex. 5   The final syllable /-son/ is not stressed and the /o/ vowel is absorbed by the /n/. **The symbol for this is [n̩], also known as a "syllabic n"**, meaning the [n̩] represents the entire syllable, vowel and all.

person	[pɝ-sn̩]	**Daw**son	[dɔ sn̩]
Mason	[meɪsn̩]	**Madi**son	[mæ dəsn̩]
Samson	[sæm sn̩]	**Wil**son	[wɪl sn̩]
Peterson	[pi tər sn̩]	**Nel**son	[nel sn̩]
Garrison	[gæ rɪ sn̩]	**Nix**on	[nɪ kn̩s]
poison	[pɔɪ zn̩]	**pri**son	[prɪ zn̩]

- Mason Peterson is watching the movie "Madison Avenue."

- Wilson and Nixon are former presidents of the United States.

- Samson and Jason are Nelson's personal connections.

- Mr. Garrison serves in the Prison Ministry at Dawson Church.

- Jason Dobson was infected by poison ivy.

Ex. 6   The final syllable /-ton/ is not stressed and the /o/ is not pronounced as a #4, but usually as a schwa, as in the names Washington, Boston, or Darlington. However, sometimes it feels more like a 'consonant to consonant' T-N blended, indicated the syllabic n [n̩]. Explore the /-ton/ sound with the syllabic n in the following words.

Bar*ton*	[bar tn̩]	**Bur***ton*	[bər tn̩]
but*ton*	[bə tn̩]	**cot***ton*	[ka tn̩]
Car*ton*	[kar tn̩]	**Clin**ton	[Klɪn tn̩]
Dalton	[dal. tn̩]	**Mil***ton*	[mɪl. tn̩]
Shera*ton*	[ʃer ə tn̩]	**Wal***ton*	[wɔl. tn̩]

Notes: ....

....

....

....

Ex. 7   Explore the /-ton/ syllable in the following sentences. Which are "ton" with a schwa and which are syllabic n? The first sentence is marked for you.

- Elizabeth Bar*ton* and George Bur*ton* got married in the Darling<u>ton</u> Hotel in Washing<u>ton</u>.

- The Barton family of Great Britain moved from Birmingham, England to Birmingham, Alabama, United States.

- Crompton Milton used to eat a lot of cotton candy when he was a toddler.

- Ms. Hampton takes the Lexington Avenue line to go to work every morning.

- The Hamilton family was given two options for their lodging during the convention: the Hamilton Hotel in Boston and the Washington Hotel in Washington DC.

- In Fort Walton Beach, the Petersons stayed in a button-hole lodge to compensate for the huge hotel bills they had run up while in five-star hotels in Boston and Washington.

Notes: ....

....

....

....

....

....

....

....

....

....

The Lip-Rounding Vowel #5[ɑ]
(The Structural Energy Vowel # 5)

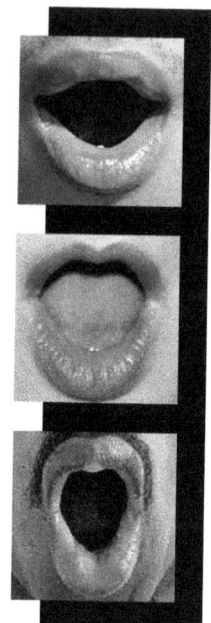

The Relaxed and Rounder [ɒ]

To create the Structural Energy Vowel #5

1. Open your mouth with rounder and more relaxed lip-corners compared to the Vowel #4. This will be a relaxed oval shape, as when the doctor asks you to stick out your tongue and say 'ah'. Add voice as you make this shape.

2. The sound that you create with this lip-opening is the Structural Energy Vowel #5.

For your information:

- The photo above can be the model for the actual lip-opening size and shape for the Structural Energy Vowel #5.

- This sound is often spelled with the /a/ or /ea/.

- Notice that the Structural Energy Vowel #5 is always in the stressed syllable in the following explorations.

Ex. 1   Explore the Structural Energy Vowel #5 [ɑ] in the following words by sustaining the sound.

/a/   car, far, bar, tar, star, tart, start, mars, smart, dart, park, spark, father, farther, farmer, gargle, garden, hard, large, pardon, parliament, pharmacy, pharmaceutical, mirage, sardine, varsity

/e/   sergeant

/ea/   heart

170

Ex. 2   Explore the Structural Energy Vowel #5 [ɑ] in the following sentences.

- A father's heart is as large as a mother's heart.

- Barb Barker barked while Mark Marker marked.

- Is Mars the farthest star from the earth?

- Farmer Parson is a man of a big heart, and just like his big heart, he owns a large garage for his many large cars that serve large communities near Fargo.

- As soon as Carl started spreading the seeds in the garden, the rain started to pour.

- Barney Marla joined the Darby County Master Garden Club this March and altered his status of farming from 'all-desire-no-knowledge' to "learning-to-serve-society."

Ex. 3   Explore the Structural Energy Vowel #5 [ɑ] in the following story by underlining the appropriate spelling and sustaining the sound. The first paragraph is marked for you.

Organic Gardening in the Heart of a City

All through my life, I have been living in places where farming or gardening was left up to farmers or garden experts. I had never thought about farming or gardening until a couple of years ago.

Since I discovered the wonderful quality of authentic Far-eastern vegetables, which cannot be easily found in Western grocery stores, and are too expensive in the Far-eastern food stores, I have decided to grow some in my large backyard near our carport.

The first year was a bumper crop as I worked whole-heartedly in my garden, giving proper nutrition and water diligently.

The second year? It was a far cry from last year! It was a heart-breaking experience, in fact. I must have trusted last year's soil and water to work hard for our garden again this year, ha! With a broken heart, I decided to start organic gardening, using the grass cuttings from our yard and food scraps from our kitchen.

After a long and hard search, I bought an Australian-engineered composter and then started putting in grass cuttings from our yard and garden, and food scraps from the kitchen. However, the kitchen food scraps collected into regular plastic garbage bags were unsightly and seemed unhygienic to be emptied into the composter.

Remembering my chemistry professor Dr. Harkins showing us the corn-based eco-friendly packing worms in one of our chemistry classes and believing that some smart people must have already invented eco-friendly plastic garbage bags with some sort of natural materials, I searched online for any eco-friendly plastic garbage bags.

Sure enough, some smart people had already invented what I was looking for—corn-based, eco-friendly plastic garbage bags that are sold by many companies. I ordered a dozen packages of 50-garbage bags and a plastic basket in which to nest the bag on the kitchen countertop.

So, with this revolutionary eco-friendly kitchen garbage collecting and composting, I hardly use the regular plastic garbage bags. So, as far as I can tell, our food scraps are placed directly into the gardening composter in the green corn-based plastic garbage bag without having to be carted out of the bags.

Because the eco-friendly plastic garbage bags are inexpensive, convenient, and pleasant to use, they have become a staple for my back-yard gardening. Also, I am happy to contribute toward a healthy environment and a happy heart through eating healthy food from organic gardening.

Through my backyard gardening experience, I realize that gardening or farming is an art form, and it takes lots of hard work. Until I started backyard farming, I never knew how farmers must work so hard to feed us. But at the same time, it is fun to have my own food that was grown by my own hard-working hands and the satisfaction of knowing what goes into my body is healthy.

Notes: ....

....

....

....

....

....

The Lip-Rounding Vowel # 51[aʊ]
(The Structural Energy Vowel # 51)

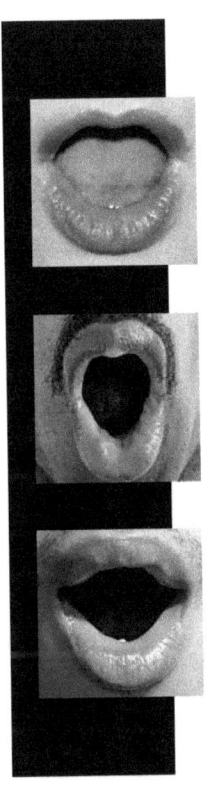

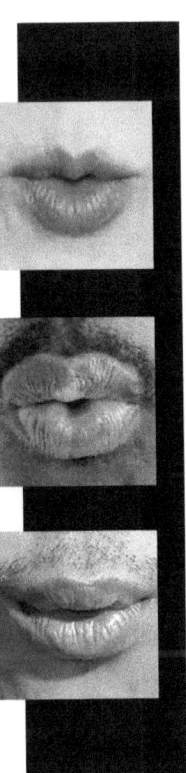

The Structural Energy Vowel #51 [aʊ] is a diphthong (a blending of two vowels) made of the **Structural Energy Vowel #5 [ɑ]** followed by the **Structural Energy Vowel #1 [u].** They both still use the same internal yawn space, but the lip opening changes from the largest to the smallest.

Note: the symbol for this diphthong in IPA is [aʊ] indicating minor differences in shaping and tongue placement. However, it is simpler to begin learning the sound with vowels you already know, such as the #5 and the #1. Doing so allows you to feel a continuation of the yawn space into that second sound, rather than collapsing the internal space. We therefore encourage *feeling* [ɑu], while we will use the standard symbol [aʊ] for IPA.

To create the Structural Energy Vowel #51:

1. Yawn into the Structural Energy Vowel #5 [ɑ], an oval shape.

2. Smoothly and gradually move to the smallest round lip opening, the #1 Vowel [u]. Maintain a spacious yawn size between your side teeth, even when moving to the #1 lip opening. Doing so encourages a tactile awareness of the forward cheek muscle movement.

3. This is your Vowel #51. The stress falls on the first sound [a]—which is pronounced **stronger, longer,** and **higher** than the [u] part.

For your information:

- Remember, even when moving into the smaller lip-opening size, you should feel your oral cavity is still open creating a small cave-like space (yawn space).

- The photos above can model the shapes and sizes for you.

- This sound is often spelled with /ou/ or /ow/.

- Notice that the Structural Energy Vowel #51 is stressed in the following exploration.

Ex. 1   Explore the Structural Energy Vowel #51[aʊ] in the following words.

/ou/   loud, out, shout, about, pout, trout, vouch, our, devour, flour, couch, cloud, proud, lousy, house, mouse, blouse, noun, count, county, council, counselor, lounge, mountain, fountain, bound, found, pound, sound, round, around, ground, compound, wound (as in 'wound up'), astound

/ow/   cow, how, wow, bow, brow, crowd, coward, power, shower, tower, flower, powder, towel, owl, down, town, downtown, gown, brown, clown, frown

Ex. 2   Compare the Vowels #1, #21, and # 51 in the following words.

#1[u]	#21[oʊ]	#51[aʊ]
knew	know	now
noon	known	noun
Loo	low	allow
fruit	follow	flower/flour
slew	slow	slouch
flew	flow	flounder
who	hoe	how
Boo	bow	bound
Sue	sow	sound
shoe	show	shower
grew	grow	ground
do	dough	down
new	no	now
sewer	slower	sour
two	tow	town
through	throw	thousand
wound	won't	wound

Notes:...
....

174

Ex. 3	Explore the Structural Energy Vowel #51 in the following *dialogue* by feeling the changes of the lip-opening from Structural Energy Vowel #5 to #1.

Abe: Now, bow your head down and shout out loud.

Babe: How much should I bow down?

Abe: Bow down, way down so that your face can squarely face the ground.

Babe: How loud should I shout as I bow down to the ground?

Abe: Shout out loud so the people downtown can hear your sound.

Babe: How can I? Downtown is way down from here!

Ex. 4	Explore the Structural Energy Vowel #51 in the following song by feeling the movement of the lip-openings from Structural Energy Vowel #5 to #1.

Amazing Grace

Amazing Grace how sweet the sound

That saved a wretch like me!

I once was lost, but now am found,

Was blind, but now I see.

Notes:...

....

....

....

....

....

....

....

....

The Lip-Rounding Vowel #6 [æ]
(The Structural Energy Vowel #6)

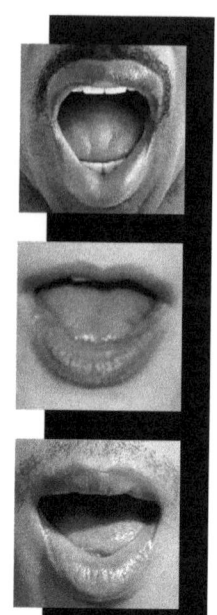

[æ] Ash Tree

The Structural Energy Vowel #6 [æ] is a single vowel. However, as the International Phonetic Alphabet (IPA) symbols [æ] suggest, the vowel #6 is the combination of the Vowel #5 [a] and the [e] sounds. But for our purposes, let's continue to think of it as a single vowel because of its shape and size.

To create the Structural Energy Vowel #6:

1. First, form the oval shape for the vowel #5.

2. Allow your tongue to relax a little forward so that the tip presses gently against the lower front teeth.

3. Slightly widen your lips to accommodate the widening tongue, and as you add voice, the sound created will be your #6 as in the word 'add'.

Useful tips:

- In the mirror, you will notice that your tongue is relaxed toward the floor of the mouth, and the tongue-tip comes forward slightly and touches the inside (back) of the lower front teeth.

- The Vowel #6 is a single sound. So, you do not want to move your tongue or lips after you create the sound. When you move your tongue or lips, you may create another sound without your intention or realization.

- For words that begin with the #6 [æ] sound, prepare the lip-opening first and then add voice. This will make a lot of difference in your confidence for the [æ] sound.

Ex. 1 Explore the Structural Energy Vowel #6 in the following words. The #6 in the single syllable words below are not underlined.

at, as, am, add, and, ant, aunt, acid, apple, animal

adjective, adverb, attitude, average, avenue

bag, bat, bank, bath, basket, band, battle, barrel

bandage, baptize, bamboo, bassoon

cat, can, campus, calendar, cattle, cabbage, casual, Canada, California

class, crab, craft, dad, dance, dandy, detract, draft, drastic

fat, fan, fantasy, fantastic, fabulous, flask

gas, grass, has, hat, hand, Japan, January

lab, land, last, latitude, map, mass, mask, mat, nap, napkin, Natalie

pad, Pam, Pat, pants, palace, rap, rack, rank, random, rattle, react

sack, sat, Sam, Saturday, sanitary, stamp, stand, Seattle, Spanish, shall,

shampoo, tan tank, thank, van, valley, value, valve, Valery, yam, yank,

wag, zap

Ex. 2 Explore the Structural Energy Vowel #6 in the following sentences. The first two lines are marked for you.

- That fat cat sat on Pat's lap and took a fancy nap.

- Janet Jacky's flannel hat is fantastically fashionable.

- Sam Pat's acid reaction; I-Pad's Apple reaction.

- On Saturday, Jan's lab manager brought his new lap-top computer to the lab.

- Jan learned that when pronouncing the word "Japan" in English, the first /a/ is pronounced as [ə] but the second /a/ is pronounced as the Vowel #6 [æ].

- However, neither [ə] nor [æ] are included in the Japanese language, and thus they are both pronounced as the Vowel #5 [a] in Japan.

Ex. 3　　　　　Explore the Structural Energy Vowel #6 [æ] in the following story. The first 4 lines are marked for you.

Mr. Happy Grasshopper and Mr. Antsy Ant

Mr. Happy Grasshopper and Mr. Antsy Ant are neighbors in the summer's green fields. However, they don't share each other's lifestyles. Contented with his carefree life, Mr. Happy Grasshopper always sings happy songs, visiting friends and neighbors, and cracking practical jokes, while Mr. Antsy Ant keeps himself busy gathering food for his family from morning till evening.

"Why do you have to work so hard all the time, Mr. Antsy Ant? Why don't you come and sing with me?" Mr. Grasshopper would ask Mr. Antsy Ant.

"Well, I have to prepare for my family's food for the winter, so we won't be hungry when cold weather arrives." Mr. Antsy Ant answered and hurriedly carried his food to his house.

"Oh, please don't act like a worrywart. Winter's far from now, and we have plenty of food in the field," Mr. Grasshopper replied.

Soon the summer ended, and the grass was covered with a thick blanket of snow. Mr. "Used-to-be" Happy Grasshopper had no food and had no place to go. He was cold and hungry.

"Why didn't I think about the fact that summer would be gone quickly, and winter would come soon?"

Holding his hand over his hungry abdomen, with a shameful attitude, Mr. Happy Grasshopper, who was not very happy anymore, knocked on Mr. Antsy Ant's door.

"Do you have any food that you can share with me?", Mr. "No-longer" Happy Grasshopper begged Mr. Antsy Ant, who was now truly happy and content.

"I am sorry, Mr. Grasshopper, as you can see, this winter will be long, and I have just enough food to last for my family."

Mr. 'No-longer' Happy Grasshopper sadly dropped his sad head and said, "Why couldn't I see that no one but I am responsible for my own happiness? I could have at least practiced my music more diligently, so I could have had contracts that would pay me to perform or have produced my own CDs and DVDs by now."

Mr. 'No-longer' Happy Grasshopper dragged his sad and heavy feet away to a place unknown and unwelcome, facing cold and an unkind winter blizzard.

(Adapted from the Aesop's Fable.[49])

Notes:..

....

....

....

....

....

....

....

....

....

....

....

....

....

....

....

....

---

[49] https://fablesofaesop.com/the-ant-and-the-grasshopper.html Adapted from Aesop's Fable, The Ant & the Grasshopper August 8, 2021

The Lip-Rounding Vowel #6y[aɪ]
(The Structural Vowel # 6y)

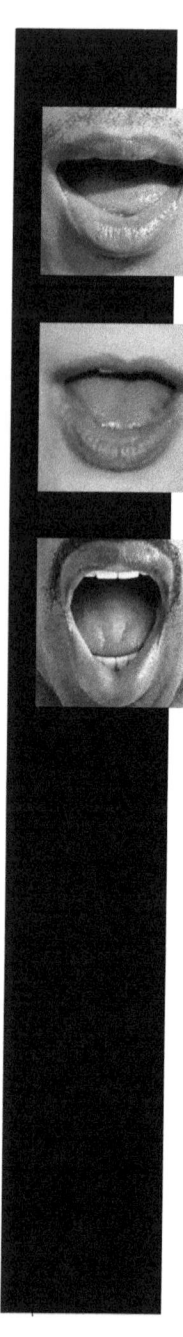

To create the Structural Energy #6y:

1. Form the #6 vowel **shape** with your lips and inner yawn space.

2. Voice the #5 vowel.

3. Then reduce the space between the side teeth slowly and finish with a brief long /e/ vowel. *This 'y' in the symbol is not a consonant Y, but an /e/ vowel.*

4. Resist the urge to spread your lips wider as you transition to the long /e/ vowel.

For your information:

• The primary stress is on the first part of the diphthong [a] using stronger tone, longer duration, and sometimes higher in pitch than the second part.

• The long /e/ is softer, shorter, and perhaps lower in pitch.

• This sound can be spelled as /ai/, /i/, /ie/, /ui/, /uy/, and /y/.

• The Structural Energy Diphthong #6y often occurs in stressed syllables as in the following experiment.

Notes: ....
....
....
....

Ex. 1   Explore the Structural Energy Vowel #6y in the following words.

/ai/   Thai, Taiwan, Taipei

/i/   I, hi, lie, sigh, nice, China, like, bike, hike, nine, line, fine, dine, sign, find, kind, mind, bind, grind, blind, dime, time, climb, ride, slide, decide, hire, fire, desire, admire, acquire, choir, five, hive, drive, survive, Brian, bite, kite, write, excite, night, light, tight, fight, sight, right, write, might, flight, quite, quiet, giant, appetite, benign, tiger, science, scientist, rhinitis, sinusitis, laryngitis, appendicitis, cholecystitis

/y/   Y, why, my, dye, sky, fly, fry, dry, cry, try, bye, dye, lye, hype, type, typhoon, dynamic, psychology, psychiatrist, Byron, Kyle, Tyson

/ie/   tie, die, pie

/ui/   guide

/uy/   guy, buy

Ex. 2   Explore the Structural Energy Vowel #6y in the following sentences or expressions.

- I like China.

- High five, low five--give me five!

- I scream, you scream, we all scream for ice cream!

- Kind Kyle White works as a tour guide in Taipei, Taiwan.

- Let's fly the kite with Ryan.

- My phone number is 555-999-5959 (five-five-five, nine-nine-nine, five-nine-five-nine).

- If you would like to have the power to hire and fire, acquire such a position instead of admiring or complaining about those who can hire and fire.

- Mr. Sire desires to be the choir director for the upcoming Messiah Concert.

181

Ex. 3   Explore the Structural Energy Vowel #6y in the following paragraph. Vowel #6y [aɪ] is underlined for you.

Brian Byron used to be a walking medical encyclopedia, hiding acute sinusitis, laryngitis, and benign fibromyalgia. And as if those were not quite enough, he lately acquired five more medical terminologies to his body--acute rhinitis, appendicitis, hepatitis, cholecystitis, and osteo-arthritis. Oh, my, oh, my, who wants to hide five to nine benign and acute medical terminologies in their fine bodies like Brian Byron did. Thanks to those high-tech medical societies and ancient Chinese formulas for fighting against all those hiders and hibernators and making Brian's body fine again.

Ex. 4   In the following words and sentences, explore the Structural Energy Vowel #6y + er [aɪ. ɚɹ], which can be spelled in many ways as shown below. The 'er' here is actually an unstressed and shortened R.

Useful tip:

Move smoothly and quickly from the consonant to the R so the Y connective is minimized.

fire, hire, lyre, mire, tire, wire, attire, entire, retire, admire, desire, require, esquire, sapphire, McGuire, liar, choir, buyer, brier, flier, prior, Meyer

Ex. 5   Now explore the #6y + er in these sentences:

- Hiring and firing people is not as desirable a job as it may seem.

- The choir director tired his choir members during the entire choir practice.

- Do they require you to wire the money or snail mail Kyle's final paycheck?

- Prior to the flight, the entire flight crew checked their night attire.

- Meyer's Esquire Shoes distributes handsome fliers to their potential buyers.

- One of Ms. Meyer's desires is to hire a gourmet chef to cook her desired food; and then, after dinner, to retire to the cushiony recliner in the living room with a cozy fire burning in the fireplace.

Ex. 6   In the following "Vowel #6y+ N" [aɪ + n] = [a + in], make sure your pronunciation smoothly transitions from the 6y to the N. This is a useful experiment for any speakers who tend to skip over the final [i] sound in the 6y.

dine	[da.in]	kind	[ka.ind]
fine	[fa.in]	find	[fa.ind]
line	[la.in]	mind	[ma.ind]
nine	[na.in	blind	[bla.ind]
pine	[pa.in]	grind	[gɹa.ind]
sign	[sa.in]	signed	[sa.ind]

Ex.7   In the following "Vowel #6y+ N" [aɪ + n] = [a + in] words, make sure you hear the [in] after the [a] sound before you proceed to other words.

- A proud but lonely mind has got to be blinded to find a fine mate for life.

- After the fine show, they will wine and dine and ride on a merry go round.

- Please kindly sign your name above this line.

- It seems that there is a fine line between a mighty leader and a wild dictator.

- I might have nine million dollars in my bank account, but I will never have enough money to pay for a fine of any sort.

- Our spinal cord is well protected by the spinal vertebra, muscles, and skin.

Notes: ....

....

....

....

....

....

The Structural Energy Vowels at a Glance

#1[u] or #y1 [ju]	#2[o]	#21[oʊ]	#3 [ɔ]	#4 [ɒ]	#5 [ɑ]	#51 [aʊ]	#6 [æ]	#6y [aɪ]
ooze/you	Osaka	oh	awe	on	alms	our	ant	ice
boo		bone	bought	bond	bar	bow	bat	buy
do/dew		Don't	dawn	Don	darn	down	dad	dine
food/few		phone	fall	fond	father	found	fan	find
Google		go	gaudy	God	gargle	gown	gas	guide
who/hue		home	haunt	holiday	harm	house	hand	hide
Jew		Joe	jaw	job	jar	jowl	Jam	jibe
cool/cue		cold	caught	cot	car	cow	can	kind
loom		low	law	lobby	large	loud	land	line
moo/mew		most	maw	Mop	Mars	mouse	man	mind
noon/new		no	naughty	nod	gnarl	now	nanny	nine
poor/pew		pole	Paul	pond	park	pound	pat	pie
room		roam	raw	Ron	Rah	round	rat	rhyme
soon		sole	saw	Sonya	sardine	sound	sand	sign
Two	Tokyo	toe	taught	stop	target	town	tan	time
Voo/view		vote	Vaughn	volume	varsity	vouch	value	vine
wood		won't	warn	waffle	Wah	wow	wag	why
you		yoke	yawn	yonder	yard	yow	yak	yikes
zoo		zone	zorgite	zombie	Zahra	zounds	Zack	Zion
choose		chose	Chaucer	chop	charm	chow	chance	China
Shoe		show	shawl	Shop	sharp	shower	shall	shine

#3 [ɔ]	#3y [ɔɪ]	3n [ɔɹ]	R [ɝ]
all	oil	oar	earth
ought	oyster	or	earn
ball	boy	bore	burn
call	coy	core	curtain
dawn	Doyle	door	dirt
fall	foil	four	fir
hall	hoist	war	hurt
law	Loy/loin	lore	lurk
mall	moisture	more	murmur
naughty	noise	nor	nurse
Paul	poison	pore/pour	purse
saw	soy	sore	surf
tall	toy	tore	turn
wall	Woy	wore	wert
choice	choice	chore	churn
shawl	Bolshoi	shore	Shirley

(Graph created by Jonghee Shadix & Nancy Krebs, based on the text *The Use and Training of the Human Voice by Arthur Lessac ©1997*)

Notes: ....

....

....

....

....

....

....

....

B. Lip-Relaxing Vowels and Neutral Vowels

1. Long EE [i] as in *easy* or *see*

2. The diphthong AY [eɪ] as in *face*

3. The Neutral Vowels:

    N1 ....[ʊ] as in *took*

    N2 ....[ɪ] as in *tick*

    N3 ....[ɛ] as in *tech*

    N4 ....[ʌ] or [ə] as in *tuck* or <u>a</u>*bove*

4. The Neutral Diphthongs

    *N1n ....[ʊɚ] as in *poor*

    N2n ....[ɪɚ] as in *peer*

    N3n ....[ɛɚ] as in *pear or pare*

*N1n– Neutral diphthong #1, N2n– Neutral diphthong #2, N3n–Neutral Diphthong #3

Introduction to Neutrals: *A Dialogue*

Jonghee:	So far, we have explored *The **Structural Energy Vowels** (The Lip-Rounding Vowels)*. Now, we are going to explore the *Lip-Relaxing Vowels*, such as the [ʊ], [ɪ], [ɛ], and [ʌ], which were named by Lessac as **Neutral Vowels,** found in the words *took, tick, tech,* and *tuck.* Also included in this lesson are the Long EE [i] as in *see*, and the Diphthong AY [eɪ] as in *fade*.
Min:	Can you explain in more depth what the differences are between the Structural Vowels and these Neutral Vowels and this other vowel and diphthong?
Jonghee:	As you know, the *Structural Energy Vowels* are those that are created through the slightly diagonally forward movement of our facial zygomatic and/or levator muscles[50] and have round or oval lip-openings. These are the major vowels. They are ideally formed by giving more space between the upper and lower side teeth (the molars)—creating a more open feel in the oral cavity–feeling similar to the space you feel when you begin to yawn.

---

[50] https://www.kenhub.com/en/library/anatomy/zygomaticus-major-muscle

Min:	Yes, I remember going over this.

Jonghee:	However, *Neutral vowels* are those that are formed with little 'yawn space' and 'neutral' or very relaxed lip openings. **Think of them as the shortest distance between two consonants.** Each of the four Neutral Vowels comes from a 'parent vowel' such as the Neutral 1–*took* comes from the Structural Vowel #1 as in the word *Tool*. Why not try this experiment–start with that word *Tool* and say it aloud with a full feeling of yawn space and that small lip opening *Tool–Tool–Tool–Tool*–say it quicker each time and reduce the space between your side teeth until you barely have any length between the T and the L then replace the L with a K–the vowel will become so short that it changes into the new vowel of [ʊ] and the word will be *took*.

Min:	(trying the experiment) Aha! It IS different–I felt it change. *Took!* Can we do another?

Jonghee:	Sure. Try it with the parent of our Neutral 2 [ɪ] which is the Long EE as in *Peel*. Say that word over and over and keep moving quicker and quicker to the L, and you will find a new vowel . You do it and let me know what you discover.

Min:	I just did it. *Pill*!

Jonghee:	Yes! Now add a K in place of the L, what do you have?

Min:	*Pick*!

Jonghee:	Wonderful. Now start with the parent for the Neutral 3 which is the [æ] like *Pal*. Repeat that word faster and faster until you find a new vowel between the P and the L.

Min:	I discovered I was saying *Pell*.

Jonghee:	Replace the L with a K, what word do you discover?

Min:	*Peck?*

Jonghee:	Yes, like a bird that *pecks* for food. And now the final one: use the parent vowel of [ɑ] as in *Palm*, and shorten that distance from the P to the M. Make sure your L is silent. What do you find?

Min:	I find *Pum*….

Jonghee:	Replace the M with a P–what do you have?

Min:	*Pup!*

Jonghee: Isn't that something?! In GA *English Neutral Vowels (Lip Relaxing Vowels)*, there are four distinct sounds: *the Short* [ɪ], [ʊ], [ɛ], and [ʌ]. And they show up in thousands of words that you will speak on any given day.

Min: I didn't know that. Right now, I most likely substitute the vowels from my First Language when I speak English.

Jonghee: That is often what takes place. As you mentioned, when we are learning to speak a new or second language, we tend to substitute the closest equivalents of the sounds from our first language to this new language.

Min: So that's why *my* English sounds different from the Americans around me. Some sounds don't actually exist in my first language, and I can see that some people don't quite understand me at times, and this can sometimes frustrate me. That is the reason why I am in this class.

Jonghee: And I'm glad that you are here. The Neutral Vowels are going to help you a lot. So, let's actually learn these Neutrals, also known as Lip-Relaxing Vowels. The Long EE and diphthong AY will also use relaxed lips. That is why I am including them in this part of our class.

Min: I am ready to start.

Jonghee: Let's begin with the Long EE [i] and move through these Lip-Relaxing Vowels.

Notes:...

....

....

....

....

....

....

....

....

....

The Long EE [i] as in *E* or *Easy*

For your information:

- The Long EE [i] exists in most languages and is most likely familiar to you. This familiarity will help you to learn the Short [ɪ] as in *sit*, which is similar but different from the Long [i], not only in its length, but also in the vertical distance or 'yawn space' between the tongue and the hard palate when the tongue is resting on the floor of the mouth.

- In this section, the Long EE [i], one of the Major English Vowels, is introduced first and will then be a good reference for the Short [ɪ], which is a Neutral Vowel.

To create the Long [i] sound:

1. Relax your tongue tip and let it gently touch the back surface of the lower front teeth and gum.

2. You will notice a very small space (distance) between the tongue surface and the ceiling of your oral cavity. This is what is known as a minimal optimal *yawn space*. This is all you need to form the sound. Relax your lips into a slight SH positioning.

3. Now, create the [i] sound by saying the name of the English alphabet letter E (A-B-C-D-*E*) and sustaining it longer –as if you are connecting two or three of them together with a little Y in between--*EE-y-EEE-y-EEEE*. You might be able to feel a small vibration on your hard palate (the ceiling of the oral cavity) near or on your upper gum ridge. This is your Long EE [i] sound. It should produce a pleasant feeling of vibrations and resonance in your head.

More information:

- When you sustain this sound the upper and lower front teeth do not touch each other. There is a little cushion of space between your upper and lower side teeth as well.

- When you sustain or voice this vowel, feel this experience in a purely personal and enjoyable way. Don't worry about being good at it, or whether it is "correct." Just sing the way you do when you sing or hum your favorite song when no one is around as you sustain the /Eeeee/.

- The Long [i] is often spelled with /e/, /ea/, /ee/, /ei/, /ey/, /i/,/ie/ and /ay/

Ex. 1

In the following words, explore the Long [i] sound by *underlining* appropriate spellings and by singing or voicing the Long [i] sound.

*Remember to sustain the sound. The words on the first lines are marked for you.

/e/   E, B, C, D, be, she, he, we, me

/ea/   easy, eat, each, pea, tea, bead, lead, read, leaf, deal, heal, seal, lean, clean, mean, wean, leave, league, colleague, beam, dream, team, teach, reach, peak, speak, peach, preach, beat, heat, meat, treat, increase, release, please, appeal

/ee/   bee, see, fee, knee, need, three, spree, seen, keen, queen, deed, seed, speed, breed, feel, peel, meek, cheek, peek, creek, keep, sleep, greet, meet, succeed

/ei/   perceive, receive, deceive

/ey/   key, osprey

/i/   naïve

/ie/   niece, chief, thief, achieve, relieve, retrieve, yield, believe

/y/   easy, busy, daily, very, clumsy, breezy, weepy, needy

/ay/   quay

Ex. 2

Explore the Long [i] vowel in the following sentences by *underlining* the spelling and sustaining the sound. The first sentence has been marked for you.

- It is easy to eat peeled peaches.

- Heath, please, lead these leaders to Group Three.

- Lee Reeves will leave shortly after she reads her email.

- The league reached the peak of the deal.

- Jean succeeded in her first team-teaching with her colleague.

- He needed to knead his knees to ease his deep knee pain.

- The dean sent out letters revealing the increase of tuition and fees.

The Short [ɪ] Neutral Vowel 2 (N2) as in *It is*

The Short [ɪ] feels as if the tongue is resting on the bottom of the oral cavity, creating the sense that there is a little more space between the tongue and the hard palate compared to the Long [i].

For your information:

- The *parent vowel* of the Short [ɪ] is the Long EE [i]. That is the reason why the Long EE [i] is introduced *before* the *Short* [ɪ] in this chapter.

- This sound is *not merely the short version of the Long EE* [i]. It is a similar but *different sound* from the Long [i]. It has its own qualities and identification.

To create the Short [I] sound:

1. Begin with the 'parent vowel' [i] EE as in *Peel* as in the dialogue above, Say it aloud and shorten the distance between the P and the L as you repeat until you feel *Pill*.

2. Replace the L with the consonant K, so that you are now saying *Pick-Pick-Pick*. This new vowel is the short [I] sound.

3. Make sure you are feeling a neutral lip-opening and make sure you move quickly from the P to the L or K sound.

The Short [ɪ] is often spelled with /i/, /e/, /ee/, /o/, /u/, and /y/.

Notes:..

....

....

....

....

....

....

....

Ex. 1   Explore the Short [ɪ] sound in the following words.

/ɪ/   if, is, in, image, income, impact, import, issue, interest, interview,
         interval, index, intimacy, incentive, incline, inflation, inflammation
         it, fit, kit, sit, city, bin, pin, twin, Quinn, win, wind, winter, hint,
         Smith, figure, finger, pixel, rinse, village, visual, did, hid, kid, lid,
         mid, rid, his, quiz, fizz, Liz, miss, sister, fill, till, pill, spill, skill,
         drill, diligent, him, simple, pink, link, think, thing, king, sing,
         six, mix, fix, quick, pick, wish, dish, polish, blemish, ticklish,
         dictionary, kitchen

/e/   pretty, college, knowledge

/ee/   been

/o/   women

/u/   busy, business

/y/   gym, mystery, symphony, syllable, syllabus, symposium

Ex. 2   Explore the Short [ɪ] sound in the following sentences.

•   Yes, it is.

•   It is in his dictionary.

•   Jim Smith found an optimal pitch in his initial singing lesson.

•   Take this pill with a sip of tepid water.

•   Tim was tickled to death by his big salary increase.

•   Dr. Min Kim hit on an interesting issue in this symposium.

Notes: ....
....
....
....

192

Ex. 3   Compare the Long [i] and (N2) Short [ɪ] in the following.

eat --------------- it   beat------------- bit
each ------------- itch   bead------------ bid
bean ------------- bin   colleague ------- college
dean ------------- din   deed------------ did
greedy ---------- gritty   feet ------------- fit
heat------------- hit   greet------------ grit
eel --------------- fill   field ------------ filled
jean------------- Jim   kneel ----------- nil
lead------------- lid   lean------------- Lynn
leave ----------- live   peel------------- pill
peach----------- pitch   queen ---------- Quinn
read ------------ rid   reach ----------- rich
meat/meet ------ mitt   neat------------- knit/nit
Pete ------------ pit   seen ------------ sin
seat------------- sit   steal ------------ still
meek ----------- Mick   team------------ Tim
teen------------- tin   wean ----------- win
wheat ---------- wit   yield------------ yin

Ex. 4   Explore the Long[i] and Short [ɪ] (N2) in the following sentences.

• Tim Steen is sitting on the seat and beating a bit of fish bones to feed his fish.

• Mr. Rich reached the rim of his life's dream.

• Pete pitches peaches with a mitted hand to Mitch when they meet each other at the peach orchard for the Peach Festival.

• It is a pity that in reality people are still stealing things from other ships in the sea.

• If Neal doesn't read his books before his classes, he will get a nil grade.

• Mr. Steve Quinn went to England to meet Queen Elizabeth.

• Keenan Kin was happy his new sneakers that his mom brought to him this weekend fit his feet.

• Keith said he will live in the dorm for the semester and leave for the summer.

The [ɛ] Neutral Vowel 3 (N3) as in *Egg*

To create this sound:

1. Start with the parent vowel in *Pal* repeating it and each time shortening the distance between the P and the L while you reduce the space between the side teeth, until you discover the neutral vowel. You find *Pell* [ɛ].

2. Replace the L with a K– *Peck-Peck-Peck*. This vowel between the P and the K is the Neutral 3 or [ɛ]*.

*This sound is often spelled with /e/, /ea/, /a/, /ai/, ay/ and /u/.

Ex. 1   Explore the Neutral 3 (N3) [ɛ] vowel in the following words. The first line is underlined for you.

     /e/   eF, eL, eM, eN, eS, egg, end, enter, echo, every, envelop, elephant, engineer, exercise, elevator, escalator, estimate, elementary, bed, berry, fed, led, leg, men, Ken, ten, pen, bet, get, let, net, met, set, wet, bend, send, bench, neck, tech, letter, fellow, Kelly, rest, test, text, next, medicine, metal, merry, method, melanin, rescue, commend, restaurant, federal, seven, sense, session, senator, several

     /ea/   head, sweat, meant, read (past tense), ready, jealous

     /a/   any, many

     /ai/   said

     /ay/   says

     /u/   bury (sounds like berry)

     /ue/   guess, guest

Notes:..

....

....

Ex. 2   Explore the Neutral 3 (N3) [ɛ] sound in the following sentences. The vowel is underlined for you.

- Esther estimated the egg dish to be about ten dollars.

- I meant to say I have not read the book "Dead Poets' Society" yet.

- The record shows Meg set seven sets of experiments for each weekend in September.

- The next test is set for the second Wednesday of the semester.

- Ken Bennett, a physical therapist, helps people to become healthier.

- Anyway, Ken says he said he could help many people in their endeavors.

Ex. 3   Compare the sounds and the shapes of the lip-openings of the Long [i], Short [ɪ] (N2) , and [ɛ] (N3) sounds in the following.

[i]	[ɪ]	[ɛ]
bead	bid	bed
lead	lid	led
read	rid	red
feed	fid	fed
heed	hid	head
weed	wind	wend
beat	bit	bet
greet	grit	Greta
meet	mitt	met
neat	nit	net
seat	sit	set
sweet	switch	sweat
deal	dill	dell
seal	sill	sell
heal	hill	hell
steam	stim	stem
team	Tim	temp
wean	win	when
peach	pitch	Petch
reach	rich	retch

Ex. 4   Explore the difference among Long EE [i], Neutral 2 (N2) Short [ɪ], and Neutral 3 (N3) [ɛ] sounds in the following sentences. Remember to keep your lips 'neutral' (relaxed) for all.

- Sealy Seth was sitting on the beach and pitched a peach pit toward the sea, but the pit did not reach the sea.

- Beatrice bet she could beat her batter a bit better than Deb did.

- Heather Heath hid her headgear beneath the heating pad.

- Sun-burned Hillary Billary will have a heck of a time with her peeling heels until they're completely healed.

- It is no sweat for sweet Sweeny Swinn to steam the stems of sweet potatoes for the steamed sweet potato stem salad.

- Winny Wilson weeded her lawn while the ground was still wet.

- Wendy Winn will wean her baby by the week after next Wednesday.

Notes: ....

....

....

....

....

....

....

....

....

....

....

....

....

Ex. 5   Compare the Lip Relaxing Vowel (Neutral Vowel N3) [ɛ] sound with the Lip Rounding Vowel (The Structural Energy Vowel #6) [æ] in the following words and sentences. Add a little more 'yawn space' between the upper and lower side teeth for the #6.

[ɛ]	[æ]
Ben	ban
head	had
den	Dan
fen	fan
pet	pat
Ken	can
set	sat
men	man
letter	latter
pen	pan
settle	saddle
ten	tan
kettle	cattle
send	sand
lend	land
mental	mantle
expensive	expansive
ketchup	catch up

- Seth sat on the sand and set up a sandcastle on the wet sand.

- Ken can catch the ketchup bottle on his head without using his hands.

- Pat said he petted his pet after getting him from the animal shelter.

- Larry's latter letter includes a picture of a lamb painted with colored pens.

- Ken, Ben's dad, banned Ben from eating food directly out of the can.

- Dan Fenton sits in the den eating a sandwich with Ben.

197

Ex. 6   In the following words, compare the Short [ɪ] with [ɛ] and [æ].

[ɪ]	[ɛ]	[æ]
it	Ed	at
bin	Ben	ban
chin	Chen	chance
din	den	Dan
fit	fed	fat
hid	head	had
kit	Ked	cat
kin	Ken	can
pin	pen	pan
pit	pet	pat
sit	set	sat
since	sense	sanction
litter	letter	latter
win	when	Wan
Kistler	Kessler	castle
mission	mention	mansion

Ex. 7   Explore the Neutral 3 [ɛ] sound in the following story. The first paragraph is marked for this vowel with a single underline.

From Red-Leaf Lettuce to Dead-Leaf Lettuce

In our GA English pronunciation class on W<u>e</u>dnesday, we made a plan to go hiking in B<u>e</u>thleh<u>e</u>m Mountain State Park n<u>e</u>xt Saturday. For the picnic lunch after the hike, there were t<u>e</u>mpting options from hotdogs, d<u>e</u>viled <u>e</u>ggs and hamburgers to Korean Spicy Pork Barbecue and ging<u>e</u>rbr<u>e</u>ad. As a chorus, everyone s<u>ai</u>d they wanted the Korean Spicy Pork Barbecue. For this ev<u>e</u>nt, I was given the h<u>e</u>lpful task of informing <u>e</u>veryone what to bring for our potluck spr<u>ea</u>d. I assigned my teacher to bring the marinated pork meat and the portable gas grill; Kaya and Hirohiko, the cooked rice and r<u>e</u>d wine; Changchun, the drinks, ice and ging<u>e</u>rbr<u>ea</u>d; and I, mys<u>e</u>lf, would h<u>e</u>lp by bringing three h<u>ea</u>ds of r<u>e</u>d-leaf l<u>e</u>ttuce and a bottle of hand-sanitizer.

So, on Thursday I went to the Publix grocery store to find red-leaf lettuce. They did not have it. So, I went to the closest Wal-Mart. They were out of that kind of lettuce also. So, I bought three large heads of romaine lettuce instead.

It was the first time for me to buy romaine lettuce, and I was energized and excited about it. I went home and washed all three heads of lettuce. Remembering my classmates' advice, I cut the heads off the lettuce. After this experience, I faced a dilemma — 'Now what?' How can I keep this lettuce fresh until Saturday?' I ultimately decided that if I froze it, it would stay fresh like the frozen vegetables I have bought; and I put those well-washed lettuce heads into the three one-gallon-sized zippered plastic storage bags and put them into the freezer section of my refrigerator.

The picnic day finally came. The weather was just gorgeous with a pleasant sun and gentle breezes. It was a treat for a summer day in the Southern United States. I was so proud of myself for the fact that I had thought about keeping the lettuce in the freezer section—What a genius I was! Even though they were not the red leaf variety, my efforts will save the day! While patting myself on the back, I took the lettuce out of the freezer, and making sure I did not forget the hand sanitizer, I went to Oak Mountain with my classmates.

The hiking was fun and pleasant. During the hike, I told my English teacher about the lettuce, and she got so upset. "You put the lettuce in the freezer?" She shook her head vigorously. I replied, "What's wrong with that?" She shook her head again and said, "Never put LETTUCE in the freezer." I had obviously never heard about that and could not believe what she said.

We continued our hiking for about an hour and a half and found a nice spot at the edge of a beautiful spring lake to eat our lunch. Everyone took their food to the picnic table.

I took my lettuce out, too. My teacher inspected my frozen lettuce and pronounced it 'DEAD.' Seeing it with my own eyes left no doubt. The beautiful red-leaf lettuce had turned into romaine lettuce and now finally into poor 'dead-leaf' lettuce! It looked terrible. It was so wet that it looked like boiled spoiled lettuce, which could never be used for taco-like shells to wrap the spicy barbecued pork with cooked rice in it. Everyone was disappointed that we missed the chance to expose ourselves to a different food culture. I felt so bad and embarrassed. But at least I learned a good lesson from it: "DON'T EVER FREEZE THE LETTUCE!"

(Adapted from an essay by Eric Winardi, Graduate Student, Department of Engineering, University of Alabama at Birmingham)

The [eɪ] Diphthong as in *Ate*

The [eɪ] is a *diphthong*, the combination of the *major vowel* [e] and the *neutral vowel* [ɪ] and is considered as *one syllable*, and therefore it is classified as a *major vowel*. The IPA symbol indicates that the second vowel is short. It is contained in this section because the lips are relaxed and there is little yawn space between the upper and lower side teeth, so it will feel much like the Neutrals.

To create the [eɪ] sound:

1. Begin with the familiar vowel we covered earlier in this section–the Long EE [i] as in *Yeast*. Start by sustaining that Long EE sound and then slide into the [ɛ] EH sound *Yee-eh–yee-eh–yee* without stopping the sound. Slowly speed up so that the tongue doesn't drop down as far as you move from *yee* to *eh*

2. Now begin with the EH and slide quickly to the EE. You have now discovered the new diphthong of Eh-y-EE   as in *Play*

*This diphthong is often spelled with /a/, /ai/, /ay/, /ea/, /ei/, /ey/.

Ex. 1	In the following list of words, explore the movement of your tongue as the sound moves smoothly from the [e] to [ɪ]

/a/ — A, ate, April, agent, base, face, race, place, space, bake, cake, take, lake, wake, brake, date, late, gate, rate, plate, state, taste, waste, create, facial, spatial, gave, wave, brave, crave, safe, came, game, same, name, frame, Dale, lane, plane, sane, membrane, change, associate, graduate, liberate, congratulate, nation, education, concentration, communication, dedication, creation, pronunciation, qualification, champagne, crazy

/ai/ — mail, bail, rail, pail, sail, tail, Gail, lain, rain, brain, drain, grain, pain, plain, remain, campaign, main, mainly, maintain, maintenance, wait

/ay/ — day, may, pay, say, way, lay, play, delay, relay, ray, gray, pray, spray

/ea/ — great, break, steak

/ei/ — eight, weight, freight, reign, sleigh, Beijing, Taipei

/ey/ — grey, prey, they, convey, survey

Ex. 2	In the following word list, by quickly moving from [e] to [ɪ] to [m], make sure to feel and recognize the [ɪ] after the [e], before you proceed to the [m]. Notice the diphthong is renotated from [eɪm] to [e.ɪm] to reinforce your Short [ɪ] pronunciation. The secret to success is making sure you recognize the Short [ɪ] sound between the [e] and [m].

aim	[eɪm] ------ [e.ɪm]		game	[geɪm]----- [ge.ɪm]
name	[neɪm] ---- [ne.ɪm]		same	[seɪm]----- [se.ɪm]
fame	[feɪm] ----- [fe.ɪm]		frame	[fɹeɪm]---- [fɹe.ɪm]
claim	[kleɪm] --- [kle.ɪm]		flame	[fleɪm] ---- [fle.ɪm]

Ex. 3	In the following words, make sure you feel and include the [n] sound after the [eɪ]. Notice the syllables are rearranged and apply the same principle given for Ex. 2.

gain	[ge.ɪn]		rain	[ɹe.ɪn]
grain	[gɹe.ɪn]		train	[tɹe.ɪn]
pain	[pe.ɪn]		brain	[bɹe.ɪn]
sane	[se.ɪn]		chain	[tʃe.ɪn]
main	[me.ɪn]		drain	[dɹe.ɪn]
maintain	[me.ɪn.te.ɪn]		explain	[ɪks.ple.ɪn]

Ex. 4   In the following, explore the movement of your tongue and lip openings for the [eɪ] diphthong.

- Fake it till you make it, and make it before it's too late.

- They say, "Eye contact can make or break communication."

- Kate Blake, an associate professor, associates with her academic colleagues.

- Dwain Maine mainly maintains the Main Building of a train maintenance company.

- Training soccer players on a rainy plain in Spain doesn't sound mundane to me.

- Some brain-drained countries are evaluating their need for the brains to return home.

- Maintaining a healthy balance between work and play is a must for Kate and Raymond.

Ex. 5   Compare the sensations in the movements of your tongue and lip-openings in [i], [ɪ], [ɛ], and [eɪ].

[i]	[ɪ]	[ɛ]	[eɪ]
beak	Bick	beck	bake
seek	sick	sec	sake
sheep	ship	chef	shape
eat	it	et	ate
beat	bit	bet	bate
neat	nit	net	Nate
meet	mitt	met	mate
Pete	pit	pet	pate
seat	sit	set	sate
meal	mill	Mel	mail/male
peel	pill	Pell	pail/pale
seal	sill	sell	sale
keen	kin	Ken	cane
mean	Min	men	main

Notes:..

....

....

....

....

....

....

....

....

....

....

Ex. 6   Compare the sensations in the movement of your tongue and lip openings in [i], [ɪ], [ɛ] and [eɪ].

- A sheep-shaped ship; and ship-shaped sheep.

- Gene ate his egg at seven, but Tina wants to eat hers later, at ten.

- Please, if you don't mind, these seats are not for sitting, but for sale.

- Heath hit the road at eight this morning because he hates driving in the heat of the day.

- Neenah's niece is making a neat, knitted necklace for Neenah.

- Hello everyone, meet this new mitten I have made.

- They named the big, beak-shaped baking pan as "The Big Beak-Baker."

- The main meal was made from the freshly milled grains mailed directly from Mel's mill.

- Ms. Sealy said she used to seal her Christmas cards with Christmas seals when she was a child.

Comparison of the [ɛn] and [eɪn] sounds

Useful tip: For the [eɪn] sound, make sure that you include the [ɪn] sound in your speech.

[ɛn]	[eɪn]
pen	pain
men	main
Jen	Jane
ten	taint
sent	saint

Notes:...

....

....

....

Ex. 7　　　　In the following, you might hear some GA speakers pronouncing the [n] as a *syllabic n* (not releasing the tongue tip from the [t] and omitting the unstressed Schwa [ə] sound spelled by the /ai/ in the /-tain/ portion of the words).

Britain	[bɹɪ.n̩]	certain	[sɝ. n̩]
curtain	[kɝ.n̩]	fountain	[faʊn.n̩]
mountain	[maʊn.n̩]	gotten	[gɒ.n̩]

Ex. 8　　　　Now read the words above aloud with the tongue tip released from the [t] place, followed by a very mild schwa [ə], and then the [n]. This pronunciation may be more familiar to you. Both are used in GA.

Notes: ....

....

....

....

....

....

....

....

....

....

....

....

....

....

....

....

Ex. 9   Explore the differences of the following vowels all felt in the front of the oral cavity.

[i]	[ɪ]	[ɛ]	[eɪ]	[æ]
heat	hit	head	hate	hat
seat	sit	set	sate	sat
Pete	pit	pet	pate	pat
neat	nit	net	Nate	Nat
beat	bit	bet	bate	bat
deed	did	dead	date	dad
feet	fit	fed	fate	fat
Jean	Jin	Jen	Jane	Jan
keen	kin	Ken	cane	can
lead	lid	led	laid	lad
meet	mitt	met	mate	mat
read	rid	red	raid	rat
see/sea	sit	said/says	say	sat
sheep	ship	chef	shape	shaft
speed	spit	sped	spade	spat
team	Tim	temp	tame	Tammy
visa	visit	vet	vase	vat
wheat	wit	wet	weight/wait	wag

Pronunciation of the Final Syllable /-ate/ in Verbs, Nouns, and Adjectives

In words with three or more syllables, the final syllable -ate is pronounced as [eɪt] when in a verb; however, it is pronounced as [ət] when found in nouns and adjectives.

Verbs [eɪt]	Nouns/Adjectives [ət]
associate	associate
estimate	estimate
graduate	graduate
separate	separate
deliberate	deliberate
appropriate	appropriate
syndicate	syndicate

Ex. 10   Explore the differences in the pronunciation of the syllable *-ate* in the following sentences. The [eɪ] or diphthong AY is italicized for you.

- K*a*te, an associate professor at Pl*ai*ns College, associates with other associate professors.

- I am a graduate of this school—I gradu*a*ted from a graduate program in M*ay*.

- The press syndicate announced that their f*a*mous editorial column is syndic*a*ted in more than 800 p*a*pers around the world.

- They estim*a*ted that the rough estimate for a new heat pump could be somewhere around $800, not $8,000. (*ei*ght)

Ex. 11   Explore the [eɪ] sound in the following paragraph. This diphthong is *italicized* for you. Remember to keep your lips relaxed and neutral.

W*ay*ne Br*ai*nie, a candidate for the st*a*te's Economic Stimul*a*tion Commission, m*a*de a st*a*tement in a press conference that people are getting increasingly imp*a*tient about seeing some real ch*a*nges that were promised by our new leader, the promises that were m*a*de during his camp*ai*gn trips around the country. Br*ai*nie m*ai*nt*ai*ned that we cannot just leave our country's status up to the federal level administr*a*tion, but each st*a*te should t*a*ke the initiative to stimul*a*te the economic growth of the st*a*te. He said that he could be an asset for m*a*king this ch*a*nge so that the people of his st*a*te can elev*a*te or at least m*ai*nt*ai*n the present standard of living.

Notes:..

....

....

....

....

....

....

....

Ex. 12   In the following poem, feel the /ain/ as [e.ɪn] whenever you say 'main' and 'pain', and note the difference between that and the pronunciation of the word "in". Remember to feel the /m/ and the /n/ fully. The /m/ and /n/ in the first few lines have been identified for you when they are final consonants.

The *Main Pain in* the Neck

Have you ever had a *pain in* your neck?
Or have you ever *BEEN* a "*main pain in* someone's neck?"
Which one is worse?
Having a *pain in* your neck?
Or BEING a "*main pain in* the neck" to someone?
I probably could have been a "*main pain in* the neck" to someone
sometime in my life.
Not just one time, or not just two times.
Perhaps, many, many times.
With endless curiosity and endless questions,
I could have given a lot of *pain in* my teachers' necks by being a "*main
pain.*"
Especially when they were tight with time to cover other content in the
classes.
Now I have a *pain in* my neck.
Really?
Yes, really!
Maybe for all the *pain* that I have given to my teachers?
Maybe, maybe not.
Perhaps, I need to *maintain* my health better
To combat the *pain in* my neck.
*A*men to that!

Notes: ....

....

....

....

....

....

....

The Schwa Sounds
The Neutral 4 (N4)

Stressed Schwa **[ʌ]** as in **fun** [fʌn], and
Unstressed Schwa **[ə]** as in func**tion** [fʌŋkʃən]

In GA English the schwa is a vowel that can be either stressed (emphasized) in a word, in which it will most likely feel and sound longer to you; or unstressed, where it will feel and sound shorter in length. IPA makes a distinction in the symbols when the vowel is in the stressed or unstressed position in a word, but the vowel is considered to be the same sound. All GA English vowels can become this Schwa [ə] sound when they are not stressed in speech. Sometimes this unstressed vowel is so short—it cannot even be identified.

To create the Schwa – Neutral 4 (N4): [ʌ] [ə]

1. Begin with saying aloud the 'parent vowel' in *Palm*–the AH [a] with a full yawn space and repeat the word while slowly reducing the yawn space while moving more quickly from the P to the M (the L is silent) until you feel the vowel shorten into a new sound. This is the schwa or [ʌ] as in *Pum*...add a P to the end of this word and you will be saying *Pump. Pump-pump-pump.* Now replace the M with just a P, *Pup-Pup-Pup.* It will sound like 'uh' not AH. Your tongue will rest on the 'floor' of your oral cavity.

For your information:

*   It is believed that about 65 percent of GA English speech contains a Schwa.

    The Schwa [ə] can be spelled with /a/, /ai/, /e/, /eo/, /i/, /o/, /ou/, /u/ and /oo/

Notes: ....

....

....

....

....

....

....

....

A Dialogue: **Pronouncing the Stressed Schwa [ʌ]**

Hiro: How do you pronounce the word 'hut'?

Jonghee: How do YOU pronounce it?

Hiro: I seem to pronounce it differently from the way my U. S. friends do. The way I say it is the same as 'hot' as we say the weather is hot. But I know they are not the same words.

Jonghee: So, you don't feel comfortable saying two different words with the same pronunciation, because you know they are different words with different meanings.

Hiro: Yes, that is true.   Now I need to know how I can say the word the way it was meant to be.

Jonghee: I understand your concern. And I have noticed that this happens to GA language learners at times. If they do not have the Stressed Schwa-like sound in their spoken languages, or an alphabet letter that can represent the exact English Schwa sound, they tend to substitute the closest vowel equivalent that they know from their languages, which is usually [a] AH (#5), for the Stressed Schwa [ʌ] UH (N4) in English.

Hiro: I find myself doing that as well.

Jonghee: Some languages do not have the Schwa sound or the Structural Energy Vowel #6 [æ]. Speakers of those languages tend to pronounce both the N4/Schwa [ə] or [ʌ] and the Vowel #6 [æ] as the Vowel #5 [a]. So, the words 'cut' and 'cat' are often pronounced as [kat]; and both "fun" [fʌn] and "fan" [fæn] as [fa̲n].

Hiro: That's true. I do that, too. So, what is the safest option for pronouncing the Stressed Schwa sound?

Jonghee: Well, as you know, in the Merriam-Webster[51] dictionary, when the Schwa sound is the only vowel or is stressed in a word with more than one syllable, the IPA symbol used is like an upside-down V. [ʌ].

Hiro: I am so glad I went through this with you. Can we go through some more example words for the Stressed Schwa sounds, please?

Jonghee: Sure. Let's concentrate on words with only one vowel or one where the schwa is present in the stressed syllable.

---

[51] https://www.merriam-webster.com/ Merriam-Webster definition

209

Ex. 1   Explore the (N4) *Stressed Schwa* [ʌ] sound in single-syllable words or found in the stressed syllable of multi-syllabic words.

up, cut, sun, bun, fun, bus, cup, gut, hut, tuck, fund, mumps, mundane under, lunch, budget, Sunday, funnel, cunning, muddle, muffler, sometimes, coming, running, humming, hungry, color, blood

And now in these sentences. The stressed schwa is in **bold** font.

- Come out of the sun before you have too much fun.

- Sunny was hungry for a dozen hot cross buns.

- Don't cut up the lunch meat for Uncle Buck.

- The country in the south was united under its Southern government.

- Sometimes cousins can act tough with one another.

Ex. 2   Now explore the (N4) *Unstressed Schwa* [ə] sound in the following words. It is even shorter than the stressed version of [ʌ], created with minimal optimal space in the oral cavity moving quickly to the following consonant. It will be *italicized*. It occurs in unstressed syllables in a word.

/a/   *a*bout, *a*bility, *a*nnounce, Chin*a*, Kore*a*, Jap*a*n, pleas*a*nt, internation*a*l

/ai/   vill*ai*n, capt*ai*n, cert*ai*n, fount*ai*n, mount*ai*n

/e/   op*e*n, tok*e*n, maid*e*n, probl*e*m, pres*e*nt

/eo/   lunch*eo*n, surg*eo*n

/i/   *a*bil*i*ty, poss*i*bility, futil*i*ty, mob*i*le

/o/   c*o*ntinue, c*o*mpare, c*o*nsumer, c*o*mputer, c*o*ntemporary

/io/   regi*o*nal, comp*e*titi*o*n, prop*o*siti*o*n, presentati*o*n, internati*o*nal

/ou/   continu*ou*s, covet*ou*s, jeal*ou*s, mischi*e*v*ou*s, right*eou*s

/u/   *u*ntil, s*u*pport, circ*u*mstance, alb*u*m

/y/   s*y*ringe, Pennsylvani*a*, *a*nal*y*sis

210

Pronunciation of the Suffix /-al/ syllable with unstressed Schwa [ə]

When an unstressed /–al/ [əl] syllable is found either in the middle of words or in word-final positions, GA speakers tend not to pronounce the Schwa [ə] but seem to depend on the voiced L to serve as both vowel and consonant even though dictionaries depict the Schwa [ə] as present. *This is known as the syllabic L [l].*

Here are some examples:

education*al*, fin*al*, met*al*, tot*al*, continent*al*, internation*al*, loc*al*, monument*al*, anatomic*al*, physic*al*, psychologic*al*, longitudin*al*, Nat*a*lie

- Anatomic*al* definitions are critic*al* to the understanding of physic*al* science.

- Nat*a*lie was tot*a*lly unhinged by the patholog*i*c*al* lying of her illogic*al* brother.

- In the fin*al* analysis, internation*al* law is of monument*al* importance to continent*al* sovereignty.

- It was not accident*al* that the met*al* tools needed by the laborer were education*al*.

Ex. 3   Explore the N4 *Stressed Schwa* [ʌ] and *UN-stressed Schwa* [ə] in the following sentences. Unstressed Schwas are underlined. Stressed Schwas are in **bold**. Remember that whether stressed or unstressed, the vowel sounds the same, just shorter in length when unstressed.

- The Sundae **fu**dge ice cream fund-raising on Monday was fun.

- Cutting the budget is not the only solution for all the company's financial problems.

- The International Studies Convention is going to be held in Seoul.

- The competition for the law school was as high as the competition for the medical school among competitors.

- I **u**nderstand that Monday is a mundane day of the week for some people.

Notes: ....

....

....

A Dialogue: **Discovering the Unstressed R-Derivative**

Cherry: Since I have started taking this class, I pay more attention to the differences between the way Americans pronounce and my usual way. I feel like my American friends pronounce the [ɝ] or R-Derivative sound slightly differently depending on whether it is stressed or unstressed, but I cannot figure out exactly what seems to be the difference.

Jonghee: It's great that you are more aware of the differences of the English pronunciation and bringing your questions to the class. There is indeed a small difference in the pronunciation of the *Stressed* [ɝ] (er) and *Unstressed* [ɚ] (er) sound.

Cherry: Ah, I see the difference in your lip-opening and the sound.

Jonghee: Be an investigator, observe and explore by saying the words 'view*er*' and 'ex*er*cise,' and feel the 'er' [ɚ] unstressed syllable in those words.

Cherry: I feel that sound of 'er' but only briefly.

Jonghee: Good observation. Now, let's explore the *Stressed* [ɝ] in 'h*er*' and '*cur*tain' and '*fur*ther.' Do you feel anything different when you experience the [ɝ] sound in those words?

Cherry: I am not sure. Can I try it again?

Jonghee: All right. The clues for the difference between the *Stressed* [ɝ] and *Unstressed* [ɚ] are in the shape of your lip-opening and the space within your mouth. Let's say them together: view*er*, ex*er*cise, h*er*, *cur*tain, *fur*ther.

Cherry: Oh, I can feel the differences now. For the Stressed [ɝ], I rounded my lips, and I gave more 'yawn space' inside my mouth than for the unstressed syllable of 'er' [ɚ], right?

Jonghee: Right. When it is stressed, this sound functions as the Structural R Derivative (ℝ) that we covered earlier. We feel an optimal yawn space inside the oral cavity like we do for all the Structural vowels and diphthongs (compound vowels), and the shape of the lips forms the #3 Structural Vowel. But when this sound is *unstressed*, we feel the minimal optimal yawn space, and the lips are neutral and relaxed. The unstressed version is also shorter in length, but it is still the same sound.

Cherry: I see. So, it's a question of relaxing both the size and the shape to 'unstress it'?

Jonghee: Yes! Here's a good example: the word 'fur**th**er' has the Stressed [ɝ] and Unstressed [ɚ] used together in one word. The first syllable is stressed, so that is our Structural version of the sound, and the second syllable is the unstressed version. Let's concentrate now on the unstressed version with neutral lips. That is why we included it among the Lip Relaxing vowels.

Notes: ....

....

....

....

....

....

....

....

....

....

....

....

....

....

....

....

....

....

....

....

....

The Unstressed [ɚ] R-Derivative (R̝)

This R colored vowel is the unstressed version of the Structural Energy Vowel **R̝**. It uses a relaxed, neutral lip positioning with minimal optimal yawn space within the oral cavity.

This sound can be spelled with /ar/, /er/, /ir/, /or/, /ure/, /ur/ and /yr/

/ar/	dollar, molar, columnar, popular, Richard
/er/	doer, drummer, exercise, further, interview, international, singer
/ir/	stir, sir, flirt, fir, elixir
/or/	color, record (n), history, victory, memory, doctor, actor
/ure/	future, nature; denture, manufacture, fixture
/ur/	femur, murmur, bulgur, jodhpur
/yr/	satyr, zephyr, martyr

Ex. 1   Explore the unstressed R Derivative (R̝) in the following sentences. These are <u>underlined</u> for you.

- The history and records of Western civilization traces their roots back to the Mediterranean and Europe.

- The drummer, the piano player and the actor were diligent workers and team players.

- The dirtier the clothes, the murkier the water will be.

- Nurture versus nature plays a bigger role and bears further observation.

- The future of the dollar is an international issue among debaters.

- Mrs. Gerber's earlier interview was an exercise in futility.

Notes: ....

....

....

The Short [ʊ] Neutral 1 (N1) as in *Took*

To create this sound:

1. Once again, begin by speaking aloud the 'parent vowel' which is the #1 Structural vowel, as in *Tool*. Feel the optimal yawn space and the small, rounded lip opening.

2. Repeat the word, moving quickly from the T to the L T*ool-T–l–T–l -Tull*. As you repeat, allow less yawn space and relax the lips.

3. Replace the L with a K, so it becomes ***Took-Took-Took***. This new vowel is the N1 [ʊ].

4. The lips will be neutral and there is reduced space between the side teeth.

The Short [ʊ] is often spelled with /u/, /oo/, or /ou/

For your information:

• The Neutral #1 (N1) [ʊ] is short in duration, as all neutral vowels are. They are all *the shortest distance between two consonants.*

Ex. 1   Explore the (N1) Short [ʊ] sound in the following words.

         /u/   full, bull, pull, push, put, pudding, bullet, pulpit

         /oo/   good, hood, stood, wood, book, cook, look, hook, nook, took, foot

         /ou/   could, should, would

Ex. 2   Explore the Short [ʊ] sound in the following sentences. The vowel is underlined for you.

     • If I could, I would. But I am not sure whether I should.

     • A good cook cooked a bowl of pudding for the hooding ceremony.

     • He took the cooked pudding and put it on the bookshelf and forgot all about it.

     • After the hooding ceremony, the cook said, "I should've kept the pudding on the stove top instead of putting it on the bookshelf!

Comparison of the Long [u] #1, Short [ʊ] N1, and Schwa [ʌ]/[ə] N4 sounds

Ex. 3 Explore the differences between the Long [u], Short [ʊ], and the schwa [ə or ʌ] sounds in the following.

Long [u]	Short [ʊ]	Schwa [ʌ] / [ə]
woo	wood/would	won
boo	book	buck
cool	could	cud
food	foot	fun
fool	full	flutter
goofy	good	gut
who	hood	hut
Luke	look	luck
pool	pull	pulse
shoot	should	shut
poodle	put	puddle
noodle	nook	knuckle
stool	stood	stud
two	took	tuck

Notes: ....

....

....

....

....

....

....

....

....

....

....

Ex. 4   Explore the differences between the Long [u], Short [ʊ], and the Schwa [ʌ] sounds in the following sentences. For your information, the Structural vowel [u] is marked **Bold**, the *Stressed Schwa* [ʌ] is <u>underlined</u>, and the *Short* [ʊ] is italicized.

- Mr. B<u>u</u>ckeye b*oo*ked himself int**o** a sp**oo**ky show.
           [ʌ, ʊ, u, u]

- It t*oo*k tw**o** h**ou**rs for <u>us</u> t**o** get t**o** Kent<u>u</u>cky.
           [ʊ, u, ʌ, u, u, ʌ]

- Y**ou** w*ou*ld if y**ou** c*ou*ld. B<u>u</u>t sh*ou*ld y**ou**?
           [u, ʊ, u, ʊ. ʌ, ʊ, u]

- P*u*t your <u>o</u>ther f*oo*t int**o** your b**oo**t.
           [ʊ, ʌ, ʊ, u, u]

- I w*ou*ld l*oo*k for w*oo*d if I kn**ew** wh<u>a</u>t w*oo*d I sh*ou*ld l*oo*k for.
           [ʊ, ʊ, ʊ, u, ʌ, ʊ, ʊ, ʊ]

- Is f**oo**ling <u>o</u>ther people f*u*ll of f<u>u</u>n?
           [u, ʌ, ʊ, ʌ]

- It l*oo*ks like today is L**u**ke's l<u>u</u>cky day.
           [ʊ, u, ʌ]

- Paul p*u*lled th<u>e</u> p<u>u</u>mp toward th<u>e</u> p**oo**l.
           [ʊ, ʌ, ʌ, ʌ, u]

- <u>A</u> st**oo**l with st<u>u</u>nning st<u>u</u>ds st*oo*d on th<u>e</u> stand.
           [ʌ, u, ʌ, ʌ, ʊ, ʌ]

- Y**ou** sh*ou*ld sh<u>u</u>t your ears before y**ou** sh**oo**t.
           [u, ʊ, ʌ, u, u]

Ex.5   Explore the difference between the (N1) Short [ʊ], and the Schwa (N4) [ʌ] / [ə] sounds in the following tongue twister. Try to assign appropriate marks according to the vowel marks in the bracket next to each sentence. The N4 is <u>underlined</u> and the N1 is *italicized*.

How much wood would a woodchuck chuck?

How m<u>u</u>ch w*oo*d w*ou*ld <u>a</u> w*oo*dch<u>u</u>ck ch<u>u</u>ck
     [ʌ, ʊ, ʊ, ʌ, ʊ, ʌ, ʌ]

if <u>a</u> w*oo*dch<u>u</u>ck c*ou*ld ch<u>u</u>ck w*oo*d?
     [ə, ʊ, ʌ, ʊ, ʌ, ʊ]

He w*ou*ld ch<u>u</u>ck as m<u>u</u>ch w*oo*d as he c*ou*ld,
     [ʊ, ʌ, ʌ, ʊ, ʊ]

and ch<u>u</u>ck as m<u>u</u>ch w*oo*d as <u>a</u> w*oo*dch<u>u</u>ck w*ou*ld ch<u>u</u>ck
     [ʌ, ʌ, ʊ, ʌ, ʊ, ʌ, ʊ, ʌ]

if <u>a</u> w*oo*dch<u>u</u>ck c*ou*ld ch<u>u</u>ck w*oo*d.
     [ʌ, ʊ, ʌ, ʊ, ʌ, ʊ]

Ex. 6   Compare the sounds and lengths of the vowels in /body/ and /buddy/, /father/ and /mother/.

body: [ɒ] The Lip-Rounding Vowel #4
        (The Structural Energy Vowel #4)

buddy: [ʌ] Stressed schwa (N4)

father: [ɑ] The Lip-Rounding Vowel #5
        (The Structural Energy Vowel #5)

mother: [ʌ] Stressed Schwa (N4)

Ex. 7   Explore the differences of the Long [u], Short [ʊ], and the Schwa [ʌ]/ [ə] sounds in the following dialogue. For your information, the Long [u] is marked **Bold**, the Stressed and Unstressed Schwas [ʌ] [ə] are underlined, and the Short [ʊ] is *italicized*. You might find some #4 and #5 Structural vowels as well.

Dialogue: **Body Shop Buddies**

Abby: So, when **do** people take their cars **to** the body shop?

Bill: They *should* **do** this when the body of the car is dented by accidents.

Abby: Uh, **do you** mean the outside of the car is somewhat ruined?

Bill: Usually.

Abby: So **you** *took* your car **to** a body shop before?

Bill: Yes. It seems like **too** many times.

Abby: So by now **you** *should* have many buddies at your favorite body shop.

Bill: **You** *could* say that. Since I have taken many cars **to** the body shop, I have found that many body-mechanics have become my buddies.

Abby: Isn't that **cool**?!

Bill: In fact, my mother and father run a **tru**ly *cushy* body shop.

Abby: Are your mother and father the mechanics in their shop?

Bill: My father and his buddy are *good* mechanics. My mother is in charge of, and very successful at keeping the *books* for the body shop.

Comparison of the Structural Vowels #21 [oʊ], #4 [ɒ], and N4 Schwa [ʌ].
If unstressed at any point, the Schwa [ə] is *italicized*.

Vowel #21 [oʊ]	Vowel #4 [ɒ]	Schwa [ʌ] /[ə]
Toby	Tom	tummy
robe	Rob	rubber
lobe	lob/lobby	love
role/roll	roster	rug
p*a*trol	trolley	tuss*le*
probe	prob*a*bly	rust
tone	tonsil	tough
owner	honor	under
own	on	*a*nother
ode/owed	odd	utter
phone	pond	pumm*el*
holy	holly	hum
know	not	nothing
go	God	gut
cone	con	cunning
stove	stop	stuff
toe	toddler	tunn*el*
toed	Todd	tub
soak	sock	suck
coat	cot	cut

Notes: ....

....

....

....

....

....

....

....

C. The Neutral Diphthongs (the lip-relaxing vowels blended together)

The lip relaxing vowels [ʊ], [ɪ] [ɛ] (*took, tick, tech*), when followed by the schwa [ʌ] (*tuck*), are known as **neutral diphthongs**. You remember that a diphthong is two vowels blended together to form one syllable. Putting them together, we get: N1n: [ʊə], N2n: [ɪə], and N3n: [ɛə][52]. These diphthongs only occur in GA English when they are followed by the consonant R.

Ex. 9   Explore the neutral diphthongs [ʊə], [ɪə] , and [ɛə] in the following words. Remember that neutral diphthongs are always followed by an R consonant.

[ʊə] (N1n)

poor	[pʊəɹ]	your	[jʊəɹ]
sure	[ʃʊəɹ]	cure	[kjʊəɹ]
pure	[pjʊəɹ]	secure	[səkjʊəɹ]

[ɪə] (N2n)

ear	[ɪəɹ]	dear	[dɪəɹ]
gear	[gɪəɹ]	hear	[hɪəɹ]
fear	[fɪəɹ]	near	[nɪəɹ]
rear	[rɪəɹ]	tear	[tɪəɹ]
sear	[sɪəɹ]	year	[jɪəɹ]
clear	[klɪəɹ]	appear	[əpɪəɹ]
deer	[dɪəɹ]	cheer	[tʃɪəɹ]
here	[hɪəɹ]	sheer	[ʃɪəɹ]
peer	[pɪəɹ]	we're	[wɪəɹ]

[ɛə] (N3n)

air	[ɛəɹ]	bear	[bɛəɹ]
care	[kɛəɹ]	dare	[dɛəɹ]
fair	[fɛəɹ]	hair	[hɛəɹ]
pear	[pɛəɹ]	rare	[rɛəɹ]
wear	[wɛəɹ]	where	[wɛəɹ]

---

[52] In IPA, the notation would be: [ʊɹ] [ɪɹ] [ɛɹ] but for our purposes, we are adding the schwa as a reminder of the diphthong.

Jonghee: So far, we have learned about the long and short vowels such as the Long [i] vs. Short [ɪ]; and the Long [u] vs. Short [ʊ].

Yun: The most important thing that I have learned, so far, is that the Short [I] is not just the shorter version of the Long [i] but rather a different sound. And the same is true for the Long [u] and Short [ʊ] comparison. Because the Short [ɪ] and Short [ʊ] do not exist in my language, I have been using the Long [i] and Long [u] in place of the Short [ɪ] and Short [ʊ].

Jonghee: Which is natural and understandable. So now you are getting used to the idea that for the Long [i], your tongue rises in the center, while the tip remains at the anchor point of the inside lower front teeth; and for the Short [I], the tongue relaxes down while the tip remains at that same anchor point resting inside the lower front teeth.

Yun: Yes! I am beginning to understand that some vowels are supposed to be short, and others are intended to be long.

Jonghee: Right. However, in addition to the fact that the Long [i] is sustained longer than the Short [ɪ] by nature, GA English vowels can become longer or shorter according to their 'environment', meaning what other sounds are around them. For example, when a vowel occurs before a voiced consonant such as g, b, d, v, z, r, l, n, m, ng, zh, it is usually sustained longer. But when the same vowel is positioned before a voiceless consonant, such as k, p, t, sh, ch, or f, the vowel is shorter in length.

Look at the examples in the following words.

Longer	Shorter	Longer	Shorter
bag	back	pig	pick
seed	seat	nod	not
bead	beat	cud	cut
chug	chuck	live	lift
laid	late	squeeze	squeak
node	note	code	coat
eyes	ice	peas	peace
prize	price	cage	case
side	sight	hum	hut

Jonghee: Now let's try the same concept in the following sentences. When the vowel or diphthong is followed by a voiced consonant, it will feel longer in duration than when it is followed by an unvoiced consonant. Feel the longer vowel/diphthong when it is italicized and feel the shorter length when it is underlined.

- The h*u*ngry ch*i*ld _o_pened h*is* *ey*es w*i*d*e*ly wh*e*n he saw the _i_ce cr*ea*m.

- He d*oe*s n_ot_ n*o*d h*i*s h*ea*d.

- The c*o*de *is* *i*n the c_oat_ p_o_cket.

- P_e_te is _at_ p_ea_ce wh*e*n he *ea*ts p*ea*s.

- The d_o_ctor n_o_ted a n*o*de *i*n h*i*s p*a*tient's thr_oat_.

- The p*ig* d*i*d n_ot_ p_i_ck _up_ the p*ea*rl th_at_ w*a*s thr*ow*n to h*i*m.

- The *i*ns*i*de *o*f the c*a*rd r*ea*ds, '_I_t w*a*s love _at_ f*i*rst s*igh*t.'

Yun: I see what you mean about the "environment" of the GA English vowels. The vowel length is significantly different before voiced sounds or voiceless sounds. I've learned a lot from this lesson and am looking forward to more. Thank you very much.

Notes:..
....
....
....
....
....
....
....
....
....
....

222

| Ex. 11 | Explore the Short and Long vowels in the following *dialogue* |

| Dialogue | *Peripheral Vision as a strategy for fluency* |

Jonghee: To help with fluency issues, I would like to share another tool with you--*peripheral vision*.

Naser: Peripheral vision? What is that, and how does that work to improve English fluency?

Jonghee: Peripheral vision is our ability to see objects and movement outside of the direct line of vision. This means, we can see what is on our left, right, above, and below our direct line of vision to some extent without moving our head. One example I can give you is that through peripheral vision, even though I am looking at the computer screen, I can also see my keyboard, telephone, walls, and the door of my office.

Naser: Ah, so you want me to use my peripheral vision to read several words ahead of the word that I am focusing on in the book.

Jonghee: Right. This way, we can prepare for the next several words—the meaning of the words, stresses, and sentence structure. This strategy can help to eliminate unnecessary stops and hesitations in our speech. We are looking ahead.

Naser: So, do you think we can use our peripheral vision to get ready for the next thought or words in our brain in order to make our speech flow more smoothly?

Jonghee: You've got the point. The human brain is fascinating, and it can be developed infinitely, if we open ourselves to possibilities.

Naser: This class is nothing like those in which we echo or mimic the teacher or practice by listening to CDs. I'm connecting to how sounds are felt on my lips, teeth, hard and soft palates, and my throat, and in the bones and muscles around my mouth, head, neck; in fact, practically my whole body! The feeling of the movement of these areas becomes my 'guide,' not how I thought I heard you say it. This is a science.

Jonghee: Yes, it is called English phonology, and as you said, it is a lot more than a 'follow-your-teacher' sort of class. You are learning to express your spoken English with universal intelligibility. The Lessac work does not rely on imitating someone else to change and improve the speech of any particular region, class, or race.

Naser: I am excited about this class and am looking forward to learning more about how to improve not only my pronunciation, but also my communication skills.

Carryover into everyday life: Now we have been introduced to all the GA English vowels and diphthongs. Take time throughout the day to focus on feeling and including these new skills in your conversations. Another strategy is to read aloud to small children from their favorite bedtime story (and focus on the vowels and diphthongs) or have a conversation with a friend or colleague during the day, again focusing your attention on these elements of GA English speaking.

Notes: ....

....

....

....

....

....

....

....

....

....

....

....

....

....

....

....

Section B:

American English Prosody

Chapter 3

The Music of Expressive Speaking

Dialogue: *Discovering Expressive Speech through Linking Syllables and Words, Vowel Length and Pitch Variety*

Kai: I have been learning or speaking GA for nearly a couple of decades since middle school, but my speech sounds choppy, disconnected, and staccato (as in music). My colleagues tell me that they can understand me, but I am not satisfied with my English.

Jonghee: I desire my students to speak English with the same or similar fluency, clarity, ease, and comfort as they do in their First Language.

Kai: I would like to do that, too. For me, clear and expressive communication is a must, and to have a generally good GA accent is a bonus.

Jonghee: We seem to have a common goal here. One of the reasons for choppiness is that when students of English are in the beginning or intermediate level of learning and speak with limited vocabulary, understanding of grammar, and sentence structure, and with limited speaking opportunities, they often translate their thoughts into English as they speak. This slows them down and causes unnecessary and frequent hesitations. So, improving your vocabulary, grammar, and the frequency of exposure to language usage are ways to improve the flow of your speech.

Kai: I've been working on this, but I know I need some more help in this area.

Jonghee: I know you have. A way of creating that flow is through a process called 'linking'. The English language uses many linking devices, which help speakers move smoothly from syllable to syllable and word to word.

        Also, many students learned English by reading and translating sentences from English into their First Languages. From this, they progressed to speaking the written forms of English, which do not deal with stress, intonation, or linking. So when you learn the linking strategies of General American English, your speech will be more smoothly connected, expressive and better understood by others.

Kai: I remember when I first arrived here, I was shocked because I could not understand Americans although I was a good student of English in my home country. To my ear, they did not speak word by word, and when they spoke, I could not understand them clearly most of the time.

Jonghee: That's the difference between the written language and the spoken one! Another contributor to choppiness is making all the vowel lengths the same and having no variation of pitch on words. As we have learned through the Structural Energy Vowels and Neutral Vowels, English contains long

226

and short vowels. For this reason, First Language GA speakers tend to communicate with generally wider ranges of vowel lengths and more pitch variation compared to someone learning GA English.

Kai: As a language learner, I also have noticed those differences.

Jonghee: But many GA English-learners speak with shorter vowel lengths and use the intonation patterns of their First Languages. When these speech patterns are repeated over and over again, the learner sounds disconnected even though he or she speaks fairly fast.

Kai: So, speaking quickly does not necessarily take care of everything, does it?

Jonghee: No, it doesn't. We need to learn to vary our vowel lengths and add pitch levels to create smooth and connected speech to express our thoughts effectively.

Kai: So, now I know why my speech has been choppy, but it's comforting to know there are remedies--I can improve the flow of my speech with connectedness and variations in vowel length and pitch levels.

Jonghee: I am glad you found new hope through this class and through what Lessac Kinesensic Training can contribute to your language learning and being able to express yourself more effectively. Variations in speed, pitch, length of vowels, linking between words and sounds, and emphasizing the words that carry meaning can help us communicate with clarity, fluidity, and confidence. And guess what? First language English speakers benefit from this sort of training as well.

Kai: I imagine that they can. I am ready for more! What is this linking you talk about?

Notes: ....

....

....

....

....

....

....

Strategies for Creating Connection Within and Between Words

1. Consonant-to-Vowel Linking

When a word ends with a consonant sound and the next word begins with a vowel sound, link (connect) the final consonant of the first word directly to the vowel of the next word without any pause or interruption, however small, between the two words. This way, that final consonant is pronounced very shortly and lightly as you connect it to the vowel beginning the next word. This is called a 'direct link'[53]. In **consonant to vowel linking**, the symbol for the direct link will be a little link or liaison (‿).

Reminder: Remember that some /e/ spellings are not pronounced or said aloud in English. In linking, we are connecting the *sounds* not the *spellings* together.

Notes: ....

....

....

....

....

....

....

....

....

....

....

....

....

....

....

....

---

[53] Direct Link: *The Use and Training of the Human Voice: A Bio-Dynamic Approach to Vocal Life, 3rd Edition* by Arthur Lessac ©1997 McGraw-Hill Higher Education Publishing, pp 114-115.

Ex. 1   Explore consonant-to-vowel linking in the following expressions.

For your information:
The *italicized 'd'* marked by an asterisk (*) in the following exploration represents a T sound which sounds more like a soft and light /d / or, in some languages, equivalent to the / r / with tongue tip touching very **lightly to** the gum ridge without lip-pursing like the Korean 리을 / ㄹ / [r], or the consonant portion of the Japanese ら[ra]、り[ri]、る[ru]、れ[re]、ろ[ro].

Written form	Linked Form
yes, it is	[jɛ.sɪ.*dɪz]
if it isn't	[ɪ.fɪ.*dɪzn.t]
men or women	[mɛ.nɚ.wɪmɪn]
boys and girls	[bɔɪ.zn.gɚlz]
bread and butter	[bɹɛ.dn.bʌ*dɚ]
ham and cheese	[hæ.mən.tʃi:z]
amount of	[əmaʊn.təv]
of another	[ʌv.ə.nʌthɚ]
get it over	[gɛ.*dɪ.*doʊ.vɚ]
with advertising	[wɪ.ðæd.vɚ.tai.zɪŋ]
and as	[æn.dæz]
this is	[ðɪ.sɪz]
for ever	[fə.ɹɛ.vɚ]
is unusual	[ɪ.zə.nju:ʒu.wəl]
guideline is	[gaɪd.laɪ.niz]
kind of	[kaɪn.dəv]
take it or leave it	[teɪ.kɪ.*dɚ.li:vɪt]
on our	[ɒ. naʊɚ]
car expenses are	[ka.ɹɛk.spɛnsɪ.zaɹ]
school of	[sku.ləv]
that's a	[ðæ.tsə]
savings and	[seɪ.ving.zænd]
come out of	[kə.maʊ.*dəv]
that's only	[ðæts.oʊn.li]
twice as	[twai.sæz]
price of	[pɹaɪ.səv]
other apples	[ʌðɚ.ɹæplz]
teachers or students	[ti.tʃɚ.zɔɚ.stu.dn̩ts]
English and Chinese	[ɪŋ.glɪ.ʃænd.tʃai.níz]
consonant or vowel	[kan.sə.nən.tɔɹ.vaʊl]

229

Ex. 2.1   Explore the following short phrases for the consonant-vowel linking practice. The little link (‿) is given to you as a visual cue to continue moving smoothly from the final consonant of the first word to the beginning vowel in the next word. These words are taken from *The Gettysburg Address* by Abraham Lincoln[54].

Written Phrase	How the link feels as you speak
fourscore‿and	[fɔɹ.skɔ.ɹænd]
years‿ago	[jɪəɹ.za.goʊ]
conceived‿in	[kʌn.siv.dɪn]
that‿all	[ðæ.dɔll]
men‿are	[mɛ.naɹ]
created‿equal	[kɹi.jeɪ.tə.di.kwəl]
consecrated‿it	[kɒn.sə.kɹeɪ.tɪ.dɪt]
far‿above‿our	[fa.ɹə.bʌ.vaʊɹ]
take‿increased	[teɪ.kɪn.kɹist]
add‿or	[æ.dɔɹ]
but‿it	[bʌ.dɪt]
it‿is	[ɪ.dɪz]
for‿us	[fɔ.ɹʌs]
died‿in	[dai.dɪn]

Ex. 2.2   Now explore the Consonant-to-Vowel linking opportunities in the following sentences by adding the linking signs (‿) and slash marks (/). The slash marks (/) indicate where you can take a breath or a pause. The first two sentences are marked for you.

Why‿and how‿is Lessac Kinesensic training for stage‿actors‿important for learning pronunciation / by people who aren't‿actors?

John was‿able to find‿out why his‿ideas weren't‿acceptable to his‿office partners, / but he didn't like‿it.

If‿I were to chase the ball‿into her garden, the home‿owner would tell me to get‿out.

Please wash‿up the dishes before you run‿off to watch‿a movie.

[54] https://www.nationalgeographic.org/encyclopedia/gettysburg-address/ August 17, 2021

2. Consonant to Consonant Linking

A. Linking Two Consonants Made at Different Contact Points: Play and Link

When linking two consonants that are made at different contact points in the mouth, either between syllables or between two words, the first consonant is completed and the transition to the next consonant is made as quickly as possible to avoid unnecessary pausing or interruption (ex. find Mary, stockpile). In the Lessac training, this is known as 'Play and Link'.[55]

- Keep in mind that the purpose of language is to move forward: Communication moves dialogue forward, ideas forward, and your goals in speech forward. If we move quickly from one consonant to the next, yet each receiving its full expression, we will naturally minimize any unnecessary vowel such as a schwa [ə] between words.

- Remember, if a vowel spelling is not written, do not add a vowel sound such as schwa [ə], as in "but-ə-the" for "but the", or "and-ə-Bob" for "and Bob".

- When the ending consonant of the first word is a sustainable sound, sustain that sound fully before proceeding to the first consonant of the second word.

- If the ending consonant of the first word is an *un*sustainable sound, briskly tap the first sound and then proceed to the second consonant.

Notes:..
....
....
....
....
....
....
....
....
....

[55] Play and Link, *The Use and Training of the Human Voice: A Bio-Dynamic Approach to Vocal Life, 3rd Edition* by Arthur Lessac ©1997 McGraw-Hill Higher Education Publishing, pp. 115-116.

Ex. 1   In the following expressions, explore the linking of *two consonants made with different contact points within each word and between words.* The first two lines are marked for you. Take your time, as many of these terms are challenging.

Remember:

1. *Double underline* the final consonant of the first word if it is sustainable. Example: *Sun ray*

2. *Single underline* the final consonant of the first word if it is unsustainable. Example: *Take tea*

3. The final /e/ is not pronounced in many English words. Because we are connecting the sounds of the words together, not the spellings, watch for the *silent /e/*. Example: give me

4. Speak each phrase fluidly, connecting the words according to your marking.

Biomedical Department	business concept
communication studies	criminal justice
departmental policy	English department
exchange program	financial management
foreign languages	Governmental Studies
middle school	human studies
industrial sociology	international studies
international study	math department
mechanical drawing	medical sociology
music department	nutrition sciences
political science	restorative sciences
social studies	hard work

Notes:..

....

....

....

....

Ex. 2   In the following list, explore more linking opportunities of the *two adjoining consonants made with different contact points*. These are medical terms and are quite challenging for most people not in the medical field!

cardiac resuscitation

correctional dentistry

dental health

naturopathic medicine

medical care

general surgery

health behavior

infusion therapy

musculoskeletal surgery

neurosurgical discovery

palliative care

Orthopedic surgery

Psychiatric study

surgical department

clinical diagnosis

critical care

dermatological conditions

health care

gastrointestinal medicine

psychiatric department

hematological survey

internal medicine

neurobiological findings

obstetrics department

pathological study

physical therapy

Radiation Therapy

Notes: ....

....

....

....

....

....

....

....

....

....

....

....

B. Linking Two Consonants made at the same or similar contact points: Prepare and Link

The consonants in these categories all share the same or closely adjacent contact points. When they are placed back-to-back, the first consonant is *prepared* meaning that there is no release of the tongue or lips, and one moves quickly to the second consonant, which will be fully completed or executed. Lessac calls this linking strategy 'Prepare and Link'[56] because the first consonant sound is considered as a preparation for the next sound. Examples will be indicated by the first of the two adjacent consonants being *italicized.*

There are three categories of Prepare and Link. They are:

1. *Identical:* The same consonant.
    Examples: D-D, N-N: Di*d* Da*n* know; M-M the sa*m*e men

2. *Cognates:* Two consonants made in the same place, one with 'voice', one without.
    Examples: D-T, V-F, Z-S, B-P   di*d* Tom, lo*v*e friends, bu*zz* saw, ca*b* pass

3. *Semi-related:* Two consonants made at *nearly* the same contact point in the mouth.
    Specifically:

    -   D or T followed by SH, TH, S, Z, N
        Examples: tha*t* these, bu*t* none

    -   B or P followed by M
        Examples: gra*b* me, sto*p* me

Exploring Prepare and Links

Reminder: When performing *any* prepare and link, do not release your tongue or lips from the point of contact of the first consonant until you have moved to the second consonant. In the following examples, the prepared consonant is *italicized.* Other consonants in 'playable' positions are marked for you.

Explore these *identical links.*

di*d* Don	no*t* Tom	since some
ha*t* trick	li*fe* force	clo*th* thrown
me*n* know	eve*n* now	no*t* Charles
fee*l* like	hel*p* pack	stick close

---

[56] Prepare and Link: *The Use and Training of the Human Voice: A Bio-Dynamic Approach to Vocal Life, 3rd Edition* by Arthur Lessac ©1997 McGraw-Hill Higher Education Publishing, p. 116.

Explore these *cognate links*. Remember: *Two consonants made in the same place, one with voice and one without voice.*

dedicate*d* to

shor*t* day

bu*zz* sy*stem*

bu*s* zo*ne*

han*d*-trade*d*

acu*te* de*nt*al issue

qui*ck* ga*me*

big ca*ke*

tou*gh* va*se*

sa*fe* venue

grea*t* day

di*d* cha*nge*

Explore these *Semi-Related links*. Remember: *Semi-related consonants are those made at nearly the same contact point in the mouth. They are:*

- D or T when followed by SH, TH, S, Z, N Examples: hi*d* those, bu*t* none

- B or P when followed by M Examples: gra*b* me, sto*p* me

an*d* so

migh*t* li*ve*

thousa*nd* thermometer*s*

bu*t* the

an*d* thi*s*

goo*d* smi*le*

re*d* zipper

tha*t* natio*n*

wha*t* they

tha*t* chur*ch*

tha*t* nu*mb*er

an*d* seve*n*

hel*p* Mi*ke*

ba*d* ju*dg*e

Notes: ....

....

....

....

....

....

....

....

Ex. 1   Explore all the consonant linking opportunities we have covered so far in the following narrative.

For your information: In this exploration of our now familiar story, all sustainable consonants are *double underlined* throughout, and 'tappable' consonants *single underlined*. Direct links are marked with a small hoop (˅) and prepare and links are marked by *italicizing* the consonant to be prepared. Watch for the *Silent L* in some words, also *italicized*. The slash / between words indicates a place for you to take a breath or pause. [ŋ] is the symbol for the NG when spelled with the N alone.

I met confidence on a Golf Course

For golfers, /a 'good' weather' means good weather to play golf./ This winter, the New Year's holidays were as warm as April in Birmingham, Alabama. / Of course, I was not about to miss these golden opportunities. / So, one day, my husband and I drove to the Oak Mountain golf course. / Here, we can play a nine-hole course for ten dollars during the week, / which is not bad at all for occasional *exercise. *ks

By the time we arrived at the pro-shop, / the parking lot was crowded with the patrons' cars,/ and the starting point was also crowded with golfers waiting for their turns. / Four teams were in front of us. / My husband and I were teamed up with a father and his teenage son/ who were waiting for their turn in their golf cart. / But I usually walk with my golf bag on my shoulders so I can pinch my pennies as well as increase the amount of *exercise. *ks

The marshal advised the golfers not to go onto the driving range/ because there was no way he could estimate how the games before us would proceed. / He said we might have to wait for about 45 minutes to an hour before we could hit our first balls. So, I started to warm up with one of the longest clubs/ for about ten minutes, / but still many people were waiting before us.

So, I started to look around and paid attention to people around me because watching people is fun to me. Compared to other days, there were more female golfers today. One of the teams before us was made up of four middle-aged ladies, and one of them caught my eye. As if

236

accommodating the unusually warm weather, she was wearing a short sleeve T-shirt and shorts. However, the one thing that caught my eye was that one of her legs was made of a shiny metal bar. She was wearing socks and golf shoes on both of her feet.

Her team members chose to walk! But none of them had any pull-carts either. This means that they were going to carry their own golf bags on their shoulders. Watching these ladies talking to each other, waiting for their turn, I applauded this special lady with her special leg.

Because of the large size of the golf course, I could not continue keeping my eyes on her, but during the entire course, I kept on thinking of her courage, confidence, and freedom.

Notes: ....

....

....

....

....

....

....

....

....

....

....

....

....

....

....

Vowel-to-Vowel linking

A. Y-insertion between two vowels

When a word ends with an /ee/[i], /ay/[eɪ], /oy/[ɔɪ], or /I/[ai], and the next word begins with a vowel, insert a [y] sound between the two connecting vowels.[57] This also takes place between two syllables within a word. Let the 'y' link you to the next syllable or word.

Ex. 1   Explore the Y-link in the following expressions.

the answer ----- the-y-answer   associate --------- associ-y-ate

association----- associ-y-ation   studying --------- study-y-ing

seeing ---------- see-y-ing   realize----------- re-y-alize

reaction -------- re-y-action   pronunciation --- pronunci-y-ation

scientist -------- sci-y-əntist   my only---------- my-y-only

sociology ------ soci-y-ology   the issue -------- the-y-issue

they exist ------ they-y-exist   we are------------ we-y-are

immediately --- immedi-y-ately   comedian -------- comedi-y-an

the easiest ----- the-y-easy-y-est   the eye is ------- the-y-eye-y-is

the boy is ------ the boy-y-is   the joy of ------- the joy-y-of

Ex. 2   Explore the Y-link in the following sentences

- The associ-y-ation said that the-y-answer was "MB-y-A."

- For sci-y-entists, any-y-odd re-y-action is worth noticing.

- Sy does not show any signs of being a sci-y-entist, but sure is the crazi-y-est artist with the high-y-est cre-y-ativity.

- We-y-offer bi-y-ology and soci-y-ology courses all year long.

- The-y-easi-y-est way to correct the problem is to tackle it immedi-y-ately.

- They-y-are immedi-y-ately at odds with the-y-issue at hand.

---

[57] Prepare and Link: *The Use and Training of the Human Voice: A Bio-Dynamic Approach to Vocal Life, 3rd Edition* by Arthur Lessac ©1997 McGraw-Hill Higher Education Publishing, pp. 111-112.

B. W-insertion between two vowels

When a word ends with an /oo/[u], /oe/[oʊ], /ow/[oʊ], and the next word begins with a vowel, insert a [w] sound between the two connecting vowels. This also takes place between two syllables within a word. Let the 'w' link you to the next syllable or word.

Ex. 3   Explore the W-linking in the following examples.

go out ------------go-w-out   going ----------- go-w-ing

go ahead ---------go-w-ahead   so easy --------- so-w-easy

borrow again ----borrow-w-again   know it--------- know-w-it

you are -----------you-w-are   do it------------ do-w-it

so old------------so-w-old   too easy -------- too-w-easy

to identify -------to-w-identify   coordinate ----- co-w-ordinate

show it -----------show-w-it   how is it-------- how-w-is it

you examine ----you-w-examine   blue is ---------- blue-w-is

cooperate- -------co-w-operate   graduate-------- gradu-w-ate

Ex. 4   Explore the W-linking in the following sentences.

- You may go-w-ahead and go-w-out of the building.

- Can you show-w-it to me first?

- This is the blu-w-est color you can get this time.

- I am a gradu-w-ate of this school: I gradu-w-ated in May.

- How-w-is it go-w-ing?

- How-w-ever, it was too-w-easy.

- What would you do when the go-w-ing gets tough?

- I don't want to borrow-w-again.

Notes:..

....

....

Ex. 5   In the following narrative, explore all types of linking strategies we have learned so far. *The first two paragraphs are marked for you.*

Marking Guide if you would like to use it:

˅ = direct link—consonant to vowel

<u>d</u> = play and link—consonant to different consonant

d = prepare and link—consonant to similar or identical/cognate consonant

-w- = 'w' connective between vowels

-y- = 'y' connective between vowels

ŋ = NG when spelled with the N alone

/ = place to take a breath or pause

The Scariest Ordeal—A Retrospective

In the summer of 2008, / I was a new gradu-w-ate student at SUNY-Buffalo./ It started as a great summer for me / because I-y-only had the course work and no research assignments in the first year of gradu-w-ate study./ I went back to China for a one-month vacation. / When I came back to New York from China, / I received an offer letter from Hamburg University-y-in Germany for an international summer school, /which would be held in September. / I was so-w-excited and planned to-w-apply for a visa to Germany. /

However, I discovered that my visa to the U.S. had *expired, /and I had to renew-w-it before applying for a visa to Germany. / There were two-w-options for me/, one was to go back to China for the visa renewal, /and the -y-other was to go to the nearest third country. / Since I had just come back from China, I didn't consider that to be my first option, and so decided to go to Canada, which was just a few-w-hours away from Buffalo.   *ks

I took the Greyhound bus to Ottawa and found a family hotel. I was nervous about the visa interview because my major, physics, could be considered a danger to the United States, according to the national security point of view. Even though I was used to this, the background-checking interview made me nervous. In the worst-case scenario, I might have had to stay a long time in Canada and not be able to go back to the U.S. immediately, which meant that I would not be able to start the fall semester on time. In Ottawa, the Visa Officer told me it could take up to 5 or 6 weeks before I could get a visa stamped on my passport.

I was so disappointed and depressed at this news. I did not know what to do. Some Chinese students advised me to go back to the U.S. if I had my passport and valid I-20 forms. I decided to follow that advice. My two new Chinese friends who stayed in the same family hotel were willing to give me a ride to Buffalo, N.Y. But, at the U.S. Customs checkpoint, I was denied entrance to the United States since my visa to the U.S. had already expired. The officer told me that if he granted a visa to me, he could lose his job. I was devastated. Buffalo lay just a few meters in front of my very eyes. I could see the highway sign to Buffalo, but I was not able to touch it, and I could not go back there. As a result, I was sent back to the Canadian Customs from the U.S. Customs. The Canadian Customs Officer called a taxi to send me back to Canada.

Trying to figure out what to do while in the taxi, I found the telephone number of one of the home-stay facilities in Toronto and called there. I took the Greyhound again to Toronto and arrived at 10 pm. I then took the subway and the transit bus to get to the home-stay place at around 11:30 pm. To my utter disappointment, I found out that the house was still under construction without any furniture—no bed either. So, with the land-lord's help, I stayed my first night in Canada at a family hotel.

During the night, I looked through the information for a 'Room for Rent' on the web and found one in Ottawa. The next morning, I carpooled to Ottawa and arrived at the place at 11 pm.

I was nervous because I had never met the landlord before traveling to this place, and I was afraid that I might face the same situation as I did the night before in Toronto. But I was very lucky this time. The landlords were very nice people with a great family. They treated me as their family member and took me everywhere during my five-week stay there while waiting for my visa.

By the time I came back to Buffalo, New York with my renewed visa to the United States, the Fall Semester at SUNY Buffalo had already begun, and my Teaching Assistant position had been awarded to another student. The director of my department informed me that I did not need to rush to the university because it was too late for me to enroll in the school. He advised me to consider applying for the Spring Semester, since I had missed too many of the classes already; and it might be too difficult to catch up. If I took that option, I might not be able to stay in the U.S. legally before the spring semester began. I insisted that I had to enroll in the university in September and persuaded the director that my academic background was strong enough to be able to catch up with the classes. Finally, I got his permission to enroll in September and received all A's in my classes. But unfortunately, catching up with all the course work prevented me from attending the summer school in Germany.

Even though I had no time to feel, cry, or even realize how dangerous it was at the time, this ordeal was one of the most exciting and scariest adventures I ever experienced in my life--a young Chinese girl in a strange foreign place where I knew not one soul—just to be able to continue my studies in the United States. When I think about it again, it still gives me goosebumps.

(Adapted from an essay by Yujiao Zou, PhD Candidate, Department of Physics, University of Alabama at Birmingham)

A dialogue: *Continuing our journey*

Jonghee: We have now covered all the Consonants AND vowels found in GA English. Now, how do you feel about your communication, Sunny?

Sunny: Linking everything together is making a huge difference. I am feeling more skilled all the time.

Jonghee: Vowels and consonants are the skeleton of the words, and now you're ready to move into how we use them, how we express ourselves while speaking by adding inflection and intonation.

Sunny: This is going to be fun!

Notes: ....

....

....

....

....

....

....

....

....

Chapter 4

Intonation
(The Music of the Language)

Dialogue:	*What is Intonation?*

Jonghee: Your understanding of English is quite advanced. Why do you think you need to take this class?

Eric: I am not at all confident about my GA English when I speak, because it seems that other people don't understand me very well.

Jonghee: What gives you that impression?

Eric: I am not sure exactly, but I can just tell that other people don't understand me at times, especially my professors when I present my papers in classes or lab meetings. In addition to that, soon I will be graduating and going to job interviews. So, I want to make sure my speech is clear enough to be understood by possible employers.

Jonghee: I see. So, what seems to be the problem with the way you speak?

Eric: I cannot pinpoint it, but maybe it is just because I come from another language background.

Jonghee: You are right that your GA speech sounds different from your American colleagues and friends because you speak a different 'first language'. Your first language can influence your GA pronunciation in so many ways, such as the individual sounds, and in the intonation patterns, which contains the music of the language.

Eric: What does "intonation pattern" or "the music of the language" mean?

Jonghee: Well, when we sing, our voice creates variations in sound waves by going up and down in pitch and being stronger or softer. These sound waves also occur when we speak, but the variations are usually not so dramatic. When we speak, we don't usually raise our pitch so high or emphasize strongly unless we are very happy or angry. We call these sound waves in speech "intonation patterns[58]."

Eric: I see. So, because each language has unique vowels and consonants, its own resonance, and its own music, we speak our version of English influenced by our own First language patterns?

Jonghee: You are correct! Sometimes, we are *aware* that we sound different from others around us. But often, we think we are speaking the same way as others do, until we compare our voices on a recording device.

---

[58] https://www.merriam-webster.com/dictionary/intonation definition of Intonation, August 10, 2021

Eric:	So, can you tell me what my differences are, and how I can work on them?
Jonghee:	As you just said, each human language has its own unique sounds and intonation patterns. So, when we learn to speak English, the influence of our first language carries over into the way we speak any form of English. This creates a unique accent or intonation pattern that shows up in our English speaking. This is often called a 'foreign' accent by Americans.
Eric:	Is there something wrong with having an accent? I know what each word I am speaking means, and I know how to say each one of them. Or at least I think so. But sometimes people don't know if I am asking a question or making a statement!
Jonghee:	Well, let's talk about accents. There is nothing wrong with having an accent, but the degree to which your accent impedes communication between you and another English speaker might cause misunderstanding and miscommunication. To some people, a foreign accent can be attractive. However, to others, it can be challenging to understand. But this class isn't about eliminating your background, or who you are. We want to give you a choice of options you can use to become clearer in your speech and feel more comfortable communicating—because this is something you *want* to achieve. Isn't that true?
Eric:	Yes, that's why I am here. So, I would like to know what kind of music people hear when I speak my GA English, compared to what they are used to.
Jonghee:	All right, let's explore some patterns of English intonation.

Notes: ....

....

....

....

....

....

....

....

....

Patterns of English Intonation

1. *Falling intonation for Statement Sentences*

Our dialogue continues…

Jonghee: As you may already know, G.A. speakers use falling intonation at the end of a statement or confirmation sentences, meaning that the pitch goes down. However, at times, we observe speakers of certain languages speak with a rising tone (pitch goes up) as shown in the following:

    Classmate A: How much did you pay for your textbook?

    Classmate B (U.S.):   **Fif**ty **do**llars [**da.**lə-rz]

    Classmate C (International):   Fi**fty** dol**lar** [dol.**lar**]

Eric: Hmmm! Student C sounds like me.

Jonghee: Or here is another example. Let's say a clerk at a Social Security Administration office asks an international student a question, and the response from this student might be as follows with a different intonation pattern as well as a different written language.

    Clerk: Can you tell me your age?

    Client A (U.S.):   I am **thir**.*dy* and my **wi**fe is thir.*dy*, **to**o.

    Client B (International):   I **am** thir**ty**, and my wi**fe is** thir**ty, too**.

Eric: Client B sounds like me. I can see right away that Client A uses a falling intonation at the end of the speech, but Client B uses the rising tone at the same place. Now it's clearer to me that there is a difference in the music of the language or intonation patterns between mine and GA speakers.

Jonghee: Or, when a native of the United States might say,

    • "the **rea**son is …"

    • "the **on**ly way we can…"

246

we might hear certain GA English learners saying,

- "the rea**son is**
- "the on**ly** way we can...."

Eric: Again, I see the different music picture of the intonation patterns in this case. Can you give me some more samples?

Jonghee: I am glad that you are beginning to recognize the differences in the patterns. So, here is another example.

When a native GA English speaker might say,

- "I'm **ha**ppy, and **you** are happy, **to**o."

a certain English learner might raise the end of the phrase as follows:

- "I **am** ha**ppy** and you **are** ha**ppy**, **too.**"

Eric: I think I might raise my pitch at the end of a phrase like this person does. I bet I've been singing unfamiliar melodies and expecting others to understand me perfectly. Now I see why they might not!

Jonghee: Let's review. When we apply the musical elements found in the English language by pronouncing the long sounds long, short sounds short; strong sounds strongly, soft sounds softly, high sounds high and low sounds low like the native or GA English speakers, people will understand us better, since everything will seem more familiar. This is important because our communication skills will impact our performance evaluations on so many levels—social and work related. So, let's continue....

Eric: I am ready. By the way, I came up with *a math formula* for the *music of the language:*

- The English language + the influence of a learner's mother tongue = Accented speech = Reduced intelligibility when speaking with my American colleagues and friends

- The English Language + Native-like Intonation = Less Accented speech = Increased Intelligibility when speaking with my American colleagues and friends

Jonghee: I like it! Now, let's explore more patterns of intonation-- the music of GA English.

2. *Falling intonation for Reference or Appositives*

Jonghee: Here is another occasion in which to use the falling intonation—for reference words, or appositives. An appositive is a noun or pronoun — often with modifiers — set beside another noun or pronoun to explain or identify it. When we have these reference words side by side, we lower the ends of both words. In this case, we refer to the relationship of these words as "appositives." We will use **arrows** to indicate up or down pitch changes. Here are some examples:

- Abraham Lincoln, ↘ the 16th president of the United States. ↘[59]

- Alice, ↘ the girl who sat next to you in English Class. ↘

- Dr. Austin, ↘ the director of the Professional Development Program. ↘

- The Chairman of the Board, ↘ Mr. Edward Hudgins! ↘

Eric: It feels good to know ↘ that I am supposed to lower the pitch at the ends of ↘ appositives or reference words. ↘

3. *Intonation for Sentences that ask questions*

A. *Rising* intonation or inflection for *Yes/No Questions*

Jonghee: You know what it means to ask a Yes or No Question. ↘ Right? ↗

Eric: I do. ↘ This is the kind of question where the responding speaker is expected to answer with a "yes" or "no" at the beginning of the response. Right? ↗

Jonghee: Right! ↘ Here, we both asked a question that required either a yes or a no. So, what happened to the tone or pitch of our voices at the end of each question? ↘

Eric: The intonation at the end of our question was raised. ↘

Jonghee: Right! ↘

---

[59] The arrow pointing up or down indicates a rising or descending pitch or note in the voice.

B. *Falling* intonation for *Who, What, Why, Where, When, How Questions*

Jonghee: However, we should use the falling intonation at the ends of questions other than those that require a yes or a no answer.... for example:

"Why do you feel like you need to take this class?"↘

"What is the music of the language– or intonation pattern?↘

"What are the elements of clear and intelligible speech?"↘

Eric: I can hear that the ends of the sentences are going down in pitch for these types of questions. Here are similar questions that I have been asking myself:

"How can I learn English pronunciation so others can understand me?"↘

"Where can I go to learn such speech?"↘

"How is it that no one ever showed me how to speak clearly before?"↘

"Why do some Americans have to take intelligibility training classes?"↘

"What's wrong with the way I speak?"↘

"Why don't they understand me when I speak English?"↘

"Which might be the right way to stress important words in sentences?"↘

Jonghee: However, sometimes these questions can use the RISING intonation when a speaker wants to confirm the statement of the previous speaker:

Mother: So, where is Egypt?↘

Allen: Europe.↘ In Europe!↘

Mother: Where?↗

Allen: In Europe.↘

Mother: (to her friend) I think my son wants to believe ↗ we live in Europe!↘

249

4. *Intonation Patterns when making a choice*

A. A choice from two items: A or B

When making a choice between two items, use a rising intonation at the end of the A, and then falling intonation at the end of the B:

Sunny:	Did you say A ↗ or B?↘
Minny:	I said B.↘
Flight attendant:	Tea ↗ or coffee?↘
Passenger:	Tea please!↘

B. A choice from 3 or more items: A, B, and C; A, B, C or D

When we choose an item from a list of three or more, we use a rising intonation at the end of each item in the list until the final item-- then use a falling intonation for that final item. This is not a hard and fast 'rule', but it is typical of speech in the United States.

Chuck:	The assignments are Explorations 1, ↗ 2, ↗ and 3.↘
June:	Explorations 1, ↗ 2, ↗ and 3.↘
Teacher:	A, ↗ B, ↗ C, ↗ D↘
Student:	A, ↗ B, ↗ C, ↗ D, ↗ E, ↗ F, ↗ G↘

Dialogue:	*At the restaurant*
Server:	What kind of dressing would you like to have on your salad?↘
Customer:	What do you have?↘
Server:	We have Vinaigrette, ↗ French, ↗ Italian, ↗ and Thousand Island. ↘
Customer:	I'll take vinegar. ↘
Server:	Sir, excuse me, ↘ what did you say you'd like to have?↗
Customer:	Vinegar. ↘
Server:	You mean Vinaigrette?↗
Customer:	Oh yes, vinaigrette!↘

Ex. 1	Explore the intonation pattern in the following *dialogue* by employing intonation patterns we have learned so far. You can draw your own arrows if that would help you.

Dialogue I1:	*At the Watch Shop*
Shopkeeper:	Good morning. May I help you?
Customer:	Well, something is wrong with my watch. It isn't working as it should. Maybe it's hungry and needs to be fed. So, maybe I should start with a new battery.
Shopkeeper:	OK, we'll start there.
	(Shopkeeper disappears for several minutes, and comes back to the counter again)
Shopkeeper:	Done!
Customer:	Wow, So quick! How much do I owe you?
Shopkeeper:	$7.99, Sir. (or Madam/Ma'am)
Customer:	That's all?
Shopkeeper:	That's all.
Customer:	Thank you!
Shopkeeper:	Thank you.

Carryover into everyday life: In this chapter we have added intonation and inflection (the music of GA English) to speech. See if you can find some time throughout your day to explore with awareness the intonation patterns and musicality of English as you converse with friends, family, and colleagues.

Notes: ....

....

....

....

Chapter 5

Word Stress
(Stressed Syllables in Words)

Dialogue:	*What we have learned so far...*

Malissa: So, let me see what I have learned so far. I have learned about the Lip-Rounding Vowels and Lip-Relaxing Vowels, which are also called the Structural Energy Vowels and Neutral Vowels. There, I have learned that the Lip-Rounding Vowels (The Structural Energy Vowels) are innately longer when stressed in words; and the Neutral Vowels (Lip-Relaxing) Vowels are shorter and often unstressed; and the appropriate lip-opening shapes and sizes are helpful for GA vowel sounds. And clear pronunciation is an important key for clear *communication*, and for being understood more easily.

Jonghee: You have learned a lot, and you should feel very proud of yourself.

Malissa: Thank you! And in the consonant chapter, I learned about voiced and voiceless consonants which can be either sustainable or unsustainable. And most importantly, I have learned about the point of contact and the manner of articulation for each consonant in English. I've also learned about intonation and linking words together.

Jonghee: What an excellent language student you are! Now, we are going to tackle Word Stress[60] in this chapter. You probably remember that you learned in your country that English words are made of syllables. Do you remember that syllables are made up of at least one vowel, or a combination of vowels and consonants?

Malissa: Yes, I do.

Jonghee: As you know, each word has a syllable that is given more stress or emphasis than others, and you have learned that this is called the 'primary stress.'

The Importance of Word Stress in English Intonation

Malissa: Yes, I am aware of **primary stress** in words. I do remember memorizing those in my English classes and I got good grades on it. But I am not sure why we had to learn about this. Why is it so important that we be reminded about Primary Stress in this class?

Jonghee: We can say that recognizing and using 'word stress' means knowing where the primary stress is in each word. That is because sentences are made of words, and words are made of syllables; and syllables are made of vowels

---

[60] https://www.englishclub.com/pronunciation/word-stress-what.htm Word Stress definition
August 10, 2021

and consonants. And the primary stressed syllable and the unstressed syllables form the small waves of speech lines called 'intonation' or 'the music of the language'. The stressed syllables are generally pronounced stronger in tone, longer in duration, and/or higher in pitch, while unstressed syllables are pronounced as weaker in tone, shorter, and lower in pitch.

Malissa: So, since sentences are made of words, 'word stress' creates small waves and those small waves become part of the big waves within phrases or sentences. And so, this is how English intonation patterns are created!

Jonghee: Correct! The GA English intonation is formed by the relationship of the vowel lengths and pitch variations through word stress and sentence stress.

Malissa: Since I learned English as an academic subject rather than to use in speaking in my everyday life, or for communicating, I didn't realize the importance of word stress which would have given me the expected intonation for speaking English. Even though I achieved high grades in my English classes, when it comes to speaking in English, I am not yet equipped to communicate as clearly as I'd like.

Jonghee: In all languages, people communicate through speech wave lines, or intonation patterns. And word stress is a part of those intonation patterns. So, it is important to learn the primary stress of each English word, because applying correct primary stress in each word is a step toward more applicable GA English intonation.

Malissa: Wow, now I understand why we learned the syllable stress when I was in Middle School in my country. Now, let me make sure that I understand: Primary Stress means that I locate the stressed syllable in each word; and all the words make small waves that become part of the big waves called sentences. If we find the primary stress in the important (= stressed) words, we can make small and big speech waves appropriately, and have more typical GA English intonation patterns.

Jonghee: You've got it.

Notes: ....

....

....

....

....

The Primary Stress in GA English Words

Jonghee: When a syllable in an English word is **stressed**, the stress always falls on a **vowel**. And the stressed vowels are pronounced **stronger in tone, longer in duration,** and **higher (sometimes lower) in pitch** than the unstressed syllables.

Malissa: So, this means, the innately long vowels such as the Lip-Rounding, or Structural Energy Vowels, are pronounced even longer when they are stressed?

Jonghee: Right. By the way, you might recall that the Lip-Rounding (Structural) Vowels are stressed in most words. And as we have learned, whatever surrounds the stressed vowel in a word, such as consonants or unstressed vowels, also affects the length of the primary stressed vowel.

Malissa: Yes, I remember, such as 'a vowel is pronounced longer when it comes before a voiced sound such as a vowel or a voiced consonant'.

Jonghee: You have a good memory!

Malissa: Do GA English speakers know all this?

Jonghee: When people speak in their First language, this phenomenon happens organically, without having to think or choose the vowel lengths or stress pattern consciously. They learned it from their parents and others with whom they grew up. When language students apply this information to their GA English speech, the spoken words become more understandable to other English speakers.

Malissa: I can't wait until that day! I am looking forward to learning more about Word Stress. But what happens if we do not pronounce the stressed vowels longer; short vowels shorter; high sounds higher; and low sounds lower, like native-born speakers do?

Jonghee: Well, people will just recognize that we are still learning English. For example, if you want to say "Pete" but make the vowel length short, your listeners might hear it as "pit," because hearers cannot see the spelling of spoken words in oral communication, Miscommunication can also happen when we do not use the appropriate stress patterns in words.

Malissa: So what you are saying is that, in addition to creating the appropriate individual sounds, knowing the location of primary stress, vowel lengths and pitch levels are also important for effective English oral communication.

Jonghee: You've got it down pat! Now let's have some hands-on practice of what we've been talking about.

Malissa: Great! I can't wait.

1. Primary Stress on Two-Syllable Words

When two-syllable words with the same meaning are spelled the same for nouns, adjectives or verbs, the following rules are observed for the **primary stress:**

a. For Nouns/Adjectives: The primary stress falls on the 1st syllable.

b. For Verbs: The primary stress falls on the 2nd syllable.

Ex. 1   In the following word list, the primary stress falls on the first syllable in nouns and adjectives, and in verbs, the primary stress falls on the second syllable.

Remember:

*   The **vowels in the stressed syllables** are pronounced **stronger, longer, and higher** in pitch.

*   You will feel the stress shift between syllables, and also feel how the shape and space of the vowels change, depending on the stress.

Nouns/Adjectives		Verbs	
checkout	[ʧɛkaʊt]	check **out**	[tʃɛkaʊt]
concert	[kɒnsəɹt]	con**cert**ed	[kənsɜɹtɪd]
conduct	[kɒndəkt]	con**duct**	[kəndʌkt]
conflict	[kɒnflɪkt]	con**flict**	[kənflɪkt]
content	[kɒntɛnt]	con**tent**	[kəntɛnt]
contest	[kɒntɛst]	con**test**	[kəntɛst]
contrast	[kɒntɹæst]	con**trast**	[kəntɹæst]
convert	[kɒnvɜt]	con**vert**	[kənvɜt]
convict	[kɒnvɪkt]	con**vict**	[kənvɪkt]
desert	[dɛzəɹt]	de**sert**	[dɪzɜt]
discharge	[dɪsʧɑɹdʒ]	dis**charge**	[dɪsʧɑɹdʒ]
envelope	[ɛnvəloʊp]	en**vel**op	[ɛnvɛləp]
export	[ɛkspɔɹt]	ex**port**	[ɪkspɔɹt]
import	[ɪmpɔɹt]	im**port**	[ɪmpɔɹt]
insult	[ɪnsəlt]	in**sult**	[ɪnsʌlt]
increase	[ɪnkɹis]	in**crease**	[ɪnkɹis]

decrease	[dikɹis]	decrease	[dɪkɹis]
interchange	[ɪntɚtʃeɪndʒ]	interchange	[ɪntɚɪtʃeɪndʒ]
makeup	[meɪkʌp]	make up	[meɪkʌp]
object	[ɒbdʒɛkt]	object	[əbdʒɛkt]
perfect	[pɝfɪkt]	perfect	[pɚfəkt]
permit	[pɝmɪt]	permit	[pɚmɪt]
pick up	[pɪkʌp]	pick up	[pɪkʌp]
present	[pɹɛzənt]	present	[pɹɪzɛnt]
produce	[pɹoʊdjus]	produce	[pɹədjus]
progress	[pɹɒgɹɛs]	progress	[pɹəgɹɛs]
project	[pɹɒdʒɛkt	project	[pɹədʒɛkt]
pronoun	[pɹoʊnaʊn]	pronounce	[pɹənaʊns]
protest	[pɹoʊtɛst]	protest	[pɹətɛst]
put down	[pʊtdaʊn]	put down	[pʊt daʊn]
recall	[ɹikɔl]	recall	[ɹɪkɔl]
record	[ɹɛkɚd]	record	[ɹɪkɔrd]
reject	[ɹidʒɛkt]	reject	[ɹɪdʒɛkt]
research	[ɹiɪsɝtʃ]	research	[ɹɪsɝtʃ]
subject	[sʌbdʒɪkt]	subject	[səbdʒɛkt]
suspect	[sʌspɛkt]	suspect	[səspɛkt]

Notes: ....

....

....

....

....

....

....

....

....

Ex. 2   Explore the word stress in the <u>underlined words</u> in the following sentences. Observe how stress patterns differentiate the **bold-font** verbs, nouns, and adjectives.

- The **<u>rec</u>ord** that the popular singer **re<u>cord</u>ed** was a **<u>rec</u>ord**-high sellout.

- **<u>Re</u>searchers** are the people who **re<u>search</u>** any significant data and results for their research.

- **<u>Re</u>bels** are a group of people who act collectively to <u>rebel</u> against their government or other larger social organizations.

- A **<u>con</u>vert** is a person who **con<u>vert</u>ed** his life to a certain way of living.

- His **<u>con</u>duct** is not acceptable. He needs to learn to **con<u>duct</u>** himself better.

- I need to <u>check **out**</u> at the **<u>check</u>out** stand.

- Would you <u>hand **out**</u> these **<u>hand</u>outs** to the class, please?

- The **<u>sur</u>vey** team went out to <u>sur<u>vey</u></u> the community for their project.

- You will <u>pick **up**</u> your order at the **<u>pick</u>up** station behind this building.

- They <u>sus**pect**</u> that the person on CCTV is the **<u>sus</u>pect**.

- That is an **<u>in</u>sult** although you did not mean to <u>in**sult**</u> me.

- Did you hear they might <u>in**crease**</u> tuition again? I cannot afford another **<u>in</u>crease** in our tuition.

- The store called "**<u>Re</u>ject**" in London's popular tourist district sells china that is <u>re**ject**ed</u> from factories of famous brand name chinaware.

Notes: ....
....
....
....

258

Ex. 3   In some words identifying people, the primary stress falls on the same syllable regardless of whether they are nouns or verbs. Explore the primary stress patterns in the following words.

Nouns	Verb	Noun	Verb
baby	**ba**by	**mo**ther	**mo**ther
father	**fa**ther	**doc**tor	**doc**tor
nurse	**nur**sing	engi**neer**	engi**neer**
friend	be**friend**ed	volun**teer**	volun**teer**
model	**mo**del		

- Don't **ba**by your **ba**by brother too much. He needs to learn to grow up.

- **Mo**thering does not necessarily come naturally to all **mo**thers.

- Jacob, the **fa**ther of Joseph, **fa**thered twelve sons.

- My **doc**tor gave me this recipe and suggested that I **doc**tor it to my liking.

- Jan, a registered **nur**se, decided upon **nur**sing her baby for over two years.

- The engi**neer**s reported that they had engi**neer**ed nuclear-engi**neer**ed soybeans.

- My **friend** told me that his professor asked the class to un**friend** him on a social network service because his students did not respond diligently to his emails.

- Volun**teer**s from all over the country volun**teer**ed to join a volun**teer** organization in order to give a helping hand to the recent storm victims.

- She **mo**deled herself as a **mo**del for a function at her child's school.

Notes:..
....
....

Ex.4   Explore the primary stress on the first syllable.

Noun	Verb	Noun	Verb
accent	accent	access	access
benefit	benefit	brainstorm	brainstorm
broadcast	broadcast	challenge	challenge
comfort	comfort	contact	contact
credit	credit	distance	distance
exercise	exercise	interest	interest
figure	figure	focus	focus
function	function	highlight	highlight
journey	journey	label	label
market	market	mirror	mirror
model	model	neighbor	neighbor
number	number	picture	picture
profile	profile	question	question
resource	resource	schedule	schedule

Ex. 5   Explore the primary stress on the second syllable.

Noun	Verb	Noun	Verb
*address	address	alert	alert
approach	approach	balloon	balloon
campaign	campaign	concern	concern
control	control	design	design
default	default	effect	effect
exhaust	exhaust	mistake	mistake
neglect	neglect	result	result
return	return	repair	repair
reform	reform	repeat	repeat
report	report		

*Address as a noun can also have its stress on the first syllable

Ex. 6   Explore the word stress in the following sentences.

- The TV **programmer progra**mmed a new **prog**ram for the new season.

- The news announcing the **int**erest rate for this quarter did not **int**erest me any longer because I am debt free now.

- My re**port** on the debt ceiling wasn't re**por**ted on the news last night.

- Our company's excellent educational **ben**efit surely can **ben**efit those who would like to take advantage of it.

- The re**pair** on the washing machine wasn't re**pair**ed properly.

- They did not **la**bel the **la**bel on this bottle in a way that everyone can read easily.

- He **dis**tanced himself from the person who came from a **dis**tance.

Notes: ....
....
....
....
....
....
....
....
....
....
....
....
....
....
....
....

2. Primary Stress in Multisyllabic Words

When a word contains several syllables, which syllable should be stressed?

Rule 1   **Prefixes are usually not stressed.**

Ex. 1   Explore the stress patterns of the following prefixes. The *italicized* syllables are the prefixes; the **bold** syllables are stressed.

/a/:   *a*loud, *a*float, *a*drift, *a*bed, *a*far, *a*nomaly

/in/:   *in*active, *in*sufficient, *in*appropriate, *in*justice

/im/:   *im*possible, *im*mature, *im*practical

/il/:   *il*legal, *il*legible, *il*legitimate, *il*logical

/un/:   *un*do, *un*able, *un*known, *un*welcome, *un*intelligible, *un*common, *un*comfortable

/de/:   *de*crease (v), *de*mote, *de*part, *de*port, *de*fend, *de*sire, *de*gree

/dis/:   *dis*courage, *dis*qualify, *dis*mantle

/pre/:   *pre*liminary, *pre*caution, *pre*scribe, *pre*pare

/pro/:   *pro*motion, *pro*claim, *pro*tect, *pro*posal, *pro*duce, *pro*bation

/re/:   *re*call, *re*form, *re*furbish, *re*creation, *re*visit

Notes: ....

....

....

....

....

....

....

Ex. 2   In the following sentences, explore the stress patterns of the words that
            have *prefixes*. Remember: Prefixes are *not* stressed. They are *italicized* for
            you.

- I was reading *a*loud as I was *a*float on a friend's boat, we were *a*drift
  and *a*far.

- He said that it is *in*appropriate, *in*sufficient, and *un*just to state that the
  *in*active stage of the cancer meant that the cancer was cured.

- Jim thinks a plan formed of an *im*mature mind is *im*possible and
  *im*practical to carry out.

- The ill-equipped *pro*posal was not only *il*legible and *il*logical but also
  *il*legitimate and *il*legal.

- *Un*intelligible speech patterns are not *un*common in speech
  communities; however, we cannot say that we are *un*able to find
  the training methods to *un*do the *un*comfortable and *un*clear speech
  patterns.

- Dean *de*parted the *de*partment after a *de*motion with *de*creased pay.

- Finding out that her *dis*mantled sculpture work was *dis*qualified from
  the exhibition, Deidra was *dis*couraged and *dis*heartened, but *re*mained
  calm.

- In the past century, the idea of *pre*fabricated buildings was not even in
  the *pre*liminary stage.

- Pat visited her clinic regularly and as a *pre*caution, but for some
  *un*known reason, her doctor *pre*scribed additional medicine.

Notes:...
....
....
....
....
....
....

Ex. 3   Explore the pronunciation of /re/ in the beginning of the words.

1. The /re/ syllable pronounced as un-stressed [ri] or [rɪ], (v) refers to a verb

*re*act	[ɹiækt]	*re*call	[rɪkɔl]
*re*ceipt	[ɹisit]	*re*cord	[ɹɪkɔrd]
*re*design	[ɹidəzaɪn]	*re*elect	[ɹiilɛkt]
*re*form	[ɹifɔɹm]	*re*flect	[ɹɪflɛkt]
*re*frain	[ɹɪfreɪn]	*re*frigerator	[ɹɪfrɪdʒɚ-eɪtɚ]
*re*furbish	[ɹifɚ-bɪʃ]	*re*gain	[ɹɪgeɪn]
*re*lieve	[ɹɪ.liv]	*re*model	[ɹimɒdl]
*re*schedule	[ɹiskɛdʒʊl]	*re*search (v)	[ɹisɝ-ʧ]
*re*solve	[ɹɪzɒlv]	*re*source	[ɹɪsɔɹs]
*re*vamp	[ɹivæmp]	*re*view	[ɹɪvju]

2. The /re/ pronounced as the stressed [ri] in the noun forms of the words.

re**call**   re**ject**   re**search**   re**flex**   re**verb**

The /re/ pronounced with the secondary stressed [rɛ].

*re*feree	[ɹɛfɚi]	*re*gistration	[ɹɛdʒɪstɹeɪʃən]
*re*creation	[ɹɛkɹieɪʃən]	resolution	[ɹɛzəluʃən]
reservation	[ɹɛzɚ-veɪʃən]	restoration	[ɹɛstɚ-eɪʃən]

3. The /re/ pronounced as stressed [rɛ]

re**cord**	[ɹɛkɚ-rd]	re**bel**	[ɹɛbəl]
re**cognize**	[ɹɛkəgnaɪz]	re**gister**	[ɹɛdʒɪstɚ-]
re**ference**	[ɹɛfɚ-əns]	re**levant**	[ɹɛləvənt]
re**sonant**	[ɹɛzənənt]	re**concile**	[ɹɛkənsaɪl]

Ex 4	Explore different pronunciations of the stressed- and unstressed /re/ prefixes in the following *dialogue*. The stressed syllables are marked in **bold**, and unstressed syllables are *italicized*.

Jenny: Hey, we seem to see each other quite **re**gularly in the *Re*creation Center.

Susie: Yes, I come to the *re*creation center **re**gularly; in fact, every day. That's **re**gular enough, isn't it? Hahaha.

Jenny: It sure is. Hahaha. I **re**cognized you in the Zumba class the other day. What other exercises are you **re**gistered for?

Susie: I **re**gularly come to Zumba classes. And Yoga absolutely is another favorite. Also, I **re**gularly attend Step classes. Am I using the **re**sources wisely, or not?

Jenny: Great *re*sponse! So how did your presentation go at the *Re*storation *Re*sort?

Susie: Well, the **re**gistrar informed me that my *re*servation for the conference on "Absolute *Re*solution" was not processed correctly during *re*gistration.

Jenny: So, how was the food at the *Re*storation *Re*sort Hotel?

Susie: Their **re**cipes for desserts were out of this world.

Jenny: Oh, I wish I could have been there. By the way, did you find out what went wrong with your *re*gistration?

Susie: They **re**cognized that the mishap occurred because of lack of **re**levant *re*cords and **re**ferences recorded in their system.

Jenny: I see. Did they finally *re*solve your *re*gistration?

Susie: Finally. The **re**gistrar informed me that they had to quickly *re*view their system and make a *re*solution of the **re**levant issues, which also prevented other people from **re**gistering. To compensate for my mishap, they **re**gistered me free of charge, and *re*funded my *re*gistration fee.

Jenny: I *re*member a saying, "The haps and mishaps of life are next-door neighbors."

Notes: ....

....

....

Rule 2   **Suffixes are usually not stressed.**

The suffixes will be in *italics*.

/-ed/   **plann**ed, **learn**ed, design*ed*, abort*ed*, receiv*ed*, **stay**ed

/-er/   **do**er, **fix**er, **mak**er, **teach**er, **speak**er, receiv*er*, design*er*

/-ing/   **do**ing, **mak**ing, **fix**ing, **teach**ing, **speak**ing, design*ing*

/-ic/   **Stress the syllable immediately before the /-ic/ ending:**

heroic, economic, **ba**sic, domestic, **com**ic, terrific, **traf**fic, Atlantic, concentric

/-ical/   **Stress the syllable immediately before the /-ical/ ending:**

economical, geographical, biological, biblical, technical, classical, logical

/-cion/, /-sion/, /-ssion/, /-tion/:
Stress the syllable immediately before /-ion/ ending:

mission, expression, impression, suspicion, invasion, nation, mansion, education, evolution, compression

/-ious/: **Stress the syllable immediately before the /-ious/ ending:**

gracious, precious, delicious, malicious, suspicious, capricious, contentious, pretentious, contagious

/-ient/: **stress the syllable immediately before the "-ient" ending:**

convenient, deficient, efficient, proficient, sufficient, emollient

For words with 3 or more syllables that end with the *-ate* or *-ize*, stress the second syllable before the suffix.

/-ate/:   educate, graduate, associate, nominate, insulate

/-ize: **1) Stress 2nd syllable before /ize/ ending:**
          realize, recognize, compartmentalize, revolutionize,

          2) Stress 3rd syllable before /ize/ ending:
          sensationalize, sectionalize, nationalize, personalize

Rule 3   **Prefixes and suffixes can be stressed when compared or contrasted.**

- I bet that any **ha**ppy and **ho**nest person could have **un**happy or **dis**honest moments at times.

- Tuitions tend to **in**crease not **de**crease; however, the students and parents celebrated when their newly elected president promised a **de**crease in tuition instead of an **in**crease.

- Is Mr. Yang **ha**ppy or **un**happy?

- The scientists are **sear**ching and **re**searching for the missing clue.

- He has been known for his **hon**esty, not **dis**honesty.

Ex. 5   Explore the vowel sounds, vowel lengths, and location of the primary stress in the following word list according to the grammatical function of each word.

Remember, the stressed syllable is *stronger, longer, and slightly higher in pitch.*

Verb (action)	actor (doer)	Noun/ Nominalization	Adjective	Adverb
analyze	**a**nalyst	a**na**lysis	ana**ly**tical	ana**ly**tically
com**pete**	com**pe**titor	compe**ti**tion	com**pe**titive	com**pe**titively
con**test**	con**tes**tant	**con**test	con**tes**ted	con**tes**tably
e**co**nomize	e**co**nomist	e**co**nomy	eco**no**mical	eco**no**mically
e**lec**trify	elec**tri**cian	elec**tri**city	e**lec**tric	e**lec**trically
his**to**ricize	his**to**rian	**his**tory	his**to**ric/his**to**rical	his**to**rically
hy**po**thesize	hy**po**thesizer	hy**po**thesis	hypo**the**tical	hypo**the**tically
linguist	lin**guis**tics	lin**guis**tic	lin**guis**tical	lin**guis**tically
musicalize	mu**si**cian	**mu**sic	**mu**sical	**mu**sically
mechanize	me**cha**nic	mecha**ni**zation	me**cha**nical	me**cha**nically
naturalize[næ]	**na**turalist [næ]	**na**ture [neɪ]	**na**tural[næ]	**na**turally[næ]
photograph	pho**to**grapher	**pho**tograph	photo**gra**phic	photo**gra**phically
practice	prac**ti**tioner	**prac**tice	**prac**tical	**prac**tically
program	**pro**grammer	**pro**gram	**pro**grammed	programmatically
sensitize	**sen**sitizer	sensi**ti**vity	**sen**sitive	**sen**sitively
signify	**sig**nifier	sig**ni**ficance	sig**ni**ficant	sig**ni**ficantly
sta**tis**tisize	statis**ti**cian	sta**tis**tics	sta**tis**tical	sta**tis**tically
technify	tech**ni**cian	tech**nique**	**tech**nical	**tech**nically

267

Ex. 6   Now, explore the vowel sounds, vowel lengths, and location of the primary stress in each underlined word in the following sentences.

- The <u>photographer</u> <u>**phot**ographed</u> many <u>**phot**ographs</u> of the wedding.

- Jan trusted her <u>photo**graph**ic</u> memory and did not study very much.

- The apprentice is <u>**prac**tically</u> <u>**prac**ticing</u> his <u>**prac**tical</u> jokes with his Master Jokester.

- <u>Electric</u> appliances consume a great deal of <u>electricity</u>.

- The lightning <u>electrified</u> a portion of the field with its formidable <u>electric</u> power.

- The country needed to <u>economize</u> its fiscal budget, but its people did not like it.

- However, we've altered our <u>economic</u> status into a positive outcome.

- In some countries, eating out is more <u>economical</u> than cooking at home.

- The oil-rich countries are still <u>economically</u> strong.

- The <u>technique</u> of the <u>technician</u> in the <u>**tech**nical</u> company is <u>**tech**nically</u> superb.

- The <u>analytically</u> oriented <u>analyst</u> <u>analyzed</u> the problems and made a quick and sharp <u>analysis</u> to solve the problem.

- <u>Statisticians</u> can't find a verb that defines the "action of <u>statistical</u> analysis."

- <u>Hypothetically</u>, we possess all the <u>technological</u> resources of the world.

- It's only <u>natural</u> that Nathan, a <u>naturalist</u>, <u>naturally</u> likes to explore <u>nature</u>, eats <u>naturally</u> grown food, wears clothes made of <u>natural</u> fibers, and uses <u>natural</u> skin care products.

- The doctor performed a <u>sensitivity</u> test on a piece of tissue because the patient usually reacts <u>**sen**sitively</u> to pollens and dust. He will <u>de**sen**sitize</u> the <u>**sen**sitive</u> allergens by injecting diluted forms of dust into the patient's body.

- Dr. Jenkins <u>hy**pot**hesized</u> regarding the influence of the language distance between a learner's first and the second languages, and her <u>hy**pot**hesis</u> has been repeatedly proven true in my pronunciation teaching experiences.

Ex. 7	Explore the primary word stresses in the following *dialogue*.

Grace: **What** is your **fa**vorite **col**or?

Barton: I like **green**. For **me, green** means **trees** in the **for**est, **new life** in the **spring**, and **fresh air** in **na**ture. So **na**turally, I like **na**tural **things** and spending **time** in **na**ture.

Grace: **Spen**ding **time** in **na**ture is an eco**nom**ical way to pro**mote** our **health, too**.

Barton: **Right**. With the e**con**omy as it **is**, I am trying to e**con**omize my **bud**get and **try**ing to make it eco**nom**ically **fit**.

Grace: The **same here**. I am trying to e**con**omize in my **life**, trying to waste **less** elec**tri**city by using fewer e**lec**trical items. For e**xam**ple, I switched my **can** opener from an e**lec**trical one to a **man**ual one, which is also a**noth**er way to use my **mus**cle-**fit**ness with**out** u**sing** electricity, **hah!**

Notes: ....

....

....

....

....

....

....

....

....

....

....

....

....

Ex. 8	Explore the syllable/word stress in the following *dialogue*.
Andy:	What is your **ma**jor?
Bill:	My **ma**jor is **me**dical sociology.
Andy:	**What** do you **ac**tually **stu**dy in that **dis**cipline?
Bill:	Medical sociology was established as a **spe**cialized **field** in the United **States** during the **1940**s. It is con**cern**ed with **so**cial **caus**es and con**se**quences of **health** and **ill**ness, and with the appli**ca**tion of sociological **theo**ry and **re**search **me**thods to the **stu**dy re**la**ted to **health** and the **health care sys**tem.
Andy:	I **see**. What **sorts** of **ar**eas are in**clu**ded in **me**dical sociology?
Bill:	The **ma**jor **ar**eas of **me**dical sociology in**clude** the **so**cial **fa**cets of **health** and di**sease**, the **so**cial be**ha**vior of **health care** person**nel** and their **cli**ents, the **so**cial **func**tions of **health** organi**za**tions and institutions, the **so**cial **pa**tterns of **health ser**vices, and the relationship of **health** care delivery **sys**tems to **o**ther **sys**tems such as e**co**nomy and **po**litics.
Andy:	For **such stu**dies, what **sorts** of as**sump**tions **take place** in **me**dical sociology?
Bill:	**Me**dical sociology as**sumes** that **so**cial **fac**tors such as **so**cial economic **sta**tus, **gen**der, ethnicity, **life**styles, and **high**-risk be**ha**vior, play a **cri**tical **role** in de**ter**mining or **in**fluencing the **health** of individuals, **groups**, and **lar**ger societies. Social **fac**tors **al**so are im**por**tant in **in**fluencing the **ma**nner in which so**cie**ties **or**ganize their **re**sources to **cope** with **health ha**zards and deliver **me**dical care to the population at **large**.
Andy:	So, what **sorts** of **job** oppor**tu**nities might the **gra**duates of **me**dical sociology look **in**to?
Bill:	Since **me**dical sociology has an ap**plied fo**cus with **re**levance for **po**licy and **health ser**vice delivery at the com**mu**nity, **re**gional, societal, and **glo**bal levels, **gra**duates from **me**dical sociology **hold teach**ing positions not **on**ly in sociology de**part**ments, but **al**so in **pub**lic **health**, **me**dical, and **nur**sing schools. In ad**di**tion, they are em**ployed** as **re**searchers in **pub**lic and **pri**vate **health a**gencies and in **health**-related **in**dustries such as insurance, and **hos**pital **ma**nagement **com**panies. **I** love **teach**ing as well as **re**search, **so** I would like to ap**ply** for **teach**ing positions in uni**ver**sities in the **fu**ture.
Andy:	**Thank** you for **sha**ring this **in**fo with me, and I **wish** you the **best** in your professional en**dea**vor.

(Adapted from Yue Cao, Graduate Student, Department of Sociology, University of Alabama at Birmingham)

Ex. 9   Explore stresses in words in the following essay.

How I began learning the English language

I started **learn**ing **Eng**lish in my **coun**try when I was thir**teen**. At **first**, I **learn**ed to **say** and **write** the **names** of the English **al**phabet letters and then continued to **learn simp**le vo**cab**ulary, **gramm**ar, and **sen**tence **struc**ture. By the **time** I finished **learn**ing **greet**ings such as '**good morn**ing,' 'good **afternoon**,' 'good **evening**,' and '**how** are **you**?', **I** thought I was **rea**dy to **con**quer the **world**, but **soon found out** that there were a **lot** more **comp**licated **things** to **learn**.

As we went **deep**er **in**to the **lang**uage, we had to **me**morize **ma**ny vo**cab**ulary **words** and learn **complex gramm**ar and **sen**tence **struc**tures by **spend**ing most of our **class time read**ing and **trans**lating **Eng**lish **texts** into our **own lang**uage. When we **read Eng**lish texts out **loud** in **class**, our **teach**ers en**cour**aged us to **read each word** correc**tly, but we did **not** have any **place** to **use Eng**lish **out**side the **class**room.

So, I **stud**ied **Eng**lish conversation on my **own** by **list**ening and re**peat**ing **af**ter the **speak**ers in **au**dio **tapes**, CDs, and **Eng**lish **broad**casting, but I could **not** really **tell whe**ther I was **mim**icking them cor**rect**ly or **not**. **No one** really **showed** me or ex**plain**ed to me **clear**ly how to pro**noun**ce the **sounds** of **Eng**lish **vow**els and **con**sonants cor**rect**ly; how **Eng**lish-**speak**ing people might **feel** the **sounds** in their **bo**dies; and **no** one was there to **give** me **much need**ed **feedback**.

After ar**riv**ing in the United **States**, I **found** that I could **not** under**stand** what Americans were **say**ing, and **they** could **not** under**stand** me **ei**ther, so **this iss**ue can **still** be **daun**ting at **times**. I ac**cept** the **fact** that I **don't speak Eng**lish like A**mer**icans **do**, but what **both**ers me is that I can**not figure out** ex**act**ly **what** I am **do**ing **diff**erently. And be**cause** I **don't** know **what** I am **do**ing that **is diff**erent, I can**not** ad**apt** my **speak**ing. **This** is im**pac**ting my per**form**ance and **con**fidence, and most **like**ly my pro**fess**ional ad**van**cement.

I sure would **like** to **see** a **day** when my **Eng**lish **speech tru**ly re**flects** my pro**fess**ional qualifications to my A**mer**ican **coll**eagues and **helps** me to com**mu**nicate **full**y with com**plete con**fidence and **ease** with **every**one I en**coun**ter.

271

Ex.10   GA syllable stress on the names of countries and the people of that country

Country adjective	Its People/	Country adjective	Its People/
Af**gha**nistan	**Af**ghan	Algeria	Algerian
United **States**	American	Argentina	Argentinean
Austria	**Aus**trian	Aus**tra**lia	Aus**tra**lian
Ba**ha**mas	Ba**ha**man	Bah**rain**	Bah**rain**i
Bangladesh	Bangla**de**shi	Bots**wana**	Bots**wana**n
Be**la**rus	Bela**ru**sian	Bo**li**via	Bo**li**vian
Bhu**tan**	Bhuta**nese**	Bra**zil**	Bra**zil**ian
Britain	**Brit**ish	Came**roon**	Came**roon**ian
Canada	Ca**na**dian	**Chi**le	**Chi**lean
Chad	**Chad**ian	**Chi**na	Chi**nese**
Co**lom**bia	Co**lom**bian	**Cu**ba	**Cu**ban
Denmark	**Dan**ish	Do**mi**nica	Do**mi**nican
Egypt	E**gyp**tian	El **Sal**vador	Salva**do**ran
England	**Eng**lish	Eri**trea**	Eri**trea**n
Es**to**nia	Es**to**nian	E**thi**opia	E**thi**opian
France	**French**	**Fin**land	**Finn**ish
Germany	**Ger**man	**Greece**	**Greek**
Greenland	**Green**lander	Gre**na**da	Gre**na**dian
Guate**ma**la	Guate**ma**lan	Guy**a**na	Guy**a**nese
Haiti	**Hai**tian	**Hol**land	**Hol**lander
Hon**du**ras	Hon**du**ran	**Hung**ary	Hun**ga**rian
Iceland	**Ice**lander	**In**dia	**In**dian
Indo**ne**sia	Indo**ne**sian	**Is**rael	Is**rae**li
I**ran**	I**ra**nian	I**raq**	I**raq**i
Ireland	**Ir**ish	**It**aly	I**tal**ian
Ja**mai**ca	Ja**mai**can	Ja**pan**	Japa**nese**
Jordan	Jor**da**nian	**Ke**nya	**Ke**nyan
Kazakh**stan**	Kazakh**stan**i	Ko**rea**	Ko**rea**n
Kyrgyzstan	Kyrgyz**stan**i	**Le**banon	Leba**nese**
Libya	**Lib**yan	Lithu**a**nia	Lithu**a**nian
Mada**gas**car	Mala**ga**sy	Ma**lay**sia	Ma**lay**sian
Ma**la**wi	Ma**la**wian	**Ma**li	**Ma**lian

272

Mauri**ta**nia	Mauri**ta**nian	**Me**xico	**Me**xican
Mon**go**lia	Mon**go**lian	Mozam**bi**que	Mozam**bi**can
Myanmar	Bur**mese**	Na**mi**bia	Na**mi**bian
Ne**pal**	Ne**pal**i	**Ne**therland	**Ne**therlander
New Zealand	**New Zeal**ander	Ni**ge**ria	Ni**ge**rian
Norway	Nor**we**gian	O**man**	O**man**i
Pakistan	**Pa**kistani	**Pa**nama	Pana**ma**nian
Paraguay	Para**guay**an	Pe**ru**	Pe**ru**vian
Philippine	Fili**pi**no/Fili**pi**na	**Po**land	**Po**lish
Qatar	**Qa**tari	Ro**ma**nia	Ro**ma**nian
Russia	**Ru**ssian	**Sau**di Arabia	**Sau**di
So**ma**lia	So**ma**li	**Spain**	**Spa**nish
Sri **Lan**ka	Sri **Lan**kan	Su**dan**	Su**da**nese
Sweden	**Swe**dish	**Swi**tzerland	**Swiss**
Syria	**Sy**rian	Ta**ji**kistan	Taji**ki**stani
Tan**za**nia	Tan**za**nian	**Thai**land	**Thai**
Tibet	**Ti**betan	**Tri**nidad	Trini**da**dian
Tu**ni**sia	Tu**ni**sian	**Tur**key	**Tur**kish
U**kraine**	U**krai**nian	**U**ruguay	**U**ruguayan
Uz**be**kistan	Uzbe**ki**stani	Vene**zue**la	Vene**zue**lan
Viet**nam**	Vietna**mese**	**Ye**men	**Ye**menite
Zambia	**Zam**bian	Zim**bab**we	Zim**bab**wean

Carryover into everyday life: Adding word stress will clarify words for your listeners. Find time during the day, such as when talking on the phone, to add word stress to multi-syllable words.

Notes: ....

....

....

....

....

....

Chapter 6

Sentence Stress
For GA English Sounding Speech
(Stressed Words in Sentences)

Dialogue: *What is Sentence Stress and why is it important?*

Jonghee: So far, we have explored GA English consonants, vowels, word stress, and thought groups. In this chapter, we will learn about **sentence stress**[61]. Knowing what *word* stress means, can you guess what *sentence* stress might be?

Sumi: Hmmm, since *word stress* means emphasizing the primary stress of an individual word, would *sentence stress* mean we need to stress important words within sentences?

Jonghee: You are right. When GA English speakers express their thoughts in speech, they tend to speak in thought groups (phrases) rather than in long sentences, with important words stressed or emphasized within those phrases.

Sumi: Are you saying that native GA English-speakers choose the length of their thought groups, and stress words within them consciously?

Jonghee: Yes and no. Often, the length of a Thought Group depends on the amount of breath a person uses to support the thought all the way through to its end; or sometimes the phrase has to be broken up further in order to take an additional breath. Some say that we can support about five to seven words comfortably in a phrase. But of course, the length of each word, and the number of words in the phrases can vary depending on the speaker's purpose and situations. People can even change their minds in the middle of a sentence—so this becomes another 'thought group', and words will be stressed depending upon which direction the conversation goes.

Sumi: What about English language students?

Jonghee: It can vary. Beginning English learners might speak more slowly and thus will include fewer words in a phrase, whereas someone with advanced proficiency might be able to speak as quickly as native speakers, thus more words in a phrase. However, I've been observing that those learning English tend to be unfamiliar with sentence stress because many of them have not had any opportunities to learn about it before.

Sumi: That is true for me, too. We learned English as an academic subject rather than using it for everyday communication.

---

61 https://magoosh.com/english-speaking/sentence-stress-in-english/ Definition of Sentence Stress
August 10, 2021

Jonghee: Well then, we can *stress* a word by raising or changing the pitch, which we call intonation, or lengthening the word, or accentuating it in other ways, which will improve our communication when speaking.

Sumi: I am ready to begin!

How to create optimal sentence stress: our dialogue continues

Jonghee: Now that we have discovered that sentence stress is important for effective English intonation, and that it involves stressing or emphasizing the important words in sentences and phrases (thought groups), let's talk about what sorts of words need to be stressed.

             Content words (key words) such as nouns, verbs, adjectives, and adverbs are stressed.

             Number words, such as *one, two, three, or first, second, third*, are stressed.

             Question words (Wh-words), such as *who, what, when, where, which, why,* and *how* are stressed.

             Negative words such as *no, not, never, don't* and *can't*, may also be stressed.

             Other categories include **transition words, words used in contrast, words of strong emotion, emphasis,** and **new information**.

             Finally, any words that need to be emphasized for any personal reason are also stressed.

Sumi: That makes sense to me.

Jonghee: However, the **function words** such as pronouns (including relative pronouns) Helping Verbs, Articles, and Prepositions are usually *not stressed.*

Sumi: Yes, I do remember learning about those kinds of words in my grammar classes.

Jonghee: Your knowledge of English grammar surely helps here. Now, I want you to know that **stress** in sentences or phrases is really about your intentions. The words that contain your topic, situation, content, and purpose, and that you want to effectively deliver to your listeners, need to be stressed.

Sumi:	That again makes sense. So, we cannot think about sentence stress without also including important word stress–and how to stress those words by raising the pitch of the word or finding a way to emphasize it!
Jonghee	Right!
Sumi:	I now can understand why some of my American colleagues had trouble understanding me at times.
Jonghee:	In your case, because you are a scientist, and the vocabulary you often have to use is made up of many multisyllabic words, it can be even more challenging for you—and for your listeners.
Sumi:	Thank you for taking the time to explain this. I am more than ready to dive deeper into sentence stress.

Notes: ....

....

....

....

....

....

....

....

....

....

....

....

....

....

....

Stressed Words in the Sentences

The following elements carry stress in the sentences:

1. Content words (key words): nouns, verbs, adjectives, and adverbs.

2. Question words: who, what, when, where, which, why, how

3. Number words: one, two, three, four, etc.; first, second, third, fourth, etc.

4. Negative words: no, not, none, don't, didn't, can't, won't

5. Transition words: first, second, finally

6. Words in contrast/comparison/corrections

7. Words expressed with strong emotion

8. Emphasis

9. New information

Useful tips:

- Sentence stresses are guided by the intention of the speaker (what the speaker intends to say) and the context of the speech.

- With good understanding of the long and short vowel lengths, optimal lip-openings for the vowels, and clear articulation of consonants, you can create beautiful music of the language (intonation and inflection) in each word and sentence easily and comfortably.

For your information:

- In this chapter, all stressed words are <u>underlined</u> and stressed vowels are marked in **bold font**. Some are raised above the line for you to raise the pitch of that syllable or word.

- Primary stress takes place only on the <u>vowel</u> of the syllable, not on the consonants.

- Stress can take place by simply raising or lowering the pitch of the word or syllable within a word you want to emphasize—or by lengthening it, or by making it stronger in tone (louder). There are many ways to stress a word.

1. Content Words (Key Words)

In the following sentences, *content words* are *nouns, main verbs, adjectives,* and *adverbs.*

a. Nouns

- I teach **Pu**blic Admini**stra**tion in the Uni**ver**sity of Bei**ji**ng.
- **John** likes apples, pears, and **or**anges.
- My umb**rel**la is **hi**ding from me.
- Chi**ca**go is in Illi**no**is.

b. Main verbs

- She **tea**ches there; she is **not** a **stu**dent.
- I will **go** with you.
- Let's st**a**y, then.
- I **ate** my lunch already.

c. Adjectives

- She teaches at a **large** university.
- The sky looks **clear** right now.
- The house needs a **new pa**int job.
- His sister is the **fast**est walker that I know of.

d. Adverbs

- Her students **re**ally love her.
- The sky looks **quite** suspicious to me.
- Don't postpone your daily practice **too** long.
- Why **so** fast?
- I am the **on**ly Chinese student in my lab.
- We are from all **o**ver the world.

2. Question Words

- So, tell me **who** wants **wha**_aat!_

- To **whom** should I address the letter?

- **What** seems to be the matter with you?

- **When** will they arrive here?

- **How** do you do that?

3. Number Words

- **Five** designer cars are ready to be escorted to the VIPs.

- Josh Carter is the **se**cond person to be awarded the prestigious scholarship.

- I finished the first **two** chapters and am ready for the **thir**d.

- The singer's new song hit over a **bill**ion views on YouTube in less than a week.

- Today in history is April **20,** **two thousand** thir**tee**n.

- He lives on **9**th Street.

4. Negative Words

- The sky **does**n't look friendly.

- **Haven't** you heard about it?

- I **should**n't pretend to know about something that I am **not** **su**re about.

- It **won't** take too long to get there.

- I **didn't** mean that.

5. Transition Words

A Recipe for "The Tea of Love"

Practice with awareness the many ways you can stress these underlined words. The stressed syllables are in **bold** font.

First, cut off the root of com**plaints** and **ang**er. Chop **fine**ly.

Second, re**move ar**rogance and pride from in**side**. Clean well and dry.

Third, peel off irri**ta**bility; dice and **ma**rinate **thor**oughly in the heart.

Then, re**move** the seeds of disa**ppoint**ment and **ha**tred com**plete**ly.

Blanch in for**give**ness water.

Next, com**bine** all in**gre**dients in the kettle, **add**ing **pa**tience and **pray**ers, and boil until no **long**er **bit**ter.

Finally, stir well with joy and thanks**giv**ing, add **sev**eral **grace**ful smiles, **driz**zle a pinch of faith and drink while warm.

(Translated from an unknown source)

6. Words in Contrast, Comparison, or Correction

- I traded in the **Sa**turn **View** 2003 for a new **Hyun**dai E**lan**tra 2012.

- The **col**or of my new car is **in**digo blue, but it looks more **pur**ple to me.

- Unlike my **old** car, my **new** car features a **war**ranty for **one hun**dred **thou**sand **miles** or **ten years**, whichever comes **first** from **head** to **tail**; and **two** hundred thousand miles or **twen**ty years for **eng**ine and trans**mis**sion.

- The **ser**vice in this restaurant is getting **bet**ter, not **worse**, with **time**.

Notes: ....

....

....

7. Words Expressed with Strong Emotion

all, only, always, never, should

*   For some reason, **all** my umbrellas are broken.

*   <u>Only</u> the first ten lucky students will get free ice cream.

*   My teacher is **always** ready for her classes.

*   It will **never** happen again.

*   So, we should **do** this—we **should**.

8. Emphasis

Any word can be emphasized, in various ways, according to the speaker's intention—you can raise or lower the pitch, lengthen the word or syllable, use a stronger voice to emphasize as you communicate.

A Useful tip:

You may take any of the sentences from sections 1-7 above and speak them with a different intention by choosing a different word to stress as your main point. Here are more examples:

*   I don't **have** to if I don't **want** to.

*   I guess she is at **work**, but not **at** work.

*   **Patty**, get **up**. We gotta **go**. **Now**! We are being invaded by a **tsunami**.

*   The **earthquake** hit that place **again**.

9. New information

New information in the spoken sentences or phrases is stressed, and previous statements are not.

Notes:..

....

....

Ex. 1   Notice how important words and new information are stressed in the following sentences.

- <u>Words</u> are **<u>un</u>**<u>derlined</u>.

- The <u>stressed</u> words are **<u>un</u>**<u>derlined</u>.

- The <u>stressed</u> words are **<u>un</u>**<u>derlined</u>, and the stressed **<u>syl</u>**<u>lables</u> are in <u>bold</u> font.

- <u>All</u> stressed <u>words</u> are **<u>un</u>**<u>derlined</u> and stressed **<u>syl</u>**<u>lables</u> are in <u>bold</u> font.

- In <u>this</u> **<u>chap</u>**<u>ter</u>, <u>all</u> stressed <u>words</u> are **<u>un</u>**<u>derlined</u> and stressed **<u>syl</u>**<u>lables</u> are **in <u>bold</u>** font.

- In <u>this</u> **<u>chap</u>**<u>ter</u>, <u>all</u> stressed <u>words</u> are **<u>un</u>**<u>derlined</u> and stressed **<u>syl</u>**<u>lables</u> are in **<u>bold</u>** font, but **<u>un</u>**<u>stressed</u> words are <u>not</u> underlined.

- In <u>this</u> chapter, all <u>stressed</u> words are **<u>un</u>**<u>derlined</u>, stressed **<u>syl</u>**<u>lables</u> are in <u>bold</u> font, but **<u>un</u>**<u>stressed</u> words are <u>not</u> underlined and **<u>un</u>**<u>stressed</u> <u>syllables</u> are <u>not</u> **in** bold font.

- Did you **<u>rea</u>**<u>lize</u> that, in <u>this</u> chapter, <u>all</u> stressed <u>words</u> are **<u>un</u>**<u>derlined</u> and stressed **<u>syl</u>**<u>lables</u> are in <u>bold</u> font, but **<u>un</u>**<u>stressed</u> words are **<u>not</u>** underlined, and **<u>un</u>**<u>stressed</u> **<u>syl</u>**<u>lables</u> are <u>not</u> in bold font?

Notes: ....

....

....

....

....

....

....

....

Words usually NOT Stressed in Sentences
(Unless they represent the main point that you are making)

Function Words such as pronouns, relative pronouns, helping verbs, prepositions, articles, and conjunctions are not usually stressed. And old information is not stressed either.

1. Pronouns and Relative Pronouns

Pronouns:	I, me, my, mine, you, your, yours, he, she, his, her, hers, they, their, them, we, our, ours, it, that, those, these
Relative pronouns:	who, what, when, where, which, that, why, how

Ex. 1   In the following sentences, stress the **bold** font words; do not stress pronouns and relative pronouns which are *italicized*.

- *I* **need** to **clean** *my* **house.**

- *It* has been ig**nore**d for so **long**.

- *He* **says** *he* **loves** *her.*

- *They* are in *their* **home** right now.

- *I* **see** *that my* **turn** has **come** now.

- *You* **know** *what I* am **say**ing.

- Can *you* **tell** *me where* the **office** is?

- The **girl** *whose* **mo**ther is **play**ing piano on the **stage** is **Masako**.

- *What I* **need** is more **prac**tice, not **buy**ing new **books** all the **time**.

- *It'll* **come** *when it's* **time** *to* come.

Notes: ....

....

....

Ex. 2   Now, stress/emphasize *the words in italics* in the above sentences and see how the meaning completely changes.

For your information:

- In Ex. 2, you might find that it seems like the focus is different for each sentence.

- All stress is related to the speakers' intention and what it is that you want or need to communicate.

2.   Helping verbs (Auxiliary verbs)

do, did, does, can, could, shall, should, will, would, has, have, had, may, might

- I *can* **tell** why **this** formula **works** here.

- *Do* you think **this** *might* work, **too**?

- I *don't know* why, but it worked there ***before***.

- I am ***not sure*** whether I *should* **do** that.

- **John's message** box *was* **full** when I *tried to* leave a **message** on his **phone**.

- Since I *may* need to attend a **meeting**, I *might have to* change my **schedule**.

3.   Prepositions: *in, on, at, for, upon, beside, along, above*

- Yes, I am *in* the <u>house</u>.

- *For* some **reason**, this room is <u>always</u> <u>cold</u>.

- I *will be in* <u>China</u> *for about* <u>four</u> <u>months</u>.

- *Over* the <u>week</u>end, I made a trip *to* <u>Panama City</u>.

- *Upon* <u>graduation</u>, she served as a <u>physician</u> in <u>underprivileged</u> <u>communities</u>.

- *I* left *my* <u>**handbag**</u> *beside the* <u>**flower**</u>pot.

Ex. 3   Now go through all of the above sentences and try to communicate **by stressing the italicized words by raising the pitch or changing it in some way.** Observe how doing this changes the meaning and the speaker's intention.

4.   Articles

Articles of speech such as *a, an, the* are usually not stressed in sentences.

Ex. 4   Explore the unstressed articles in the following sentences.

- How true is *the* saying "*An* **apple** *a* **day** keeps *the* **doctor away**"?

- *The* **reason** for *the* **low** prices on *the* **goods** is *the* fierce **competition**.

Dialogue:

S: I saw **Elizabeth** today.

J: Elizabeth?

S: Yeah, **Elizabeth!**

J: Elizabeth **who**? I know more than **one** person with that **name**.

S: _**The**_ [ði] Elizabeth **Tay**lor, the **mo**vie **star!**

J: Oh! **That** Elizabeth! I wish **I** had been there **too**!

5.   Conjunctions: *and, but, for, or, so, yet* are generally not stressed.

- The **taste** of the apples *and* **pear**s cannot be compared *but* con**tra**sted. **(In this case, as a verb, the second syllable is emphasized).**

- Since a se**vere wea**ther alert is on, we'd better **pack** *and* **leave** this place.

- *But* who **cares** if you **live** *or* **leave** here?

- It's kind of **cold** today, *so* I will wear my **coat** *yet*.

- The **deal** is already **made** whether we **like** it *or* **not**.

- You **earned** your de**gree**, *for* you worked **hard** to **achieve** it.

286

Stressing Multi-Word Phrases

A. Noun phrases (Compound Noun Phrases)

A compound noun is a noun made up of two or more nouns. The primary stress of the compound noun falls on the first noun.

1. Compound nouns in one word (without a space between words)

   battlefield, **in**door, **out**door, **desk**top, **char**coal, **thumb**tack, **home**work, **stair**case, **cup**cake, **foot**ball, **base**ball, **room**mate, **bed**room, **door**bell, **fire**place, **lap**top, **desk**top, **hair**brush, **hand**cart, **key**board, **news**paper, **high**chair, **pin**point, **police**man, **chair**person, **back**bone, **black**berries, **straw**berries, **rasp**berries, **state**wide, **text**book

2. Compound nouns in two words (with a space between words)

   Ex. 5   In the following, on each two-word compound noun, explore the stress pattern by single-underlining the stressed word (the first noun), and reading the stressed syllable (**bold** font) out loud without pausing between words (handling two words as one). Raise the pitch where the accented syllable or part of the compound noun should be.

   <u>**ac**cent</u> training   ac<u>**co**unt</u> number   <u>**air**</u> conditioner

   a<u>**mi**no</u> acid   bl<u>**ood**</u> pressure   <u>**cash**</u> register

   <u>**cell**</u> phone   <u>**class**</u> time   <u>**cho**colate</u> cake

   <u>**Christ**mas</u> gift   <u>**coun**try</u> music   com<u>**pu**ter</u> screen

   <u>**cus**tomer</u> service   <u>**desk**</u> top   <u>**di**ning</u> room

   <u>**dri**ver's</u> license   <u>**dri**ving</u> school   <u>**ex**it</u> number

   <u>**gra**duate</u> school   <u>**gra**mmar</u> rules   <u>**hand**</u> carry

   infor<u>**ma**tion</u> center   into<u>**na**tion</u> pattern   <u>**jour**nal</u> club

   <u>**lab**</u> meeting   <u>**law**</u> firm   <u>**life**style</u>

living room   **lunch** box   **nur**sing school

office supply   **or**ange juice   **or**der form

paper clip   **park**ing lot   **phone** number

problem solver   **pub**lic health   **pulse** rate

quality control   regis**tra**tion desk   **re**search center

room number   **se**same chicken   **sta**tion wagon

satellite station   **sen**tence stress   **space** ship

steering wheel   **street** sign   **store** front

student center   **text** message   **tra**ffic light

3. Compound nouns in three words

Air conditioning unit   **Air**port transportation systems   **hand** carry it

Customer service desk   **cell** phone number   **o**ffice supply store

com**pu**ter screen cleaner   **desk** top computer   **dri**ving test center

steering wheel cover   **back** seat driving   **wind** shield wiper

citizenship interview test   infor**ma**tion desk clerk   **di**ning room table

living room furniture   **gro**cery shopping list   **ice** cream cones

orange juice bottle   **car**pet stain remover   **lunch** box specials

lifestyle changes   **state**-wide response   **jour**nal club topics

quality control team   **back**pack design   **port** security office

Powerpoint presentation   **knock**-out mice   **wild** type mouse

288

course work schedule

take-home exam

payroll tax

Money Market Account

radi**a**tion therapy center

healthcare center

health-related industries

hospital management company

4   Compound nouns in four words

five-year survival rates

boneless **chicken** wings

lab meeting **sche**dule sheet

Greyhound **bus** station

smart phone sales agent

com**pu**ter screen **clean**ing kit

English pronunciation **class** schedule

writing center **Message** board

drug-resistant tuberculosis research

Homeland Security officer

health care information center

United States Immigration Services

5.   Compound nouns in five words

smart phone sales agent training

Homeland security officer exam

Oral proficiency interview testing schedule

Airport passport control officer kiosk

Notes:..

....

....

....

....

289

B. Set Phrases

American dream	drive-through	elementary school
middle school	high School	graduate school
Social Studies	final exam	mid-term
White House	civil activity	drunk driving
driving school	dining table	hard drive
soft material	warehouse	hot tub
hot dog	small intestine	large intestine
blue jeans	foreign affairs	International House
compound noun	set phrase	white collar

Notes: ....

....

....

....

....

....

....

....

....

....

....

....

C. Phrasal verbs (verb + prepositional phrases)

Phrasal verbs are verbs made of two or more words with verb + preposition or a verb + adverb form. Most phrasal verbs are stressed on the adverb or preposition, which is the second word. However, in some rare cases, the verb is stressed.

1. Two-word phrasal verbs with the stress on the verb

count on	**look** at	**look** for
care for	**care(s)** about	**pay** for
rely on	**stick** to	**talk** about

- You can *count on* me--I can do the job in no time.

- I have been *looking for* the pen that I was holding in my hand all this time.

- Who *cares about* it?

- We have to *rely on* our savings for a while.

- *Look at* this flower, it is so pretty.

- If you want it, you have to *pay for* it.

- Make the plan and *stick to* it.

- Did you *talk about* me?

Notes:...

....

....

....

....

....

....

....

2. Two-word phrasal verbs with the stress on the preposition

break **down**	break **out**	break **up**
bring **down**	bring **out**	bring **up**
drive **through**	find **out**	fill **in**
get **up**	get **on**	get **back**
get **out**	get **around**	get in
go **out**	go **around**	go **back**
look **up**	look **back**	look **around**
look **down**	look **after**	look **over**
pick **up**	pick **out**	put **on**
put **off**	put **away**	put **down**
rip **off**	roll **up**	write **down**
send **in**	send **out**	send **off**
settle **down**	take **in**	take **out**
take **away**	take **off**	take **up**
turn **on**	turn **off**	turn **around**

- Let's *drive **through*** the ***drive-through*** window.

- Don't *look **down*** on that employee; you might have to *look **up*** to him some day.

- This is our ***take-out*** menu that you can *take **out*** with you.

- They *found **out*** that they could stay a few days longer.

- If you think they *ripped* you ***off***, that deal is a ***rip-off*** to you.

- I will *look **around*** here to see if I can find a spot for our picnic.

- She *broke **down*** into tears when her dog recognized her and *ran **up*** to her.

- The celebrity couple *broke **up*** their 15-year relationship.

- We are going in the wrong direction: We need to *turn **around*** and *go **back***.

- *Hurry **up***. We need to *get **up***, *get **in****to our car, and *go **away*** from this place.

- She *broke **out*** with a rash all over her body.

3. Three-word phrasal verbs with the stress on the first preposition

add **up** to

come **down** with

cut **back** on

get **away** with

get **around** to

look **for**ward to

look **up** to

come **up** with

made **up** of

do **away** with

get **back** into

grow **out** of

look **out** for

put **up** with

- We cannot completely *do **away** with* our weekend duties.
- We need to *cut **back** on* our expenses.
- I will take a look at it again when I can *get **around** to* it.
- He *grew **out** of* his first blue jeans.
- The rebels decided they could not *put **up** with* their dictator anymore.
- No, I am sorry, but you cannot *get **away** with* it.
- The bill *added **up** to* $50 dollars.
- He thinks he has *come **down** with* the flu.
- I *came **up** with* an idea that might work for us.
- A compound noun is *made **up** of* two or more different nouns.

Notes: ....

....

....

....

....

....

....

....

D. Emphasis "dialogues"

Explore emphasis in the following *dialogues*. Stress the words that are especially important and that need to be emphasized according to the situations, contexts, and speaker's intention. The *stressed* words are <u>underlined</u> and the stressed *syllables* are **bold** font. Divide long sentences into manageable shorter phrases if that is helpful.

Dialogue I	*Lunch with Grace*

Nina: Are you having lunch with <u>**Grace**</u> today?

Harry: I <u>called</u> Grace but she sent me a <u>text **me**</u>ssage <u>**say**</u>ing that she <u>**can**not</u> have <u>**lunch**</u> with me today. I didn't know <u>where</u> she was. She was at <u>work</u>, but she was not <u>at</u> work, I guess.

Dialogue II	*Venus and Mars*

Venus: My <u>car</u> doesn't want to <u>start</u>.

Mars: <u>**Real**ly</u>? I wonder whether it has a <u>low **bat**tery</u>. Did you try to <u>turn on</u> and <u>off</u> the lights?

Venus: It <u>worked</u> until <u>**yes**terday</u>. I don't know <u>why</u> it <u>**sud**denly</u> <u>won't</u> <u>start</u>.

Mars It's a <u>**se**rious **prob**lem</u> if it's an <u>**en**gine</u> problem. But <u>first</u>, <u>check</u> the <u>**bat**tery</u>. Did you check the <u>lights</u>?

Venus: What am I going to <u>do</u>? I have an <u>ap**point**ment</u> and I gotta have the <u>car</u>.

Mars: I <u>know</u>. Calm down. Were you able to <u>turn on</u> the <u>lights</u>?

Venus: Ohhhhh Myyyyy, it <u>**def**initely</u> was <u>all</u> <u>right</u> <u>**yes**terday</u>!

Mars: I <u>hear</u> you. <u>But</u> did the <u>lights</u> work <u>all</u> <u>right</u> <u>**yes**terday</u>?

Venus: <u>Why</u>?

Mars: Uhmmm, if the <u>lights</u> didn't <u>work</u>, it could <u>**in**dicate</u> a <u>low</u> <u>**bat**tery</u>.

Venus: So <u>what</u> are you trying to <u>say</u>?

Mars: Just that it could be a <u>**bat**tery</u> <u>**prob**lem</u>. I'm <u>**tell**ing</u> you. You should <u>check</u> that.

Venus:	Are you <u>mad</u> at me now?
Mars:	<u>No</u>, I am <u>not mad</u>. <u>Try</u> it.
Venus:	You <u>sound</u> angry. <u>What</u> did I do <u>wrong</u>?
Mars:	You **didn't** do anything wrong. It's <u>ok</u>. Go ahead and <u>try</u> it.
Venus:	<u>What</u>'s OK?"
Mars:	I am **tr<u>y</u>ing** to tell you about the **battery**.
Venus:	<u>Who</u> said the <u>car</u> is the <u>im**por**tan</u>t <u>issue</u> <u>right</u> <u>now</u>?
	(Translated from an unknown source.)

Dialogue III	*Summer Intensive Classes*
Jenny:	So, you **finished** the <u>Inten</u>sive?
Masako:	Yeah, **al**<u>most</u>.
Jenny:	You <u>don't look</u> like someone who just <u>survived</u> a <u>cram</u> **graduate** course in a month. You look <u>re**fresh**ed</u>.
Masako:	I just had the **final** **exam** **yes**terday for this <u>one</u> course.
Jenny:	Ah, <u>that's</u> the **rea**son. I'll <u>bet</u> you are **relieved**!
Masako:	I **sure** am, but I <u>still</u> have a **take**-home exam to **finish**.
Jenny:	You had a **final** exam, and a **take**-home exam, too?
Masako:	<u>Yeah</u>. I was taking <u>two</u> classes.
Jenny:	<u>Two classes</u> in a <u>month</u>, while working at a full-time job? I don't know how you did it.
Masako:	<u>I</u> don't know how I did it **either**. I had to <u>work</u> for <u>eight</u> hours at my <u>job</u>, and <u>then</u> took **classes** for <u>four</u> hours a day.
Jenny:	And you had to **study** for your **classes** and do your **homework** assignments <u>after</u> that!?

| Masako: | Yes, I had to **study** and do <u>assignments</u> for the classes, which left very little <u>time</u> for <u>sleep</u>. |

| Jenny: | Oh, my…. But you <u>don't</u> look <u>tired</u> at <u>all</u>. You look so <u>refre</u>shed!. |

| Masako: | <u>Thank</u> you. I <u>feel</u> very <u>well</u> **physically** and feel pretty <u>good</u> about <u>my**self**</u>, in <u>fact</u>. |

Dialogue IV   *At the Bank*

| Clerk: | Hi, how may I <u>help</u> you? |

| June: | Well, I have a <u>few</u> <u>items</u> that you might be able to <u>help</u> <u>me</u> with. |

| Clerk: | OK. <u>What</u> are <u>those</u>? |

| June: | <u>First</u> of all, on my **state**ment, I **noticed** that the <u>bank</u> <u>charged</u> a <u>ten</u> **do**llar <u>ser</u>vice <u>fee</u> to my **Money Market account**. So I came to see **Cus**tomer **Ser**vice a few <u>days</u> ago. And the **lady** who was sitting at <u>that</u> desk <u>told</u> me that because my **balance** was **below** a certain **amount**, they <u>charged</u> the fee. I <u>understood</u>. But it would take <u>several</u> <u>months</u> for me to **accu**mulate the <u>required</u> **balance**, so I <u>asked</u> her to <u>close</u> the **account**. She said she <u>would</u>. And the **money** from that **account** was <u>depo</u>sited to my **check**ing account. <u>However</u>, **yester**day, I **noticed** that my **Money** Market account had some **activity**, which I did <u>not</u> **expect**. I would like to <u>know</u> what is **going** <u>on</u>. |

| Clerk: | I <u>see</u>. <u>Let</u> me <u>check</u> your account now. OK. **Apparently**, your account is <u>not</u> closed at this <u>point</u>. So, let me **really** <u>close</u> it for you now. <u>OK</u>. <u>Now</u> it is **really** closed, and I will <u>print</u> out the **clo**sing **sta**tement for you. <u>Here</u> it <u>is</u>! Thanks. This does <u>not</u> show the <u>depo</u>sit amount but shows the **result** of that <u>deposit</u> as you can <u>see</u>. |

| June: | <u>Yes</u>, I <u>see</u> it. <u>Thank</u> you very <u>much</u>. |

| Clerk: | You are **wel**come. Do you have <u>another</u> issue? |

| June: | I <u>know</u> that our **cur**rent bank is <u>incor</u>porated into the <u>new bank</u>, I have been reading the <u>information</u> about it and <u>figured out</u> that since I have <u>already</u> <u>logged</u> <u>myself</u> into the <u>new bank</u>, at <u>this point</u>, I <u>don't</u> have to take any <u>other action</u>, <u>right</u>? |

| Clerk: | <u>Right</u>, **unless** you pay bills <u>online</u>. |

June:	We <u>do</u> pay our bills online.
Clerk:	Since we are moving <u>all</u> our **ban**king systems to the new bank this **week**end, and the <u>new</u> bank has a **different online** bill **pay**ment **op**tion, if you <u>pay</u> the <u>bill</u> <u>online</u> <u>this</u> **week**end, your <u>bill</u> payment might be <u>lost</u> or **rou**ted incor**rec**tly. So, <u>wait</u> until <u>next</u> week to pay any bills.
June:	<u>Next</u> week meaning from next **Monday**?
Clerk:	<u>Right</u>.
June:	<u>Got</u> you. Now here is my **final** question. Since I <u>don't</u> <u>deposit</u> money to my **Money Market account** any**more**, and since the **interest** rates at the bank are <u>so</u> <u>low</u>, I am thinking of in**ves**ting my **mo**ney in something <u>else</u>. Do you have any **program** in your <u>new</u> bank where I can <u>deposit</u> a **certain** <u>amount</u> of **money** <u>regularly</u> to invest in <u>stocks</u> or **mutual** funds?
Clerk:	We sure <u>do</u>. In <u>fact</u>, I am doing the <u>same</u> <u>thing</u> you are **talking** about. <u>Once</u> our bank **finishes** **moving** the **bank**ing business to the <u>new</u> <u>bank</u>, I should be able to <u>help</u> you with it. So <u>come</u> sometime after <u>next</u> week and let's <u>talk</u> about it.
June:	You have **an**swered <u>all</u> my **ques**tions. <u>Thank</u> you very <u>much</u>. Have a <u>good</u> <u>day</u>.
Clerk:	Thank <u>you</u>. You have a good day, <u>too</u>. <u>Bye</u>.

Dialogue V	*Boneless Chicken Wings*
Server:	Hi <u>my</u> name is **Les**lie. Would you like to order something to <u>drink</u> first?
Lisa:	Yes, I would like to have some **water** with only a <u>few</u> <u>cubes</u> of <u>ice</u>, please.
Larry:	Do you have **un**sweetened <u>iced</u> <u>tea</u>?
Server:	Yes, we <u>do</u>. (Disappears into the kitchen).
Lisa:	(Looking at the menu) Well, <u>what</u> to eat for lunch today! Hmm… the **Boneless Chicken Wings** sound good. It comes with **Buffalo wing** sauce or **honey-mus**tard. 8 pieces for $<u>9.95</u>. I will order <u>this</u> one.
Larry:	Let me see. The <u>Grilled Tilapia</u> with **lemon** and **pepper** sounds good.

297

Server: (Comes back with the **water** and iced tea). Here you go—water and **un**sweetened iced tea. Are you guys **rea**dy to order your food or do you need more time to think?

Lisa: I'm ready. I'd like to have the **Boneless Chicken Wings**. Do you have more **cho**ices for the sauce?

Server: Yes, we have sweet and **spic**y sauce as well.

Lisa: That sounds good. I will take that.

Larry: I'd like to have the Grilled Tilapia, please.

Server: All right. Anything else?

Lisa: That's all.

            *(The Server disappears to the kitchen. Lisa and Larry have been waiting for a long time, an **unusually** long time.)*

Lisa: I wonder what is taking so long. They **should'**ve had my kind of food already fried, and all they have to do is to **reheat** them and pour the sauce over. It **shouldn't** take this long.

Larry: Maybe the **chickens** are not hatched yet. This is the "**slow**est" fast-food restaurant, ha, ha, ha.

            (After a while, the Server brings the food to the table.)

Server: Here you go, the **Boneless Chicken Wings** for you, and the Grilled Tilapia for you.

Lisa: Oh, they look so good.

Larry: Thank you.

            (The Server disappears once more into the kitchen.)

Lisa: (Bites a piece of "Boneless Chicken Wing" with anticipation) Oh, no! These are not chicken wings. This is breast meat. **Actually,** chicken **nu**ggets coated with sauce.

Larry: It **sure is**.

            (The Server approaches Lisa and Larry's table again.)

Server:	How's everything? Do you need anything else?
Lisa:	Good, except I **ordered Boneless Chicken Wings**, but these are not wings.
Server:	Yes, they are wings.
Lisa:	No, they are not wings. You can see this is breast meat. These are, in fact, chicken **nuggets** coated with sauce.
Server:	Sorry, they are chicken wings. I am sorry--they are.
Lisa:	I don't mean to be **difficult**, but these are not chicken wings. I ordered **bone**less chicken wings for its particular taste, not the breast.
Server:	I am **sorry**, but they are our chicken wings.
	(Server disappears into the kitchen again)
Lisa:	Larry, do you think I was being **difficult**?
Larry:	Well, they are **bone**less, but they are not chicken wings. I guess, in this case, **servers** tend to feel that they are being personally attacked.
Lisa:	I **understand** what you're **saying**, but I did not mean to be a **problem**. How's your **Lemon-pepper tilapia**, by the way?
	(Months after this incident, Lisa and Larry are in another restaurant.)
Lisa:	(Reading the menu) OH MY!
Larry:	What?
Lisa:	They have **Boneless Buffalo Wings**, too. But, **listen** to the description: **Boneless Buffalo Wings, hand**-breaded all white meat **chicken** tossed in your choice of mild or hot sauce and served with **celery** and blue cheese dressing." So, the boneless chicken wing IS white meat! I gave that poor **server** a hard time for nothing.
Larry:	Yeah, we were not **educated** then, but now we know better. You know what? **Buffaloes** don't have wings either.

Carryover into everyday life: You have explored linking consonants, which led to linking of words in phrases and sentences, adding fluidity to your speech. Adding up or down inflection and using word stress helps to carry meaning and intent to your listener. Choose a time today to converse with someone you know, focusing on the skills you discovered in this chapter.

Chapter 7

Thought Groups

Dialogue:	*Dividing Long Sentences into Meaningful phrases*
Mika:	I feel much more comfortable pronouncing GA English words in short sentences or paragraphs. But I am not quite confident in reading or speaking in longer sentences or paragraphs. Can you tell me how I can increase my confidence while speaking or reading longer sentences or phrases clearly?
Jonghee:	When GA English speakers express their thoughts in speech, they usually divide long sentences into phrases or thought-groups[62] to deliver their thoughts to the listener as they intended.
Mika:	Do they divide their speech consciously?
Jonghee:	Consciously and unconsciously.
Mika:	Sometimes, when the sentences are long and complex, and loaded with unfamiliar context and vocabulary, I get lost. I cannot understand what I am reading about. And I know when that takes place, my listeners cannot grasp what I am reading or speaking about.
Jonghee:	I understand.
Mika:	When the sentences are very long, at times, I cannot decide where I should pause in phrases; whether a certain word should go at the end of one phrase or move to the beginning of the next phrase.
Jonghee:	I realize that there are many things to overcome in order to use the English language like First language speakers when we are conversing. To make the long sentences clearly understood, we need to create uniquely GA English intonation patterns by keeping the following tips in mind:

1. First, divide long sentences into manageable thought groups (phrases).

2. Identify important words in each group.

3. Out of the important words, identify at least ONE most important word.

4. Identify the primary stress in the important word (= stressed word)

5. Pronounce the primary stress of the stressed words stronger, longer, and "higher in pitch"

In this chapter we are going to review what you might have already learned: how to divide long sentences into manageable phrases (thought groups).

---

[62] https://tfcs.baruch.cuny.edu/thought-groups/ Definition of Thought Group, August 10, 2021

Thought grouping (Phrasing)

Many students have already learned how to divide long sentences of English—when they translated English into their own first languages in their early education. So, this concept is not a new one, but one that needs more focus at this point for better communicating in GA English.

Ex. 1   In the following, familiarize yourself with the sense of thought grouping (phrasing) according to the grammatical structures of the sentences.

Grammatical Functions	Examples
Noun phrases (noun + modifiers)	my major; medical sociology; specialized field; United States; social causes and consequences; health and illness; application of sociological theory; research methods; healthcare system
Verb phrases (verb + modifiers)	was established; is concerned; related to; are included; include the social facets of health and disease; take place; are important; would consider; are employed; would like to apply; love teaching
Relative clauses	what I study is; which is related to health; that are concerned; which include the social facets of health and disease; which social factors are at play
Prepositional phrases	in that discipline; as a specialized field; in the United States; during the 1940s; with the social causes; of health and illness; with the application of theory; at the community; to other systems

Notes: ....

....

....

....

302

Ex. 2	Explore Thought Grouping in the following *dialogue*. Thought groups are marked by slash lines and the stressed syllables are marked by **bold** fonts.

Yue: What is your **ma**jor?

Connie: My major is **Medical Sociology**.

Yue: What is **me**dical sociology, /and what do you **study/ in** that **dis**cipline?

Connie: **Me**dical sociology was established/ as a **specialized** field/ in the United **Sta**tes/ during the 19**40s**. /It is concerned with the **so**cial **cau**ses and **con**sequences of health and illness, / and with the **appli**cation of sociological **the**ory/ and **re**search methods to the **stu**dy/ related to **heal**th and the health care **sys**tem.

Yue: I see. / What **sorts** of **a**reas are in**clu**ded/ in medical sociology?

Connie: The **ma**jor areas of **me**dical sociology include the **so**cial facets of **heal**th and disease,/ the **so**cial behavior of **health** care person**nel** /and their **cli**ents, /the **so**cial **func**tions of **health** or**ga**nizations and institutions,/ the **so**cial patterns of **heal**th services,/ and the relationship of **health** care delivery systems to **o**ther systems /such as e**co**nomy and po**li**tics.

Yue: For **such stu**dies, /what sorts of as**sum**ptions take place?

Connie: **Me**dical sociology as**sumes** that **so**cial factors,/ such as **so**cial economic **status,/ gen**der, /**eth**nicity,/ **life**styles/, and **high**-risk be**ha**vior,/ play a **cri**tical **role** in deter**mi**ning/ or **in**fluencing the **health** of indi**vi**duals, groups, and **lar**ger so**cie**ties. Social factors are **al**so im**por**tant in **in**fluencing the **man**ner/ in which so**cie**ties **or**ganize their re**sour**ces/ to **cope** with **health ha**zards/ and deliver **me**dical care/ to the **popu**lation at **large**.

Yue: So what sorts of **job** opportunities would you consider upon graduation?

Connie: Since **Medical Sociology** has an applied **fo**cus/with **re**levance for **po**licy/ and **health** service delivery at the com**mu**nity, /**re**gional, /so**cie**tal, /and **glo**bal levels, / **gra**duates from **me**dical sociology hold **tea**ching positions/ not **on**ly in sociology departments, /but **al**so in **pub**lic health, / **me**dical, /and **nur**sing schools. In ad**di**tion, they are em**ployed** as re**sear**chers in **pub**lic and **pri**vate **health a**gencies /and in **health**-related **in**dustries/ such as insurance, /and **hos**pital **ma**nagement **com**panies. /I love **tea**ching as well as **re**search,/ so I would like to apply for **tea**ching positions /in uni**ver**sities in the **fu**ture.

Yue: **Thank** you for **shar**ing this **in**fo with me, /and I **wish** you the **best** for your pro**fes**sional ende**a**vors.

(Adapted from Yue Cao, Graduate Student, Department of Sociology, University of Alabama at Birmingham)

Ex. 3   Explore thought-grouping in the following passage. Add *slash lines* if you need them to take a breath or a pause. The first paragraph is slashed for you.

I started learning English in my country /when I was twelve./ At first,/ I learned to speak and write the names of the English alphabet letters/ and then continued to learn simple vocabulary/, grammar,/ and sentence structures./ By the time I finished learning greetings/ such as 'good morning'/ 'good afternoon,'/ 'good evening,'/ and 'how are you?'/ I thought I was ready to conquer the world,/ but soon found out that there were a lot more complicated things to learn. /

As we delved deeper into the language, we had to memorize many vocabulary items and learn complex grammar and sentence structures by spending most of our class time reading and translating English texts into our own language. When we read English texts out loud in class, our teachers encouraged us to read each word correctly, but we did not have any place to use English outside the classroom.

So, I studied English conversation on my own by listening and repeating after the speakers in audio tapes, CDs, and English broadcasting, but I could not really tell whether I was mimicking them correctly or not. No one really showed me or explained to me clearly how to pronounce the sounds of English vowels and consonants correctly, how English-speaking people might recognize through sensation how different sounds were made, and no one was there to give me much needed feedback.

After arriving in the United States, I found that I could not understand what Americans were saying, and they could not understand me either, and this issue or problem still haunts me at times. I accept the fact that I don't speak English like Americans do, but what bothers me is that I cannot figure out exactly what I do differently. And because I don't know what IS different, I cannot adapt my English speaking. This impacts my performance and confidence, and maybe eventually my professional advancement.

I sure would like to see a day when my General American English speaking reflects my professional qualifications and I have the choice to communicate fully with complete confidence and ease with everyone I encounter.

Carryover into your everyday life: Look at all the skills and strategies you are acquiring as you progress through this manual! To continue to grow, focus on one or two aspects a day—such as 'today I want to focus on exploring my consonants and vowels' (or my intonation, my thought grouping, or linking my words together, etc.). It is your choice as to how you want to use your skills to gain greater confidence in speaking GA English. In our next chapter, we'll put it all together.

Chapter 8

Putting It All Together

Dialogue:	*Connecting Your Speaking to Emotional Expression*
Chun:	I really have learned so much in this class.
Jonghee:	I'm glad! So, can you share what you learned from all these lessons?
Chun:	First, I've learned that I have acquired so many options that enable me to speak GA English more clearly.
Jonghee:	To speak *vowels* clearly, what do we need to know?
Chun:	We need to use the *optimal shapes and sizes* for each vowel, and we can achieve this by sensing the different shapes and sizes of the Structural Energy Vowels.
Jonghee:	What do we need to do for consonant clarity?
Chun:	We need to feel, sense, and recognize *the movement of the articulating system*--the tongue, lips, the ceiling of our mouths (soft and hard palates), throat, facial muscles, etc. and *the points of contact* that create the friction, impedance, or obstruction that defines a consonant.
Jonghee:	So those are reminders as to how to create individual GA English sounds. What else do we need for clear speech?
Chun:	The ideal *intonation patterns*, knowing how and why to emphasize certain words as I speak.
Jonghee:	What are the elements of the ideal intonation patterns? How do you know which words to emphasize?
Chun:	We need to know where to divide long sentences by dividing them into *Optimal Thought Groups*. Then we emphasize the *primary stress* of our important words within each Thought Group by raising the pitch, or by lengthening the word. Then we connect nearby words and sounds for more smoothly flowing speech.
Jonghee:	Yes. When these strategies become more comfortable for us, it will be easier to communicate, people will understand us better, and we will be able to express our feelings as well.
Chun:	Do you mean that someday I won't have to think about all of this as I speak?

Jonghee: Absolutely. It will take time and awareness on your part, but soon you will feel as if you can use all these skills and possess a more expressive voice which shares with the world around you how you are feeling and what you are thinking.

Chun: How do I get to that point? That sounds like just what I want!

Jonghee: Well, let's experiment....

Notes: ....
....
....
....
....
....
....
....
....
....
....
....
....
....
....
....
....
....
....

When speaking becomes sharing

Perhaps when you first encountered English, it was taught as an academic subject rather than something with which you could communicate. Now, as you have worked through this training manual, you are discovering that by using the tools that you have been exploring, you are acquiring choices, not just for the broad strokes of speaking GA English, but discovering the subtleties of expression as well within context. Now it is time to 'put it all together'.

Often, when someone is learning to speak another language, there is a period of time in which the language learner is actively translating in his or her head—not just what is heard, but what response he or she should make. It will take time to make the transition to speaking without that translation. An individual has to be patient with the process—it will come.

In the meantime, all the skills that have been explored in the journey we have taken through this 'workshop' can be used to acquire clearer language and a more 'GA' musicality in your voice when you so choose. Each chapter is meant to help the student of GA English learn skills cumulatively—so that by now, those skills are ready to assist you as you live your life day by day, whether you are in a professional situation or interacting with friends and family. It is never a question of reducing an accent you may already possess but adding the GA accent to your already prodigious storehouse of language skills.

Once you have gone through each chapter repeatedly until you feel you have gained more confidence in the skills each gives you, the final hurdle is to use those skills in conversation—not just focus on 'exercises' in a book, but actively using each skill as you speak within context and with conscious choice. You have experienced the *feel* of the sensations associated with each vowel and consonant in GA English, learned how to change your pitch depending on whether a syllable or word is more important, or lengthened or strengthened a syllable or vowel or consonant, so that some words stand out more than others. This gives life to speech, and *vocal life*[63] to your communication. Using all these skills gives you the confidence and freedom to speak GA English.

Notes: ....

....

....

....

....

....

---

[63] 'Vocal Life' is a term used by Arthur Lessac in *The Use and Training of the Human Voice: A Bio-Dynamic Approach to Vocal Life, Third Edition* ©1997 McGraw Higher Education Publishing, pg. ix

So, let's experiment with becoming more expressive in conversational contexts, using some of the dialogue examples found in earlier chapters.

Experiment 1: If you have someone with whom you can share the dialogues below, it will be enjoyable to choose either Christy or Yumiko, and then switch so that you can play the other. In this dialogue below—

1. Go through your role's 'lines' (sentences) and focus on playing <u>consonants</u> like you have learned to make sure that you are clear and intelligible.

2. Repeat from the beginning, this time focusing on the <u>vowels</u> with their distinct shapes and sizes.

3. Start at the beginning again and link all the syllables and words together.

4. Repeat from the beginning again, this time turning your attention to <u>word and sentence stress.</u> Find the thought phrases and group them together. Remember to use pitch variety for those stressed/emphasized words or syllables.

5. Repeat one more time from the beginning—and just enjoy the <u>conversation</u> by communicating with your partner. *Really* ask the question, exclaim if there is an exclamation point, get excited, mean what you say.

6. If you are alone, or just want to do this by yourself, play both C and Y, alternating between the lines, using the same steps above.

In these dialogues the <u>underlined</u> words will need stress/emphasis, and the stressed syllables will be in **bold** font once again.

Dialogue I   *Summer Intensive Classes*

Christy: So, you **fin**ished the Summer <u>**Inten**sive Course</u>!

Yumiko: Yeah, <u>al**most**</u>.

Christy :   You <u>don't</u> <u>look</u> like someone who just <u>survived</u> a <u>cram</u> <u>**grad**uate</u> course in a <u>month</u>.

Yumiko: I just had the <u>**final**</u> <u>**exam**</u> <u>**yes**terday</u> for this <u>one</u> course.

309

Christy: Ah, that's the **rea**son. I bet you are relieved!

Yumiko :   I sure am, but I still have a take-home exam to **fi**nish.

Christy :   You had a **final** exam, and a take-home exam, too?

Yumiko: Yeah. I was taking two classes.

Christy :   Two classes in a month, while working at a full-time job? I don't know how you did it.

Yumiko: I don't know how I did it **either**. I had to work for eight hours at my job, and then took **cla**sses for four hours a day.

Christy :   And you had to **study** for your **classes** and do your **home**work assignments after that!?

Yumiko: Yeah, I had to **study** and do assignments for the classes, which left **very** little time for sleep.

Christy :   Oh, my…. But you don't look tired at all. You look so **refre**shed!

Yumiko: Thank you. I feel very well **phy**sically, and feel pretty good about myself, in fact.

Notes:..

....

....

....

....

....

....

....

....

....

....

Experiment 2:   A different scenario—a more professional, business-like conversation. Once again, if you have a partner, divide the scene between you. Read through your role's 'lines' (sentences) focus on playing <u>consonants</u> like you have learned to make sure that you are clear and intelligible. (If you are doing this alone, you can take both roles.)

1. Repeat from the beginning, this time focusing on the <u>vowels</u> with their distinct shapes and sizes.

2. Once again, <u>link</u> all the words and syllables throughout the dialogue.

3. Then, find the <u>thought phrases</u> and group them together.

4. Repeat from the beginning again, this time turning your attention to <u>word and sentence stress.</u> And again, remember to use pitch variety for those stressed/emphasized words or syllables.

5. Repeat one more time from the beginning—and <u>communicate</u> with your partner, either as the banker or as the customer. This time there will be no exclamation points or excited conversation, instead try using a more 'matter of fact' tone and this time your intention is to get or provide answers.

Dialogue II   *At the Bank*

Clerk: Hi, how may I <u>help</u> you?

Customer: Well, I have a <u>few</u> <u>items</u> that you might be able to <u>help</u> me with.

Clerk: OK. <u>What</u> are <u>those</u>?

Customer: <u>First</u> of all, on my **statement**, I **noticed** that the <u>bank</u> <u>charged</u> a <u>ten-dollar</u> <u>ser</u>vice fee to my **Money** Market account. So, I came to see **Customer** Service a <u>few</u> <u>days</u> ago. And the <u>lady</u> who was sitting at the <u>desk</u> over <u>there</u> told me that because my <u>ba</u>**lance** was <u>below</u> a certain **amount**, they charged the <u>fee</u>. I <u>understood</u>. But it would take **several** **mon**ths for me to **accu**mulate the <u>required</u> **balance**, so I <u>asked</u> her to <u>close</u> the account. She <u>said</u> she <u>would</u>. And the **money** from that <u>account</u> was <u>deposited</u> to my **check**ing account. <u>However</u>, <u>yesterday</u>, I <u>noticed</u> that my **Money** Market account had some <u>activity</u>, which I did <u>not</u> **expect**. I would like to <u>know</u> what is going <u>on</u>.

311

Clerk:	I see. Let me check your account now. All right. Apparently, your account is not closed at this point. So, let me really close it for you now. OK. Now it is **REALLY** closed, and I will print out the **clo**sing **sta**tement for you. Here it is. This does not show the deposit amount but shows the result of that deposit as you can see.
Customer:	Yes, I see it. Thank you very much.
Clerk:	You are welcome. Do you have another issue?
Customer:	Since we learned that our **cur**rent bank is incorporated into the new bank, I have been reading information about it and figured out that since I have already logged myself into the new bank, at this point, I don't have to take any other action, right?
Clerk:	Right, unless you pay bills online.
Customer:	We do pay our bills online.
Clerk:	Since we are moving all our **ban**king systems to the new bank this weekend, and the new bank has a different online bill payment option, if you pay the bill online this weekend, your bill payment might be lost or routed incorrectly. So, wait until next week to pay any bills.
Customer:	Next week means next **Monday**?
Clerk:	Right.
Customer:	All right. Now here is my final question. Since I don't deposit money to my Money Market account anymore, and since the interest rates at the bank are so low, I am thinking of investing my money in something else. Do you have any program in your new bank where I can deposit a certain amount of money regularly to invest in stocks or mutual funds?
Clerk:	We sure do. In fact, I am doing the same thing you are talking about. Once our bank finishes moving the banking business to the new bank, I should be able to help you with it. So, come sometime after next week and let's talk about it.
Customer:	You have answered all my questions. Thank you very much. Have a good day.
Clerk:	Thank you. Have a good day, too. Bye.

Experiment 3:   This third *scenario* contains three characters, a husband and wife, (or two good friends) and the Server of a restaurant. Each person has a different attitude and personality. Their names can be changed if you and your scene partners wish.

1. Once again, if you have a partner or there are three of you, divide the scene among you. Read through your role's 'lines' (sentences) and focus on playing <u>consonants</u> like you have learned to make sure that you are clear and intelligible. (If you are doing this alone, you can take all three roles.)

2. Repeat from the beginning, this time focusing on the <u>vowels</u> with their distinct shapes and sizes.

3. Repeat from the beginning, focusing on linking all the <u>syllables</u> and <u>words</u> together.

4. Repeat from the beginning again, this time turning your attention to <u>word and sentence stress.</u> Discover the thought phrases. And again, remember to use <u>pitch variety</u> for those stressed/emphasized words or syllables.

5. Repeat one more time from the beginning—and <u>communicate</u> with your partner(s). Try to place yourself in an imaginary restaurant. If you are playing Lisa, she has an attitude that develops as you go deeper into the scene. What is that attitude? How can your voice and body reflect and communicate that attitude shift along the way? What about Larry? Does he try to make light of the situation, does he commiserate with Lisa? What about the Server? How can your voice communicate anxiety or frustration? Have fun playing with the real-life scenario. Pretend that you are not just reading, but really talking with each other.

6. Switch roles to focus on different lines if you have partners.

Dialogue III   *Boneless Chicken Wings*

Server: Hi <u>my</u> name is **Les**lie. Would you like to order something to <u>drink</u> first?

Lisa: Yes, I would like to have some **wa**ter with only a <u>few</u> <u>cubes</u> of <u>ice</u>, please.

Larry: Do you have **un**sweetened <u>iced</u> <u>tea</u>?

Server: Yes, we <u>do</u>. *(Disappears into the kitchen).*

Lisa:	(*Looking at the menu*) Well, <u>what</u> to eat for lunch today! Hmm…the **Bone**less **Chi**cken Wings sounds good. It comes with **Bu**ffalo <u>wing</u> sauce or **honey-mus**tard. 8 pieces for $<u>9.95</u>. I will order <u>this</u> one.
Larry:	Let me see… The <u>Grilled Tilapia</u> with <u>le</u>mon and **pepper** sounds good.
Server:	(*Comes back with the water and iced tea*). Here you go—**wat**er and **un**sweetened iced tea. Are you guys **rea**<u>dy</u> to order your <u>food</u> or do you need more time to <u>think</u>?
Lisa:	I'm ready. I'd like to have the **Bone**less **Chi**cken <u>Wings</u>. Do you have more **cho**ices for the <u>sauce?</u>
Server:	Yes, we have <u>sweet</u> and **spicy** sauce as <u>well</u>.
Lisa:	That sounds <u>good</u>. I will take <u>that</u>.
Larry:	I'd like to have the <u>Grilled Tilapia</u>, please.
Server:	All right. Anything <u>else</u>?
Lisa:	That's <u>all</u>.
	(*The Server disappears into the kitchen. Lisa and Larry have been waiting for a long time, an <u>unusually</u> long time.*)
Lisa:	I wonder what is taking <u>so</u> <u>long</u>. They **should'**ve had <u>my</u> kind of food already **fried**, and <u>all</u> they have to <u>do</u> is to **reheat** them and <u>pour</u> the <u>sauce</u> over. It **shouldn't** take <u>this</u> long.
Larry:	Maybe the **chickens** are <u>not</u> <u>hatched</u> yet. This is the "**slow**est" <u>fast</u>-food restaurant, ha, ha, ha.
	(*After a while, the Server brings the food to the table.*)
Server:	Here you go, the **Bone**less **Chi**cken <u>Wings</u> for you, and the <u>Grilled Tilapia</u> for <u>you</u>.
Lisa:	Oh, they look <u>so</u> good.
Larry:	Thank you.
	(*The Server disappears once more into the kitchen.*)

Lisa:	(Bites a piece of "Boneless Chicken Wing" with anticipation) Oh, no! These are not chicken wings. This is breast meat. Actually, **chicken nuggets** coated with sauce.
Larry:	It **sure is**.

(The Server approaches Lisa and Larry's table again.)

Server:	How's everything? Do you need anything else?
Lisa:	Good, except I **ordered Boneless Chicken Wings**, but these are not wings.
Server:	Yes, they are wings.
Lisa:	No, they are not wings. You can see this is breast meat. These are, in fact, chicken **nuggets** coated with sauce.
Server:	Sorry, they are chicken wings. I am **sorry**--they are.
Lisa:	I don't mean to be **difficult**, but these are not chicken wings. I ordered **bone**less chicken wings for its particular taste, not the breast.
Server:	I am **sorry**, but they are our chicken wings.

(Server disappears into the kitchen again)

Lisa:	Larry, do you think I was being **difficult**?
Larry:	Well, they are **boneless**, but they are not **chicken wings**. I guess, in this case, **servers** tend to feel that they are being personally attacked.
Lisa:	I **understand** what you're **saying**, but I did not mean to be a **problem**. How's your **Lemon-pepper tilapia**, by the way?

(Months later after this incident, Lisa and Larry are in another restaurant.)

Lisa:	(Reading the menu) OH MY!
Larry:	What?
Lisa:	They have **Boneless Buffalo Wings**, too. But, listen to the description: **Boneless Buffalo Wings**, hand-breaded all white meat **chicken** tossed in your choice of mild or hot sauce and served with celery and blue cheese dressing." So, the boneless chicken wing IS white meat! I gave that poor **server** a hard time for nothing.

Larry: Yeah, we were <u>not</u> **educated** <u>then</u>, but <u>now</u> we <u>know</u> better. You know what? **Buffaloes** <u>don't</u> have <u>wings</u> <u>either</u>.

Final Dialogue: Feeling positive about my journey....

Sunny: I feel positive about my GA English now. I no longer fear speaking English in public, and I possess many strategies learned in this class. I will continue to explore them in my communication. Thank you, Jonghee!

Jonghee: It is I who want to thank you, Sunny, for your willingness to experiment with each of them. Don't be a stranger. Come back and visit and meanwhile—enjoy what you've learned…and keep experimenting!

Sunny: I certainly will.

Conclusion

Now that you have taken your skill level into real-life situations through these scenarios, it won't be a difficult leap to carry what you have acquired into your own daily life—whether in a professional, collegial, or business setting, or just sitting around the kitchen table having conversations with friends and family. However, it is always your choice to make these shifts within the context of your communication. The more you engage with what you have learned from this 'workshop', the more success you will have. The more success you enjoy, the more you may want the option to employ all the strategies introduced in this book as you communicate with others. Your consonant skill will make the words more distinctive, so your communication will be clearer to your colleagues and friends. Your recognition of how GA English vowels and diphthongs are produced will do the same and will carry melody and expression. Your linking of syllables and words will make your GA English flow smoothly and fluently. Your use of word and sentence stress will provide musical inflection and continuity to your thought phrases. All of these options will vary in usage depending on context. It all works together, nothing stands alone.

You will always have a unique sound to your voice and speech, which is something to celebrate. But with continued awareness and growth from this point onward, your skills will blossom, and you may acquire a more GA English sound *if that is what you want.* Your speech will become clearer to your listener, whether that consists of one person or a large group, which will increase your confidence.

Thank you for taking this journey with us. We wish you every success.

References

Archibald Opie, I., Oxford Dictionary of Nursery Rhymes 1951 Clarendon Press, Rub-a-Dub-Dub, August 3, 2021

Black Spiritual (African American), American Folk Song, early 1900s, When the Saints Go Marching In, copyright: Public Domain

Blesing, A. Illustration: 2020 based on an original illustration Laubach Literacy International 1989 https://library.syr.edu/digital/guides/l/laubach_lit.htm August 6, 2021

Cao, Y, Graduate Student, Department of Sociology, University of Alabama, Birmingham, adapted from an essay

Chen, J. Graduate Student, Department of Chemistry, University of Alabama, Birmingham, adapted from an essay

Curry, C. M., Clippinger, E. E. Children's Literature, *A Textbook of Sources for Teachers-Training Classes*, Peter Piper, English Nursery Rhyme 1920

https://fablesofaesop.com/the-ant-and-the-grasshopper.html Fables of Aesop August 8, 2021

https://educationdata.org/international-student-enrollment-statistics August 3, 2021

https://en.wikipedia.org/wiki/First_language First Language, August 2, 2021

http://www.self.gutenberg.org/articles/eng/General_American_English August 1, 2021

https://www.britannica.com/science/phonetics Human Vocal Organs and Points of Articulation August 9, 2021

https://www.merriam-webster.com/dictionary/intonation Definition of Intonation, August 10, 2021

https://wikimili.com/en/John_Jacob_Jingleheimer_Schmidt American/Canadian Children's Song. John Jacob Jingle Heimer Schmidt, Late 19th century American/Canadian August 1, 2021

https://magoosh.com/english-speaking/sentence-stress-in-english/ Definition of Sentence Stress August 10, 2021

https://www.nationalgeographic.org/encyclopedia/gettysburg-address/ The Gettysburg
 Address August 17, 2021

https://tfcs.baruch.cuny.edu/thought-groups/ Thought Group, August 10, 2021

https://www.englishclub.com/pronunciation/word-stress-what.htm Word Stress definition
 August 10, 2021

https://www.classicfm.com/discover-music/row-row-row-your-boat-lyrics-history-
 nursery-rhyme/ origin of *Row, Row, Row Your Boat*

Jones, J. & Oliphant, T, *Welsh Melodies, Vol. 2,* compiled by John Thomas, 1862 *Deck
 the Halls*, August 8, 2021

Lessac, A. *Body Wisdom: The Use and Training of the Human Body*, re-printed by Lessac
 Training and Research Institute, June 21, 2019

Lessac, A. 1997. *The Use and Training of the Human Voice: A Bio-Dynamic Approach to
 Vocal Life 3rd Edition* McGraw-Hill Higher Education Publishing

Lyte, E. O. composer or adapter, Row, Row, Row Your Boat, Traditional English Nursery
 Rhyme, 1852, 1881 August 8, 2021

Munro, M. Ph.D, South African Lessac Intensive, Pretoria S.A. 2017

Naser, N., Department of Vision Sciences, University of Alabama, Birmingham, adapted
 from an essay

Newton, J. Words 1779. last verse author unknown, before 1829. Music: 'New Britain'
 James P. Carrell and David L. Clayton, 1831 *Amazing Grace,* Copyright: Public
 Domain August 1, 2021

O My Darling Clementine, Attributed to Montrose, P. & Bradford, B. 1884 https://
 en.wikipedia.org/wiki/Oh_My_Darling,_Clementine August 3, 2021

Rideout, P. M. IPA symbols (International Phonetic Alphabet) *The Newbury Dictionary of
 American English* Heinle & Heinle Publishers 1999

Robbins, C. Lessac Master Teacher, Associate Adjunct Professor Theatre Department,
 Santa Monica College

https://www.classicfm.com/discover-music/row-row-row-your-boat-lyrics-history-
 nursery-rhyme/ origin of *Row, Row, Row Your Boat*

Schmidt, R, & Richards, J. *Dictionary of Language Teaching & Applied Linguistics 3rd Ed.*, 1995, Longman Publishing Group

Shadix, H. Birmingham, Alabama

SLA Second Language Acquisition https://ebrary.net/7402/health/speech_language_ acquisition

U.S. Department of State https://educationdata.org/international-student-enrollment-statistics, Open Doors, May 15, 2021

wikipedia, the free encyclopedia July 20, 2021

Winardi, E. Graduate Student, Department of Engineering, University of Alabama, Birmingham, adapted from an essay

Woodward, G.R. 1924 *The Cambridge Carol Book: Being Fifty Two Songs for Christmas, Easter and Other Seasons* (London: Society for Promoting Christian Knowledge, 1924), Ding Dong Merrily on High, co-edited with Charles Wood

www.lessacinstitute.org July 20, 2021

www.thefreedictionary.com › General+American+English July 21, 2021

Zengul, F., Graduate Student, Health Services Administration, University of Alabama, Birmingham, adapted from an essay

Zou, Y. PhD Candidate, Department of Physics, University of Alabama, Birmingham, adapted from an essay

About the Authors

Jonghee Shadix, MA-TESOL, RN-BSN

JONGHEE SHADIX was born and educated in South Korea and worked as a registered nurse both in the National Medical Center in Seoul, Korea, and at the Children's and Maternity Hospital in Jeddah, Saudi Arabia under a Korea-Saudi Government collaboration, and then lived in Saudi Arabia for 15 years with her family. Later, after moving to the United States, she decided to further her education by earning a BSN (Bachelor of Science in Nursing) degree at the University of Alabama at Birmingham (UAB) and obtained an MA-TESOL (Master of Art-Teaching English to Speakers of Other Languages) degree at the University of Alabama (UA). To better prepare herself for the MA-TESOL program at UA, she completed an English Pronunciation Training program and also a teacher-training program in a Speech-Language Training program. Toward the end of her second year in the MA-TESOL program, she was offered a position teaching English Pronunciation to international graduate students and scholars in the UAB Graduate School, which she held for over 15 years.

While cross-pollinating in search of a better teaching method for English pronunciation, she discovered the Lessac Kinesensic Voice & Body Training—and began her collaboration with her mentor and co-author, Nancy Krebs.

She continues to serve her community as an English Korean Medical and Educational Interpreter in the Birmingham, Alabama region.

Nancy Krebs, Lessac Master Teacher

NANCY KREBS has been a Lessac Master Teacher since 2002, and has had an extensive career as an actor, singer, musician, songwriter, instructor, and Vocal/Dialect Coach for professional theater companies throughout the Mid-Atlantic region of the U.S and beyond. For the past 12 years, she has been the Resident Voice/Dialect Coach for the Classic Theatre of Maryland. She has taught the Lessac Kinesensic Training since 1982 and has led or participated as faculty for numerous international/national Intensive workshops since 1995 and operates her own private voice studio, *The Voiceworks*. She was on the theatre faculty of the famed Baltimore School for the Arts for 39 years and continues to teach and coach. As an author, she has contributed articles for various professional journals, notably *Play with Purpose: Lessac Kinesensics in Action* (Marth Munro, Sean Turner & Allan Munro) and *Collective Writings on the Lessac Voice & Body Work: A Festschrift* (Munro, Turner, Munro and Campbell) as well as *Voice and Speech Training in the New Millenium: Conversations with Master Teachers* (Nancy Saklad). As a singer/songwriter, she has released 7 original Christian meditational CDs since 1998. For more information: visit her website at www.nancykrebs.com

www.ingramcontent.com/pod-product-compliance
Lightning Source LLC
Chambersburg PA
CBHW041508120626

46551CB00018B/2349